teach yourself...

EXCEL FOR
WINDOWS 95

John Weingarten

MIS:
PRESS

A Subsidiary of
Henry Holt and Co., Inc.

First Edition—1995

Printed in the United States of America.

Library of Congress Cataloging-in-Publication Data

```
Weingarten, John.
    teach yourself--Excel for Windows 95 / John Weingarten.
      p.  cm.
    ISBN 1-55828-443-5
    1. Microsoft Excel for Windows 95.  2. Business--Computer programs.
    3. Electronic spreadsheets.  I. Title.
  HF5548.4.M523 W455    1995
  005.369--dc20                                          95-025019
                                                                CIP
```

10 9 8 7 6 5 4 3 2

MIS:Press books are available at special discounts for bulk purchases for sales promotions, premiums, fund-raising, or educational use. Special editions or book excerpts can also be created to specification.

For details contact: Special Sales Director
                         MIS:Press
                         a subsidiary of Henry Holt and Company, Inc.
                         115 West 18th Street
                         New York, New York 10011

Editor-in-Chief: Paul Farrell   **Managing Editor:** Cary Sullivan

Development Editor: Judy Brief   **Technical Editor:** John Wiemann

Copy Edit Manager: Shari Chapell   **Copyeditor:** Gwynne Jackson

Production Editor: Maya Riddick   **Asst. Production Editor:** Patricia Wallenburg

ACKNOWLEDGMENTS

This book was a team effort, and I want to thank everyone who helped make it possible. If I've left anyone out of the following list, please know that you are appreciated.

Matt Wagner, of Waterside Productions, is more than just a great agent. I can't thank him enough for his encouragement and guidance.

Ron Varela, who spent countless hours pouring over the manuscript to make sure I didn't say anything too stupid, helped with many suggestions and endless encouragement. He's a great guy and I'm honored that he is my friend.

Thnk you to Earl Moore for drafting many of the revised chapters and to Janice Mitchell for additional contributions.

Judy Brief, of MIS:Press, shepherded this project from beginning to end. Her wonderful sense of humor made working with her a joy. Her hard work and genuine concern for the quality of the product have been inspiring.

Patty Wallenburg applied great skill and dedication to make this a great looking book. Maya Riddick, of MIS:Press, handled last-minute changes with amazing grace and humor.

John Wiemann helped to ensure the technical accuracy of this book. His help and suggestions were greatly appreciated.

Gwynne Jackson handled the copyedit in a speedy and professional way. She is to be commended for her fine work under pressure.

Special thanks to Arturo Torres, June Stewart, Randy Manion, Leslie Fuke, and the rest of the gang at Gonzaga University School of Law Library. They make it a joy to come to work every morning at the finest Law School in the beautiful Pacific Northwest.

Finally, my wife Pam, and children, Sarah and Joshua, provided love and encouragement. For their support and patience, they deserve the most thanks of all.

TABLE OF CONTENTS

CHAPTER 1

EXCEL: THE BIG PICTURE (A LITTLE PERSPECTIVE)

CHAPTER 2

GETTING STARTED—EXCEL AND WINDOWS 95 BASICS

CHAPTER 3

CREATING A WORKSHEET 35

CHAPTER 4

EXPLORING MORE EXCEL FUNCTIONS .67

CHAPTER 5

MODIFYING A WORKSHEET 99

CHAPTER 6

ENHANCING AND ANNOTATING YOUR WORKSHEET 127

CHAPTER 7

CHAPTER 8

CHAPTER 9

CHAPTER 10

CHAPTER 11

PROOFING AND ANALYZING WORKSHEET DATA 247

CHAPTER 12

AUTOMATING YOUR WORK WITH MACROS 275

CHAPTER 13

CHAPTER 14

CHAPTER 15

SWITCHING AND CUSTOMIZING TOOLBARS **339**

CHAPTER 16

CUSTOMIZING WINDOWS **361**

CHAPTER 17

USING EXCEL WITH OTHER PROGRAMS 379

APPENDIX A

FOR LOTUS 1-2-3 USERS 407

APPENDIX B

KEYBOARD SHORTCUTS 411

APPENDIX C

CHAPTER 1

EXCEL: THE BIG PICTURE (A LITTLE PERSPECTIVE)

- ◆ Spreadsheets: how the computer revolution started
- ◆ What spreadsheets are (and aren't) good for
- ◆ What sets Excel apart from the competition
- ◆ Graphing and data management
- ◆ What You See Is What You Get
- ◆ Windows 95 overview

1

SPREADSHEETS: HOW THE COMPUTER REVOLUTION STARTED

The spreadsheet is a formidable computer tool that lets you record the past, analyze the present, and predict the future. Spreadsheets allow for easy preparation of accounting records and financial statements, as well as budgets and forecasts.

Because of their ability to use mathematical formulas and functions to calculate results when numbers are changed, spreadsheets are marvelous facilities for playing what if. In a business, you might want to know the answer to, "What if our supplies costs increase by ten percent next year?" or "What if we increased our selling price by three percent?"

Before the development of the first spreadsheet program about 15 years ago, few people thought of computers as personal. Large corporations used huge mainframe computers, often costing millions of dollars, for very specific accounting applications such as accounts receivable and inventory control. The only contact most corporate workers had with these computers was by way of printed reports, or perhaps entering data through terminals.

When the first spreadsheet program (Visicalc) appeared on the scene shortly after the introduction of the first Apple personal computers, small and medium-sized businesses quickly realized that they now had the ability to have greater control over their business. They could do budgeting and forecasting on their own desktop computers.

Computers and software have come a long way since those early Visicalc days. Other categories of software, such as word processing, database, and desktop publishing programs, now share spots on the software best seller lists along with spreadsheets. But spreadsheets remain one of the primary reasons for the tremendous proliferation of personal computers.

WHAT SPREADSHEETS ARE (AND AREN'T) GOOD FOR

Almost any task that requires numeric calculations is a good candidate for spreadsheet consideration. Budgeting and forecasting are the tasks that come to mind first when thinking about what spreadsheets are good for, but virtually anything requiring the storage and manipulation of data can be done with a spreadsheet. This includes such tasks as database management, drawing and graphics, charting, word processing, and more. However, a spreadsheet is not necessarily the best tool for any of these tasks.

It has become increasingly difficult in recent years to choose the most appropriate software category for a particular task. Many word processing programs offer spreadsheet-like features, and database programs include the ability to work with data in rows and columns, which makes them look like spreadsheets. Take Excel 95, for example. You can use Excel for several primary functions:

♦ Financial analysis

♦ Database management

♦ Charting and graphing

♦ Drawing and graphics

♦ Forms processing

♦ Word processing and text layout

There is no program better than a spreadsheet for financial analysis and numeric graphing. This is the primary function of a spreadsheet. If the work you need to perform is heavily text-oriented, where reporting on certain aspects of the document's contents isn't required, a word processing program is likely your best bet. If your task requires heavy manipulation of graphics and the ability to draw detailed images, then a dedicated graphics program is what you need. A database program would make more sense if:

1. You need to share your information with many other people but don't want two people updating the same data at the same time.

2. You want to be able to restrict the types of data being entered, as in an inventory control system.

3. Your database contains more than 10,000 records.

4. You need to combine two or more databases into one "front end" software system.

As we explore Excel, you'll see that you can accomplish most basic word processing and database tasks with this powerful spreadsheet program, but the fact that you can do it doesn't always mean you should do it. The examples in this book will give you a good idea of the types of applications where Excel...excels. Here are a few more examples:

♦ Budgets and personal financial statements

♦ Expense reports and summaries

♦ Financial projections with charts and graphs

♦ Inventory control

♦ Job estimates and cost sheets

♦ Printing and storing business forms

♦ Customer and client lists

♦ Creating and updating tables of data for documents

♦ Database statistical analysis

WHAT SETS EXCEL APART FROM THE COMPETITION

Excel 95 includes virtually every feature and refinement you could imagine a spreadsheet containing. You'll find a wide variety of powerful functions for almost any type of business, with financial or scientific calculation. Charting and database facilities, as well as proofing tools such as spell checking and spreadsheet analysis, round out Excel's impressive capabilities.

However, none of these features truly sets Excel apart from the competition. There are several other products that include practically the same feature set. So what does set Excel apart? Ease of use and integration.

Excel 95 includes a number of features that make the program easier to use, and to troubleshoot when you run into problems. These ease-of-use features—such as Tip Wizards, tabbed dialog boxes, tool tips, and tracing—are covered in detail later in the book.

For those seeking ease of use, there is the ability to switch easily to other types of computers without having to spend a great deal of time learning a new program. Excel is practically identical on both IBM-compatible computers and Macintosh computers. If your business uses both types of machines, you'll be able to use Excel on either without giving a thought to which machine you're using.

Excel works smoothly with other Windows applications, especially other Microsoft applications. Microsoft, the company that makes Excel, has gone to great lengths to make Excel work like its other Windows programs. An example of this is the similarity of menu structure between Excel and Microsoft's word processing program called Word. Excel is one of the first applications to support the new standard for sharing data with other Windows programs, OLE 2.0. OLE is discussed later.

CHARTING AND DATA MANAGEMENT

When you think of spreadsheets, you generally think of the rows and columns of text and numbers that create a worksheet document. Back in the early days of spreadsheet programs that was the only capability they had.

Most modern spreadsheet programs include at least basic facilities for turning numbers into charts and graphs and for performing database functions and manipulation. Many programs include charting and database facilities that rival the most powerful stand-alone programs in these categories.

No spreadsheet program has gone further in these areas than Excel 95. Excel's competitors cannot create a wider variety of charts and graphs or customize them in such seemingly endless ways. The data management capabilities (including easy creation of lists and almost automatic sorting) let you do more with your normal worksheet data, and may prove powerful enough to save you the dollar and time investment of a standalone database program.

WHAT YOU SEE IS WHAT YOU GET

Thanks to advances in both computer hardware and software, it's much easier to create great-looking documents than it once was. In the old days, if you wanted to print your documents with special fonts, characters, and graphic embellishments, you had to enter arcane printer codes into the spreadsheet program. As if that wasn't bad enough, you often didn't see the results of these codes until you actually printed your document. The result was a sense of flying blind, requiring repeated experimentation, as well as wasted time and paper, until you attained the desired results.

With the introduction of computers that displayed reasonably accurate representations of what would be on the printed page, you no longer had to guess at what would come out of your printer. It was right there in front of you on your screen.

The acronym WYSIWYG (What You See Is What You Get) has become as meaningless as the ubiquitous user-friendly. Many programs claiming to be WYSIWYG don't provide a very accurate view of the printed output. In this area, as in many others, Excel has raised the standard by providing a greater measure of accuracy and detail than was available before.

WINDOWS 95 OVERVIEW

Excel 95 is the new version of Excel for Windows 95. While you can use the previous versions of Excel inside Windows 95, the new version is designed to take full advantage of the Windows 95 features. Here is a summary for those familiar with earlier versions of Excel.

♦ **Updated dialog boxes**. Excel 95 includes a host of new dialog boxes that present options in an easy-to-understand way. Most noticeable will be the new Open and Save dialog boxes, which adhere to the new Windows 95 standards.

♦ **Faster operation**. Excel 95 is optimized to run as fast as possible under Windows 95.

♦ **Better memory management**. Excel and Windows 95 operate more smoothly with the available memory than previous versions. You will rarely encounter memory management errors or system crashes due to lack of memory.

♦ **New Help system**. Windows 95's new Help system is available through Excel. This is explained in more details in the next chapter.

♦ **Long file names**. Windows 95 lets you use long file names for your documents—as opposed to the old, eight-character names from DOS/Windows days. Instead of typing BUDGET95.XLS for your Excel document, you can type *Budget for 1995*.

A FINAL THOUGHT

This chapter set the stage for a better understanding of Excel's place in the computing world. While you can certainly use Excel productively without this information, this background should help shed some light on the big picture.

CHAPTER 2

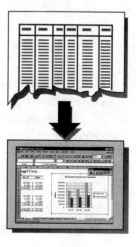

GETTING STARTED—EXCEL AND WINDOWS 95 BASICS

- ◆ What Windows 95 can do for you
- ◆ Starting and navigating Windows 95
- ◆ Recognizing Windows 95 types
- ◆ Using the mouse and the keyboard
- ◆ Starting Excel
- ◆ Touring the Excel screen
- ◆ Using menus and dialog boxes
- ◆ Using Toolbars
- ◆ Navigating the worksheet
- ◆ Using Excel's Help facility
- ◆ Exiting Excel

7

WHAT WINDOWS 95 CAN DO FOR YOU

As mentioned in the previous chapter, Windows 95 lets you accurately see what your printed documents look like before you print them. But, what the heck is Windows 95?

Glad you asked. Windows 95 is a software program in your computer that creates an environment that is friendly, intuitive, and graphical. Windows 95 is called a *GUI* (pronounced "gooey"), Graphic User Interface. Friendly and intuitive means you can choose commands from menus and dialog boxes by simply pointing and clicking with a mouse, without typing anything on the keyboard.

Windows 95 also displays everything on your screen as a graphic image and can use visual images and cues to lead you through the use of the application you're working with.

Finally, Windows 95 makes your computing life easier by providing a consistent user interface. The user interface is just a fancy term for the way you and your computer interact. Without Windows 95, you normally communicate with the computer by typing commands on the keyboard. Aside from making it easier to enter commands, the user interface makes it easier to learn new programs.

Most Windows 95 programs adhere, more or less, to the same structure of menus and other tools for communicating with Windows 95. Once you learn how to use one Windows 95 program, you've already gone a long way toward learning the next program. For example, the procedures for opening, closing, and saving documents are virtually identical from one Windows 95 program to another.

Windows 95 can increase your productivity by allowing you to run more than one program at a time and share information among them. This may seem trivial, but imagine you are working in your word processing program on a report that requires a portion of a worksheet from Excel. The ability to move between the two programs without having to exit one before starting the other saves time and effort.

N O T E   If you're used to the old-style user interface, it may feel as if Windows 95 is getting in your way and slowing you down. Let me assure you that, as you become familiar with the myriad shortcuts available to you, you'll be flying through Windows 95 commands as quickly as you used to enter them without Windows 95.

The next few sections provide a brief tutorial for using Windows 95. I know you want to dive right in and start using Excel, but please work through the tutorial if you're not familiar with Windows 95 basics. You'll find that learning Excel and other Windows 95 programs is much easier if you have a good understanding of the Windows 95 environment. Keep in mind that the following sections just scratch the surface of what Windows 95 has to offer. If you want to learn more of the ins and outs of Windows 95, take a look at *Teach Yourself...Windows 95* from MIS:Press, or use the Windows 95 tutorial included with Windows 95.

FINDING YOUR WAY AROUND WINDOWS 95

When you start your computer, Windows 95 should be up and running on the screen, which will look something like Figure 2.1. In this chapter, you'll learn the basics of getting around in the Windows environment.

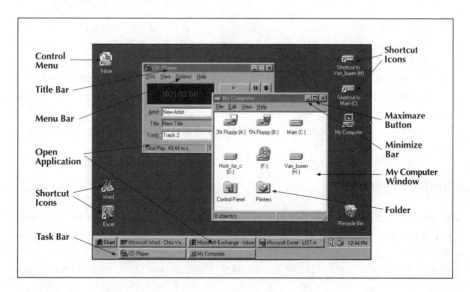

FIGURE 2.1 THE WINDOWS 95 ENVIRONMENT.

Telling Windows 95 What to Do

You communicate with Windows 95 using either the keyboard, the mouse, or both. In this book, the mouse method is emphasized, but that doesn't mean it is always the most efficient way to carry out an operation. Where there is a keyboard method that is clearly a shortcut, I'll point it out. However, most people who are new to Windows 95 find the mouse action more intuitive and easier to remember.

The mouse pointer on the screen moves as you move the mouse on the surface of your desk. In addition to moving the mouse to reposition the pointer, there are several basic mouse operations you need to master:

♦ **Dragging**—moving the mouse while holding down the left mouse button.

♦ **Clicking**—pressing and releasing the left mouse button.

♦ **Right-clicking**—pressing and releasing the right mouse button.

♦ **Double-clicking**—clicking the left mouse button twice in rapid succession.

As the mouse is moved over various portions of the screen, its shape changes to indicate the sort of action that can be performed. As the pointer is positioned over the border on the side of a window, it changes to a double-headed arrow. That indicates that you can change the height or width of the window by dragging the mouse in one of the directions the arrow is pointing. Placing the pointer over one of the corners of a window transforms it into a diagonal double-headed arrow, indicating that you can change both the height and width at the same time.

Running Programs

One of the first things you'll want to do in Windows 95 is run your programs. There are many ways to run programs and we'll discuss a few of them here. The simplest way is to locate the program's name in the Program Launcher that appears on the Windows Task Bar. This is the button that contains the word *Start..*

1. Click once on the **Start** button.
2. Move to the Programs option.
3. Move to the Microsoft Office option. The screen should look like Figure 2.2.
4. Click on the **Microsoft Excel** program.

   This launches the Microsoft Excel program, which should now be on your screen.

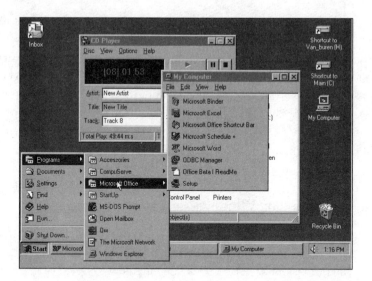

FIGURE 2.2 USING THE LAUNCHER.

You can also launch a program by locating its icon in the appropriate place on the C: disk drive. Later in this chapter, you'll learn how to open and close Windows. We'll explore how to locate the Excel icon at that time.

Putting Programs Away and Quitting

With Excel on the screen, you might find it difficult to get back to your Windows environment to perform other activities there. Actually, you can simply put Excel (or any program) away temporarily, so you can access other things going on with your computer.

1. Locate the Minimize button on the Excel screen. This appears in the upper-right corner of the screen as a button with a horizontal line at the bottom. (It's the left button in the series of three buttons at the top-right of the screen.)

2. Click the **Minimize** button.

    This temporarily closes the Excel program window and places its name in the Task Bar at the bottom of the Windows 95 screen. You can display the Excel program again by clicking on its name in the Task Bar. Try this to get Excel back on the screen.

3. Click on the **Microsoft Excel** button in the Task Bar. Excel will reappear on the screen.

   Note that programs that appear in the Task Bar are still running. They are not *completely* put away. Clicking on a window's Minimize button merely gets the window out of view. If you want to completely quit the program and close the window, you'll need to double-click on the program's **Control** menu, or click on the **Close** button.

4. Double-click on Excel's **Control** menu to completely quit the program for now. We'll run Excel again later in this chapter.

Opening and Arranging Windows

Windows 95 displays just about everything in...what else?...windows. A *window* is an area in Windows 95 that displays information. Figure 2.1 shows the basic parts of a window. The first task in Windows 95 is knowing how to open, close and arrange windows. After that, we'll explore how to change a window's size and shape.

1. Point to the **My Computer** icon on the screen and double-click. This will open the My Computer window (if it's not already open).

2. Double-click on the icon marked **Main C:**. This will open a window displaying the contents of the C: drive.

3. Double-click on the **Office 95** folder icon. (This may also be called **MSOFFICE**.) This will display the files inside the Office 95 folder. Your screen will look something like Figure 2.3.

   You may find it convenient to have several windows opened at once so you can easily refer to the programs you want to use. This can create a problem. With several windows opened, the screen can become a little cluttered. Let's open a couple of additional groups to create the problem and learn how to fix it.

   Notice that the new opened window overlaps the other windows and its title bar is dark, indicating that it is the *active window*. This means it's the window you can work with now. Also notice that although most of the other windows are obscured, a small portion of each is still visible behind the Office 95 window. Windows 95 provides several ways to get at the buried information:

♦ Click on any visible portion of a window to make it the active window.

♦ Move the windows around on the screen to arrange them in a more appropriate fashion.

♦ Move the active window so it doesn't cover as much of the window it's obscuring.

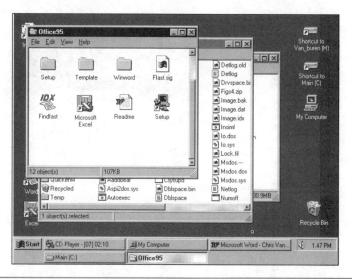

FIGURE 2.3 OPENING THE C: DISK DRIVE WINDOW AND DISPLAYING THE CONTENTS OF THE OFFICE 95 FOLDER.

4. Position the pointer in the title bar of the active window and drag it out of the way, as displayed in Figure 2.4.

FIGURE 2.4 DRAGGING A WINDOW.

5. Release the mouse button to complete the repositioning of the window, as shown in Figure 2.5.

FIGURE 2.5 THE REPOSITIONED OFFICE 95 WINDOW.

For the remainder of the book, when a step tells you to use a menu command, you'll be instructed to choose the command. For example, if you were being told to tile your window, the instruction would look like this: "Choose **Window, Tile**." In this way, the choice of keyboard or mouse access is left to you.

N O T E — Inside the Office 95 window you will notice the Excel program icon. You have now found the location of this program—inside the Office 95 folder, which is inside the Main C: disk drive. If you double-click on the Excel program icon, you will run the program, just as you did earlier in this chapter through the Start button. This is a second way to run programs and, as you'll discover, more tiresome because you have to constantly open the windows in which the icons are located. The following section describes a third way to run a program.

Creating a Shortcut Icon

If there are programs you use frequently, you might find it convenient to create shortcut icons for these programs. A shortcut icon is simply a duplicate of the

original icon that is located in a more convenient place. Let's try adding a shortcut of the Excel icon onto the main Excel screen.

1. Press the **Ctrl** key and hold it down.

2. Click and drag on the **Excel** icon located in the Office 95 folder.

3. Drag to a clear part of the Windows background, as shown in Figure 2.6.

FIGURE 2.6 CREATING A SHORTCUT OF THE EXCEL PROGRAM ICON.

4. Release the mouse to create the shortcut icon.

You can move the icon around if desired. You might want to close some windows to make more room first.

Resizing a Window

Let's try changing the size of the Office 95 window.

1. Position the mouse pointer over the right border of the window, as displayed in Figure 2.7.

2. Drag the mouse to the left, as shown in Figure 2.8.

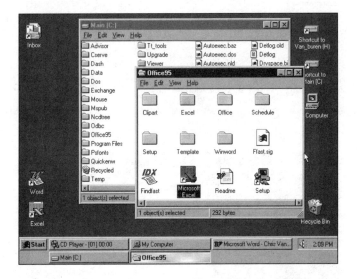

FIGURE 2.7 MOVING THE MOUSE INTO POSITION FOR RESIZING THE WINDOW.

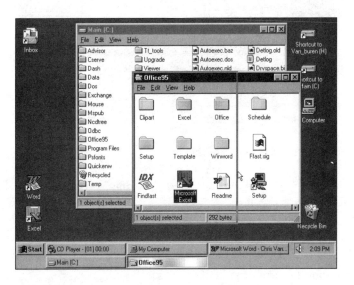

FIGURE 2.8 THE OUTLINE OF THE NEW RIGHT BORDER'S POSITION.

3. Release the mouse button to complete the resizing process.

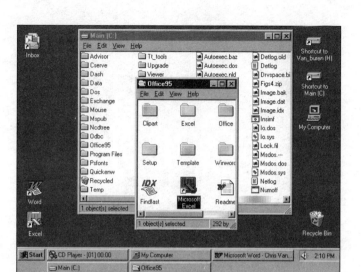

FIGURE 2.9 THE RESIZED PROGRAM MANAGER WINDOW.

Because the window is no longer large enough to display all the group icons in their current positions, Windows 95 adds scroll bars to allow navigation to portions of the window that aren't currently visible.

Depending on its size, your Office 95 window may have already had scroll bars, or you may need to reduce it further to make the scroll bars appear. If you don't have scroll bars, follow the steps above to reduce the window's size until you do have scroll bars.

Using Scroll Bars

Changing the view of the window's contents so you can see a portion of the window that isn't currently visible is easily accomplished by clicking on the scroll bar buttons, the scroll bar itself, or dragging the scroll box.

The scroll boxes let you know where your view of the window's contents is currently. For example, if the scroll box on the horizontal scroll bar is at the far left, there are no more icons or other objects further left.

1. Drag the horizontal scroll box until it is in the middle of the scroll bar and release the mouse button, as shown in Figure 2.10.

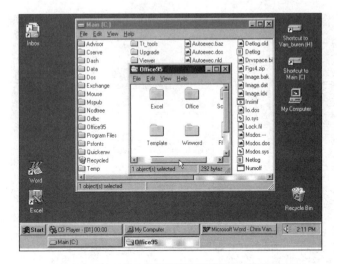

FIGURE 2.10 THE SCROLL BOX IN THE MIDDLE OF THE SCROLL BAR.

The scroll box in the middle of the scroll bar tells you that you have scrolled about halfway over in the window. Now, use the scroll button to scroll all the way to the right.

2. Point to the right scroll button and click several times until the scroll box is on the right side of the scroll bar (see Figure 2.11).

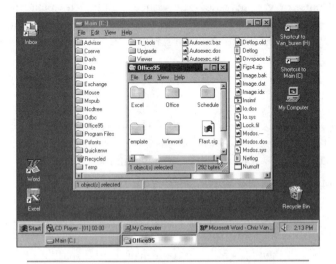

FIGURE 2.11 THE SCROLL BOX AT THE RIGHT SIDE OF THE SCROLL BAR.

The contents of the window has shifted to the left, so you are viewing what's on the right. Clicking in the scroll bar itself on either side of the scroll box also causes the scroll box to be repositioned.

 You'll find the scroll bar an invaluable tool for navigating large worksheets in Excel and large documents in other applications. If you feel that you need more practice with scroll bars, don't worry, you'll get N O T E lots of practice when we get to work in Excel shortly.

Closing Windows

When you no longer need to work with a window, you may wish to close it to reclaim some screen real estate for the windows you are currently working with.

To close the active window, you open the Control menu by clicking on the Control menu box in the upper-left corner of the window. Let's close all of the windows we opened so far.

1. Click on the **Control** menu box of the Office 95 window. See Figure 2.12.

FIGURE 2.12 THE CONTROL MENU.

2. Choose **Close**.

SHORTCUT

The fastest way to close a window is a single click on the **Close** button.

3. Close the other group windows you have opened.

Your screen should now look the way it did when you first started Windows 95.

STARTING EXCEL

The big moment has arrived. It's time to start Excel and get this show on the road. Starting Excel, or any other program in Windows 95, is done through the program Launcher as described earlier. Since we created a shortcut icon on the Windows screen, let's try using that to launch Excel this time.

1. Locate the Excel shortcut icon you created in the previous section.
2. Double-click on the icon.

After a few seconds, the main Excel screen appears on your screen, as displayed in Figure 2.13.

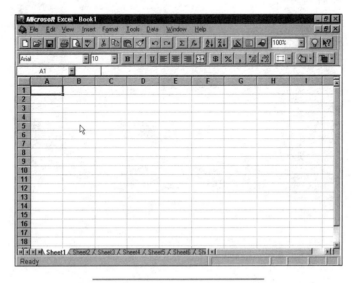

FIGURE 2.13 THE OPENING EXCEL SCREEN.

A QUICK TOUR OF THE EXCEL SCREEN

Many of the elements in the opening Excel screen should seem familiar to you. The title bar, menu bar, control menu box, and scroll bars all work the same way as they did in the Program Manager. There are also a few new screen elements that are discussed shortly.

When Excel is first started, you see a worksheet called Sheet1, that is actually contained in a document window. If the document window is maximized to fill the entire available area, as in Figure 2.13, there is a Restore button in the upper-right corner of the worksheet. Clicking on the Restore button reduces the size of the window and gives you sizing borders. However, it's often more efficient to work with your worksheet maximized to give you maximum visible area.

The worksheet consists of lettered columns and numbered rows. The intersection of a column and a row is called a *cell* and its name is the column letter followed by the row number. The active cell is surrounded by a border and its name is displayed in the cell reference area. The hollow cross on the worksheet is the mouse pointer and it changes shapes as it moves to different parts of the worksheet.

USING DIALOG BOXES

Many Windows 95 applications, including Excel, use dialog boxes to allow more detailed or efficient communication with the program than menus alone can provide. There are many types of dialog boxes providing various kinds of input.

Some dialog boxes appear automatically if you make some sort of mistake or ask Excel to do something that requires confirmation. They appear as a result of choosing a menu command that requires additional input. You can tell which menu commands produce dialog boxes because they are followed by an ellipsis (...). Let's examine one of the more complex dialog boxes to see how they work.

1. Choose **Tools** to display the Tools drop-down menu (see Figure 2.14).

   Notice that several of the menu commands have triangles next to them. These commands have submenus with additional commands. Submenus are used later. Other menu commands are followed by an ellipsis, indicating that choosing that command produces a dialog box.

2. Choose **Options** to produce the Options dialog box, shown in Figure 2.15.

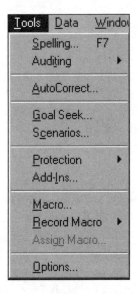

FIGURE 2.14 THE TOOLS DROP-DOWN MENU.

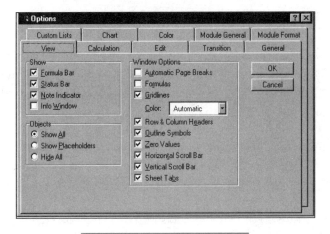

FIGURE 2.15 THE OPTIONS DIALOG BOX.

Most dialog boxes don't have as many options as the Options dialog box. This is a good example of what you'll encounter in various Excel dialog boxes. Option buttons allow you to choose only one of the options in a category. Check box categories can have multiple boxes checked. List boxes let you select a choice from a list.

Tabbed dialog boxes let you switch among various sets of options by clicking on the tab. As displayed in Figure 2.15, the View tab is highlighted. Let's take a look at another set of options in the same dialog box.

3. Click on the **General** tab.

   This set of options includes one more input method—a text box into which you can type information.

4. Click on the **Cancel** button on the right side of the dialog box, or press the **Esc** key to clear the dialog box.

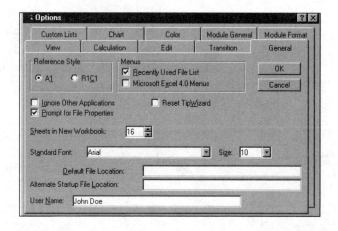

FIGURE 2.16 THE OPTIONS DIALOG BOX WITH THE GENERAL TAB HIGHLIGHTED.

USING THE TOOLBARS

You've learned that there are often keyboard shortcuts for accomplishing certain tasks. Excel's toolbars are like shortcut keys that are accessible by clicking on them with the mouse. Another advantage of the toolbars is that they keep the shortcuts visible. so they are easier to remember than keyboard shortcuts.

Excel supplies predefined toolbars for a variety of situations. Figure 2.13 displayed the two default toolbars that automatically appear when you start Excel. *Default* refers to the way things are set automatically. The top toolbar is the Standard toolbar and the one on the bottom is the Formatting toolbar.

Each toolbar button is an icon (picture) that represents a command or series of commands. Some of the icons are fairly self-explanatory, but you may be wondering how you'll be able to figure out what the rest of those cryptic little pictures mean. Never fear. Excel provides an easy way to determine what each of the toolbar buttons does. By simply moving the mouse pointer over one of the buttons, the status bar displays a description of what the button does and a tool tip pops up just below the mouse pointer with the button's name. Let's try this out.

1. Without clicking, position the mouse pointer over the **Print** toolbar button. It's the fourth button from the left on the Standard toolbar (see Figure 2.17).

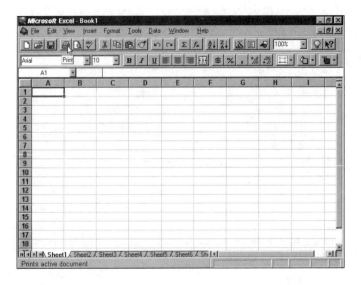

FIGURE 2.17 THE MOUSE POINTER ON THE PRINT TOOLBAR BUTTON.

The tool tip says Print, and the status bar tells you that clicking on this would cause the active document to print.

2. Move the pointer over some of the other toolbar buttons. Look at the tool tip and status bar to get an idea of what some of the other buttons can accomplish.

Throughout the book, we'll be working with various toolbars and toolbar buttons. You will learn later how to choose which toolbars you want to appear on screen, how to change their position, and even how to customize them to create special toolbars to meet your own requirements.

NAVIGATING THE WORKSHEET

As you start entering and editing data in worksheets, you need to know how to move about. There are quite a few ways to navigate the worksheet using either the keyboard or the mouse. The simplest method is clicking the mouse pointer on the cell you want to move to, or using the **Arrow** keys to move to the cell you want to be active.

1. Use the **Arrow** keys to move to several different cells. The cell reference area tells you what the active cell is.

2. Use the mouse to click on several different cells.

   While this method works well for moving short distances, it's very inefficient for moving long distances. Some of the more useful long-distance navigation techniques involve keyboard combinations (see Table 2.1).

   TABLE 2.1 THE MOST COMMON NAVIGATION SHORTCUTS

Key	Result
PageUp	Moves up one screen.
PageDown	Moves down one screen.
Alt+PageDown	Moves right one screen.
Alt+PageUp	Moves left one screen.
Ctrl+Backspace	Moves to display the active cell.
Ctrl+Home	Moves to A1.
Ctrl+End	Moves to the last used cell.

   You can also move long distances by using the scroll bars. Use the same techniques you learned earlier to scroll to different parts of the worksheet:

   ◆ Click on the scroll bar buttons to move a row at a time.

   ◆ Drag the scroll box to move to a distant location.

   ◆ Click in the scroll bar above or below the scroll box to move one screen up or down.

Using the scroll bars doesn't change the active cell, it only changes the portion of the worksheet you are looking at. Once you've moved to the desired location using the scroll bars, click in the cell you want to become active.

One of the most useful ways to move around is to use the Go To dialog box. With the Go To dialog box, you can enter the cell address you want to move to and, zap! You're there. Let's try it.

3. Choose **Edit**, **Go To** (or press **F5**). The dialog box appears, as shown in Figure 2.18.

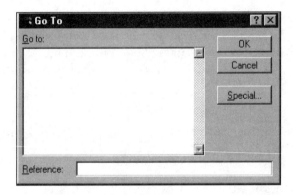

FIGURE 2.18 THE GO TO DIALOG BOX.

As we work through the book, we cover a number of ways to use the Go To dialog box. For now, let's just move to a new cell. Notice the vertical line in the Reference text box. This is called the *insertion point* and indicates that this is where you can start typing. If the insertion point isn't in the Reference text box, just click in the Reference text box and the insertion point is there.

4. Type **Z45** and click **OK** to make Z45 the active cell.

USING EXCEL'S HELP FACILITIES

One of the most important skills you can learn is how to get yourself unstuck when you run into difficulty. Fortunately, Excel provides some very useful tools for getting help. It even includes electronic demonstrations of many aspects of the program.

Let's explore Help's contents to see what's available.

1. Choose **Help** and then click **Microsoft Excel Help Topics** to produce the Help screen shown in Figure 2.19.

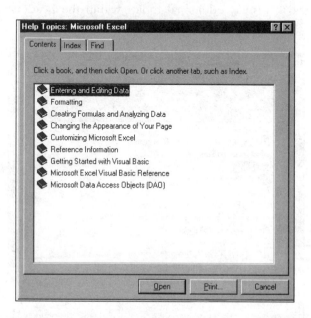

FIGURE 2.19 THE MICROSOFT EXCEL HELP WINDOW WITH THE CONTENTS DISPLAYED.

N O T E The Help window is an application window. You can tell that it is an application window because it has its own menu bar, separate from Excel's menu bar, to control it. Help is an application, or program, that runs concurrently with Excel. You can keep Help running and switch between the Help window and the Excel window by pressing **Alt-Tab**.

Help is segmented into logical groups. The first group, *Entering and Editing Data*, leads you to more sections about creating worksheets. *Formatting* leads to screens that tell you how to format your work for better visual presentations. *Creating Formulas and Analyzing Data* provides examples of using formulas within Excel's cells. Other sections lead to more information about related topics.

You can move to any of these sections by moving the mouse pointer over one of the underlined headings (also in green on color screens) and clicking. Let's try moving to one of the help sections now.

2. Position the mouse pointer over the **Entering and Editing Data** heading and click to display additional topics within the heading, as shown in Figure 2.20.

FIGURE 2.20 THE ENTERING AND EDITING DATA HELP WINDOW.

We can now choose from further headings, which contain more selections. Notice that the top choice has a question mark beside it. This indicates that clicking on this topic will provide an actual help screen—not more topics. In other words, it's the end of the line. Let's try clicking on a help topic.

3. Move the mouse pointer over the **Deciding which Office application to use...** category, and double-click to display a help screen as shown in Figure 2.21. Notice that these items are underlined with dashed underlines. A dashed underline means that you can click on that item to display a definition of the item.

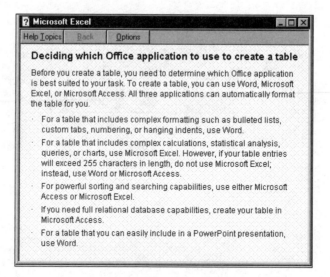

Microsoft Excel

Help Topics | Back | Options

Deciding which Office application to use to create a table

Before you create a table, you need to determine which Office application is best suited to your task. To create a table, you can use Word, Microsoft Excel, or Microsoft Access. All three applications can automatically format the table for you.

· For a table that includes complex formatting such as bulleted lists, custom tabs, numbering, or hanging indents, use Word.

· For a table that includes complex calculations, statistical analysis, queries, or charts, use Microsoft Excel. However, if your table entries will exceed 255 characters in length, do not use Microsoft Excel; instead, use Word or Microsoft Access.

· For powerful sorting and searching capabilities, use either Microsoft Access or Microsoft Excel.

· If you need full relational database capabilities, create your table in Microsoft Access.

· For a table that you can easily include in a PowerPoint presentation, use Word.

Figure 2.21 A help window.

You can use the buttons just below the menu bar to move to other portions of Help. For example, you can use the **Back** button to retrace your steps, one screen at a time, or the **Help Topics** button to return to the contents page. The **Options** button provides a list of options that you can perform with the Help information on the screen, such as printing the topic.

4. Click the **Help Topics** button to return to the Contents page.

You can search for specific information when you don't know what topic you need. This is like using the index in a book to find a specific word. Do this by accessing the Index page of the Help window.

5. Click on the **Index** page tab to view the index window, as shown in Figure 2.22.

You can either scroll to a category item in the list or just start typing the name of the feature you need help with in the text box above the list. As you type, the category items starting with those letters will appear in the list. When the category item you want is visible, you can click on the **Show Topics** button, or just double-click on the item.

Suppose you want more information about using Help. Let's try searching for help on Help now.

FIGURE 2.22 THE HELP INDEX.

6. Type **h** in the text box and notice that the list jumps to the first features that start with the letter h.

7. Type **help** and the Help category comes into view. Double-click on this topic to show the additional topics found, as shown in Figure 2.23.

    Now you can double-click on any of the topics offered to view the corresponding help information. After you have found the help screen you are looking for and read the information, you can close the Help window by choosing **File**, **Exit**, or double-clicking on the control-menu box. You can close a How To window by clicking on the **Close** button.

8. Choose **File**, **Exit** from the main Help window to exit Help.

Using the TipWizard

Not only does Excel make it easy to find and use Help for the topics you are struggling with, the TipWizard can even make suggestions about better ways to perform tasks after you have done them. Excel is a smart program.

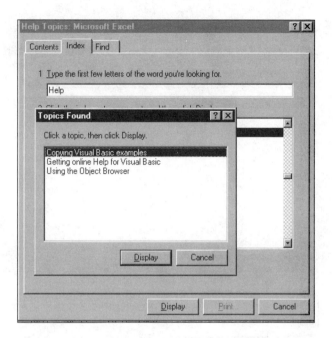

FIGURE 2.23 THE SEARCH DIALOG BOX WITH THE PRINT AREA TOPICS DISPLAYED.

When the TipWizard has a suggestion for you, the TipWizard button lights up. *Lighting up* means turning yellow on a color screen or just highlighted if you don't have color.

N O T E

When you start Excel, the TipWizard lights up before you've done anything. This lets you know that it is ready to give you the *tip of the day*, which is a random hint or shortcut for performing some commonly used Excel task.

To display the suggestion the TipWizard has for you, just click on the **TipWizard** button. To clear the suggestion, click on the **TipWizard** button again. The TipWizard button is lit because, aside from offering us a tip of the day, it has a suggestion for a more efficient way to move to a new cell than the Go To box we used to move to cell Z45 in the last section. Let's take a look at the suggestion, as well as the tip of the day.

1. Click on the **TipWizard** button to display the tip between the Formatting toolbar and the Formula bar, as shown in Figure 2.24.

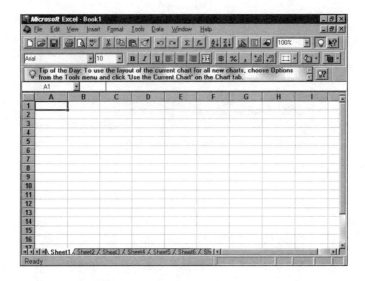

FIGURE 2.24 THE TIPWIZARD'S TIP OF THE DAY.

Just to the right of the tip text are Up and Down Arrows for moving to the previous or next tip. There is no next tip, so let's move to the previous tip.

2. Click on the **Up Arrow** to the right of the tip text to display the tip of the day.

You can leave the TipWizard open to display suggestions automatically, or you can close it and then just open it when you want to see a suggestion. For now, let's leave it open and perform a task in a less-than-optimally-efficient manner. Even though there is nothing in the active cell (Z45), we'll tell Excel that we want to cut (delete) the cell contents using the menu.

3. Choose **Edit**, **Cut** to display a suggestion for cutting using a toolbar button, as displayed in Figure 2.25.

Because Excel uses a great deal of intelligence for providing tips, you may see a different tip. Don't worry, Excel is just trying to give you the best suggestion for your particular situation.

N O T E You'll also discover that Excel only provides a tip once in an Excel session unless you perform the task inefficiently three more times.

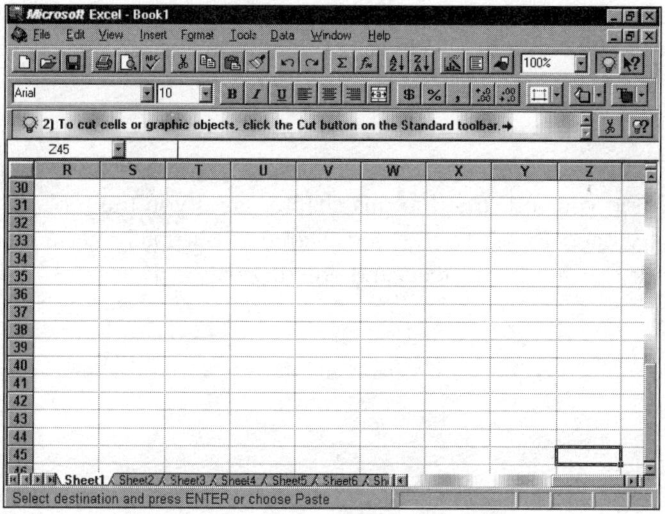

FIGURE 2.25 THE TIP FOR USING THE CUT TOOLBAR BUTTON.

If the tip suggests that you use a toolbar button, the button will be displayed to the right of the Up and Down Arrows, as you see for this tip. There is also a Tip Help displayed for tips so that you can jump directly to a help screen for more detailed information about the procedure.

We won't keep the TipWizard displayed for the figures in the remainder of the book, since it does take up some valuable screen real estate. However, don't hesitate to display it as you work through the book to see if there are better ways of accomplishing what you are doing. Of course, just because the TipWizard suggests something, that doesn't mean it's the best approach. It's just giving you a suggestion. Use your own judgment.

   4. Click the **TipWizard** toolbar button to remove the TipWizard.

EXITING EXCEL

When you are ready to leave Excel, you can do so in the same manner as closing any other window.

   ◆ Choose **File**, **Exit**, or double-click on the control menu box.

   Excel closes and returns to the icon you started from. If you have made changes to a worksheet, Excel is considerate enough to ask you if you want to save the changes. If you see such a message at this point, just click on the **No** button to finish exiting Excel.

A FINAL THOUGHT

The information you've learned in this chapter gives you the tools to get around in Windows 95 and Excel. In the next chapter, you finally get a chance to put Excel to work creating worksheets and entering data.

CHAPTER 3

CREATING A WORKSHEET

- ◆ Planning a worksheet
- ◆ Building a text framework
- ◆ Entering text
- ◆ Editing text
- ◆ Entering numbers
- ◆ Cell reference notes
- ◆ Creating formulas
- ◆ Understanding and using functions
- ◆ Saving your worksheets

PLANNING A WORKSHEET

The *worksheet* is where you enter the information you want to store and manipulate. Like almost anything you build, a worksheet is more useful, efficient, and understandable if you take the time to plan before you dive in and start entering data willy nilly.

The first step is to decide what the purpose of the worksheet is. For example, if the worksheet is to contain a monthly budget for the next year, then the purpose is to forecast and gain greater control over inflows and outflows for your business.

Give some thought to the level of detail you want to include in the worksheet. Too little detail may render the worksheet useless by omitting critical information required to make decisions based on the analysis of data entered into the worksheet. Too much detail can make the worksheet unwieldy and mask the results, not letting you see the big picture.

You may also find it useful to use paper and pencil to sketch out the overall design of your worksheet. This lets you see how the worksheet looks to the user (whether that user is you or someone else) before you take the time to enter data.

One more planning tip to keep in mind: Remember that the ultimate result of most worksheets is a printed report of some sort. Many things that seem obvious to you as you create or edit a worksheet can easily be obscured or invisible in the printout. For example, formulas you create to perform calculations can be revealed in the worksheet, but are generally not part of the printed output. The printed report is often only a small portion of the entire worksheet, so the context that might make the worksheet understandable on-screen might not be a part of the printout.

Building a Text Framework

The most common, and often the most practical, way to start putting together a worksheet is to enter titles, column and row headings, and any other text elements that provide a structure for your worksheet as you enter the data. There are no hard-and-fast rules for the text framework but, traditionally, columns contain time periods such as hours, days, and months and row headings contain categories such as rent, insurance, cost of goods, and similar headings.

We are going to create a budget worksheet for a small locksmith business that also sells bagels. The Spokane Locks and Bagel Corporation decided to use

Excel to create a budget worksheet to compare budgeted amounts with actual figures down the road. Figure 3.1 depicts the initial text framework for this budget worksheet.

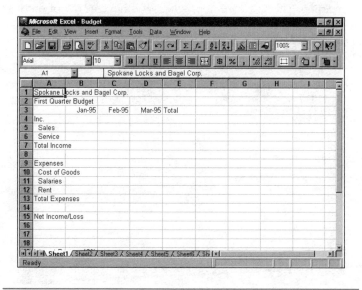

FIGURE 3.1 THE TEXT FRAMEWORK FOR THE SPOKANE LOCKS AND BAGEL CORPORATION.

ENTERING TEXT

To enter text into an Excel worksheet, simply move to the cell in which you want to enter the text and start typing. As you type, the text appears in both the cell and the formula bar. Let's start entering the text as displayed in Figure 3.1.

1. Start Excel if you don't have it on your screen. Refer to Chapter 2 if you don't remember the steps for starting Excel.

2. Be sure A1 is the active cell. Look at the cell reference area to double-check that you are in the right place.

3. Type **Spokane Locks and Bagel Corp.** Press **Enter**. Type **First Quarter Budget**.

As you start typing, notice that a flashing vertical line, called an *insertion point*, appears to the right of the text, as displayed in Figure 3.2. The insertion point lets you know where text is to be entered or deleted. As soon as you start a cell entry, three new icons appear on the left side of the formula bar. From left to right, these icons are the **Cancel**, **Enter**, and **Function Wizard** box. Also notice that pressing **Enter** moves you to the next line, where you can enter the next part of the heading. This is convenient when you have a row of entries to type.

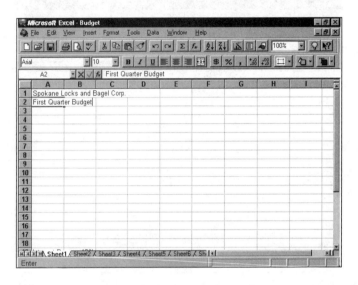

FIGURE 3.2 THE BEGINNINGS OF A CELL ENTRY.

If you make a mistake while typing, simply press the **Backspace** key to erase the character to the left of the insertion point. If you've really messed up, you can click on the **Cancel** box or press **Esc**.

While you are entering text in a cell, you cannot press the **Left Arrow** or **Right Arrow** keys to reposition the insertion point for editing. Pressing an arrow key causes Excel to complete the cell entry with what you've typed so far and move in the arrow's direction to the next cell on the worksheet.

The text you typed in cell A1 has apparently spilled over into the adjacent cells in columns B, C, D, and E. But do those other cells really contain part of the information? No. The entire worksheet title is in A1. The cell reference area says you are in A1 and the formula bar displays the whole title. If you were to move to B1, you'd see from the formula bar that B1 contains no data. In fact, it is because B1,

C1, D1, and E1 are empty that the contents of A1 are allowed to spill over. If these cells contained data, even a space, the entry in A1 would be truncated.

To see how this works, let's enter something in B1. There are several ways to complete a cell entry, including clicking on the **Enter** box, pressing the **Enter** key, or moving to another cell. The last method is usually the fastest since you often need to make entries in other cells.

1. Press the **Up Arrow** and **Right Arrow** keys to move to cell B1. Notice that cell B1 is empty.

2. Press the **Spacebar** and then click on the **Enter** box. The text in A1 is limited to what fits in the current column width. Now let's get rid of the space in B1 to restore the title.

3. While B1 is still the active cell, press the **Delete** key to allow the title to flow across the columns.

N O T E Column widths can be changed to allow for the amount of text entered in the column. Changing column widths, which is covered in the next two chapters, is usually the preferred method for accommodating long text entries.

---

4. Click on cell B3 to make it the active cell. This completes the entry in cell A1.

5. Now that the worksheet title is in place, enter the column headings. In cell B3, type **Jan**.

T I P Now, you could move to cell C3 and type **Feb** and then type **Mar** in D3, but there's an easier way. In the lower-right corner of the box surrounding the active cell is the fill handle. The *fill handle* allows you to perform several copying actions. For now we'll use the fill handle to take advantage of Excel's intelligence. By dragging the fill handle to the right so that the outline extends through cell D3, Excel automatically enters **Feb** and **Mar** for you.

---

6. Position the mouse over the fill handle until the mouse pointer turns into thin cross-hairs. Drag it to the right until the cell outline extends to cell D3, as displayed in Figure 3.3.

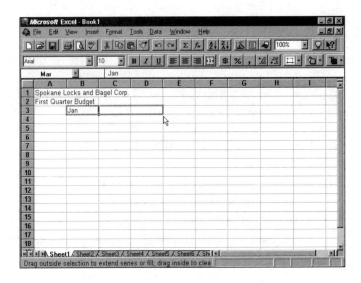

FIGURE 3.3 THE FILL HANDLE BEING DRAGGED.

7. Release the mouse button to complete the fill (see Figure 3.4).

If a cell contains **Mon**, dragging the fill handle increments the days of the week as **Tue**, **Wed**, **Thu,** and so on. A cell containing text and a number, such as **1st Period**, fills as **2nd Period**, **3rd Period**, and so on.

N O T E

You can also use the fill handle to increment a series by dragging to the right or down. If you want to use the fill handle to decrement a series, drag to the left or up. If a cell contained **Jan**, dragging left or up would fill as **Dec**, **Nov**, **Oct**, and so on.

N O T E

8. Click in cell E3 and type **Total**.

9. Move to cell A4 and type **Income**.

If you're entering several contiguous cells in a column, pressing the **Enter** key is the most efficient way to complete a cell entry since it causes the next cell in the column to become the active cell.

T I P

10. Press the **Enter** key to complete the entry and move to the next cell in the column.

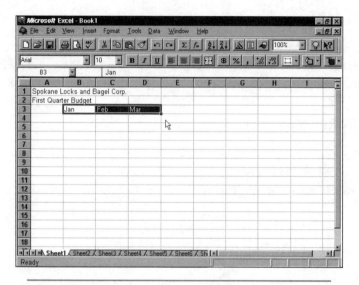

FIGURE 3.4 THE RESULTS OF THE FILL AFTER RELEASING THE MOUSE BUTTON.

In Figure 3.1, the next two entries in the column are indented just a bit. This was accomplished by preceding the entries with two spaces.

NOTE

11. Press the **Spacebar** twice and type **Sales**. Then press **Enter**.

12. Enter the following text:

```
A6   Service
A7   Total Income
A9   Expenses
A10  Cost of Goods
A11  Salaries
A12  Rent
A13  Total Expenses
A15  Net Income/Loss
```

Refer to Figure 3.1 to be sure your screen matches the figure.

EDITING TEXT

Making your worksheet look the best it can with accurate data is very important. Consequently, you'll probably spend a great deal of time editing and revising your worksheets. Let's take a look at some of the methods used to make editing easy.

Editing by Retyping

One of the easiest ways of editing cells that contain very little data is to simply click on the cell and begin typing. The new information you type will replace the data that was originally there. This works great for cells with little data. Let's try it.

1. Click on cell A4, which contains <u>Income</u>.
2. We want to abbreviate it to read <u>Inc.</u> so simply type **Inc.**
3. Press **Enter**.

That was pretty easy. <u>Inc.</u> has now replaced <u>Income</u>.

   But now you decide that it looked better spelled after all. Let's change it back.

1. Click or arrow to cell A4, which contains <u>Inc.</u>
2. Type **Income** and press the **Enter** key.

Editing Entries in the Cell

You may want to make revisions to a cell that contains more than one or two words or data. Your cells may contain sentence-long and paragraph-long data. You may, however, need to revise only one word or number and you may want not to retype the whole entry. For example, suppose you decide that you want to spell out the word *Corp.* in your worksheet title. This can be done with a few keystrokes.

1. Click on cell **A1**.
2. Use your **Right Arrow** key to position your cursor between the letter *p* and the period in *Corp.*

3. Press your **Delete** key once and type **oration**.

4. Press **Enter** to accept the change.

Try out some of editing commands in Table 3.1 when revising or editing entries in a cell or formula bar (see below concerning formula bars) that contain a lot of data.

TABLE 3.1 EDITING COMMANDS

Action	Result
Arrow	Moves cursor in the direction of the arrow
Home	Moves cursor to the beginning of the current line
End	Moves cursor to the end of the current line
Control-Arrows	Moves cursor to the beginning of a word or segment in the direction of the arrow
Control-Delete	Deletes data to the right of the cursor
Shift-End	Highlights data to the right of the cursor
Shift-Arrows	Highlights data in the direction of the arrow
Delete	Deletes data to the right of the cursor
Backspace	Deletes data to the left of the cursor

Editing Entries in the Formula Bar

You can also edit information in the formula bar rather than in the cell itself. The *formula bar* is the area at the top of the screen that displays the information in the cell. Suppose you've changed your mind again and decide that you really want the word *Corporation* abbreviated after all. These are the steps you would use to edit the title using the formula bar.

1. Click on cell A1.

2. Click between the letters *p* and *o* in the word Corporation inside the formula bar and, while holding down the mouse button, drag to highlight the rest of the word. See Figure 3.5.

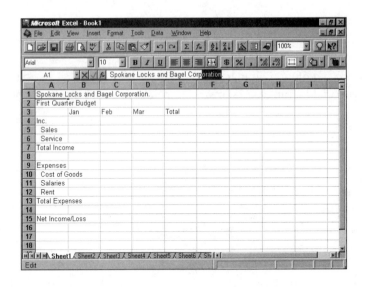

FIGURE 3.5 EDITING AN ENTRY INSIDE THE FORMULA BAR.

3. Tap the **Delete** key to delete the highlighted letters (**oration**).

4. Press **Enter** to accept the change.

See Chapter 5, "Modifying a Worksheet," for more editing functions such as copying and moving.

ENTERING NUMBERS

Entering numbers is done in the same way as entering text. What you see on-screen depends on what sort of number you enter. For example, if you enter **100**, the screen displays 100. If you enter **100.43** the screen displays 100.43. But if you enter **100.00**, the screen displays 100 without the decimal point or trailing zeros. Here's another example. Suppose you enter **100000000**. It is displayed as 1E+08. Hey, what the heck is going on here?

Let me reassure you that Excel isn't actually changing the number you enter, just the way it is displayed. The actual number you enter in the cell is used in any calculations Excel performs. Now, here's what's happening. Excel formats numbers using what it calls *General formatting*. General formatting doesn't display trailing zeros after a decimal point and converts very large numbers to scientific notation, which uses exponents.

The way numbers (or text, for that matter) are formatted can be changed to suit your taste and requirements. The techniques for changing cell formatting are covered in the next chapter.

N O T E

Let's start entering the numbers displayed in Figure 3.6 in the budget worksheet.

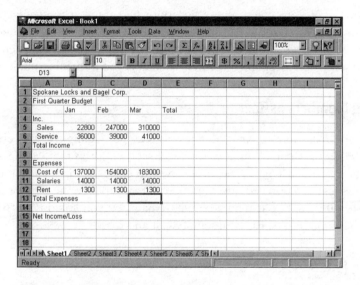

FIGURE 3.6 THE BUDGET WORKSHEET WITH ITS INITIAL NUMBERS ENTERED.

1. Move to cell B5 and type **228000** and press **Enter**.

The text entries you made earlier were aligned at the left side of the cell. Excel aligns numbers at the right side of the cell. Just like most settings in Excel, these default settings can be changed; you will learn how in the next chapter.

N O T E

2. Fill in the remaining numbers in the appropriate cells as shown in Figure 3.6.

Characters Used when Entering Numbers

When entering numbers you may use any numeric characters from **0** to **9**. You may also use the following special characters:

```
+ - ( ) , / $ % . E e
```

For example, you can type a minus sign prior to a number to create a negative number. A percent sign after the number makes it a percentage value. These characters will be discussed in more detail later in this chapter, when we talk about formulas, and in Chapter 4, when we talk about formatting numbers.

Entering Numbers as Text

At times, you may want to enter numbers as text. For example, if you enter a zip code of **05468** in General number format, Excel will drop the leading zero and display the zip code as 5468. The easiest way to enter the zip code (or any other number) as text is to precede the number with an apostrophe ('). For example, if you enter '**05468**, the leading zero will remain. Or you could type "**05468**" to achieve the same results. Go to an empty cell and try it.

Entering Fractions

Fractions must be entered as *mixed numbers*—that is, as integer values that contain fractions. For example, if you wanted to enter one-third, you would enter **0 1/3** not **1/3**. If you were to enter **1/3**, Excel 95 would think that you are entering a date of January 3. If you were to enter **5/95** for five–ninety-fifths, Excel 95 would think that you are entering a date of May 1995. Always enter fractions as mixed numbers to prevent unwanted results.

You can also enter fractions as decimal values. For example the fraction 2/5 equals .4 in decimal value. If you enter the fraction **0 2/5** into a cell, the formula bar will display the value .4 for that cell. This shows you both the fraction and the decimal value. Excel converts the fraction automatically for its own purposes.

Entering Dates and Times

Excel 95 recognizes certain entries as date entries as seen above. Date entries can be used in various mathematical calculations. For example, you can determine the number of days between one date and another or you could calculate 30 days from a date to a new date.

Excel 95 uses a serial numbering system for calculating dates. The dating system begins with January 1, 1900; its serial number equals 1. The serial number of January 2, 1900, equals 2, and so on.

Because mathematical calculations can be performed on dates, it's important to look at the date format Excel uses when you type them. You can go to a blank area of your worksheet and try various ways of inputting dates and see how Excel treats them.

Table 3.2 shows Excel display of formatting dates.

TABLE 3.2 EXCEL DATES

You Type This	Excel Displays
June 15, 1995	15-Jun-95
6/15/95	6/15/95
15 June 95	15-Jun-95
15-June-95	15-Jun-95
June-95	Jun-95
Jun-95	Jun-95
6-95	Jun-95

N O T E   Once you've chosen a format, the cell will remember it, and any other value you enter in the cell will adhere to that format unless you change it manually using the **Cell** command in the Format menu and options on the Number tab. Therefore, when you experiment with these dates, make sure you use a fresh cell for each one.

Excel handles times in a similar manner to dates. Just as a date entry is stored as a serial number, a time entry is stored as a time serial number. The serial number is a decimal fraction of a 24-hour period beginning at midnight (12:00 a.m.). Therefore, noon (12:00 p.m.) is one-half of the day and the time serial number would be .5.

Enter the following times in separate blank cells and see how Excel handles them:

```
17:32
5:32
5:32:25
17:32:25
5:32 PM
5:32 AM
12 am
```

NOTE

The default format for time in Excel is 24-hour format. Therefore, 9.30 p.m. should be entered as either **21.30** of **9.30** with the **pm** at the end.

In the sample worksheet, the column headings Jan, Feb, and Mar are not technically date values; they are text labels. You know this because they align themselves with the left side of the cell, as all text entries do. Date values entered in one of the date formats in Table 3.2 align themselves with the right side of the cell, as do numbers. Try replacing the text entries with date values in the sample worksheet as follows:

1. Move to cell B3 and type the date value **Jan-95**. Don't press **Enter** (or move back to cell B3 if you do).

2. Click on the lower-right corner of the cell (the fill handle) and drag it to cell D3.

The cells now contain date entries and are aligned with the right sides of the cells. See Chapter 4 to learn how to use date and time functions.

TIP

If you want to see the actual numbers Excel is using to keep track of dates and times, you can format the cells to General format instead of the default date format. Chapter 6 covers formatting cells.

CELL/REFERENCE NOTES

At times, you may want to write yourself a note on your worksheet and you don't want to have it cluttering your work area. It could be a note about a particular formula, a comment about formatting, or anything else.

Entering Notes

With Excel 95 you can write extensive notes and not have them clutter your worksheet. Let's see how this works.

1. Click on cell B15.
2. Select **Note** from the Insert menu.
3. Type **This value will equals the total income minus the total expenses** and click **Add** and then click **OK** (see Figure 3.7).

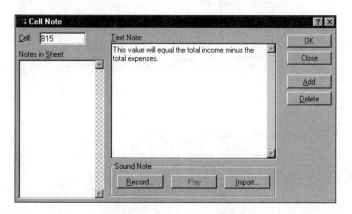

FIGURE 3.7 ENTERING A NOTE IN EXCEL 95.

4. Now select cell B3.
5. Select **Note** from the Insert menu.
6. Type **I learned how to produce months without having to type each one** and click **Add** and then click **OK**.
7. Press your **Right Arrow** key twice.

You should see a red dot in Cell B15 and Cell B3 which indicates a note exists in those cells. To view the notes, simply move the cell pointer onto the cell containing the red dot. Do not click the mouse button, just move the arrow pointer to the cell. Soon the note will appear, as shown in Figure 3.8.

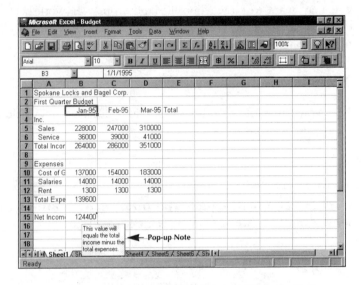

FIGURE 3.8 DISPLAYING A CELL NOTE.

If you want to change the note, follow these steps:

1. Select **Note** from the Insert menu.
2. Click on the cell you want to view from the Notes in Sheet box.
3. Edit the note in the Text Note box, then click **OK**.

The note will be displayed in the Text Note box, and your changes will appear in the worksheet when you view the note.

Turning On/Off Note Indicator

The red dot in the upper-right-hand corner of a cell indicating a note can be turned off (or on) by following these simple steps:

1. Select **Options** from the Tools menu.
2. Select the **View** menu tab.
3. Click on the **Note Indicator** to toggle between selecting and deselecting.

4. Press **Enter**.

NOTE

This does not delete the note. It only removes the note indicator from the cells.

Deleting Notes

To delete notes:

1. Select **Note** from the Insert menu.
2. Select the cell containing the note you want deleted. The cells appear on the left side of the dialog box.
3. Click on **Delete**.
4. A message appears saying the note will be permanently deleted.
5. Click **OK** to delete and then **OK** to exit Cell Note.

CREATING FORMULAS

Formulas are a spreadsheet's *raison d'etre*. If all we needed to do was to put text and numbers in rows and columns, just about any word processing program would fill the bill. Formulas allow us to perform calculations using values from any cells and to have the result appear in the formula cell.

You build formulas using the four mathematical operators:

◆ The plus sign (+).
◆ The minus sign (–).
◆ The asterisk (*) for multiplication.
◆ The slash (/) for division.

You always start a formula by moving to an empty cell where you want the results of the formula to appear and typing the equal sign (=), which tells Excel to get ready for a formula. For example, you could type the formula **=2*2** in a cell and, after completing the cell entry, the cell would display the result of the formula as 4, but the formula bar displays the formula.

At this point, you know how to use your fancy spreadsheet program like a pocket calculator. Big deal, you say. Well, the real power of formulas comes into play when you use cell referencing. Instead of entering a formula using values, you can enter a formula using cell references, such as **=C12*D14**. If 2 is the value in both C12 or D14, the result is still 4. However, if the values in C12 and D14 change, the result automatically changes as well.

Let's create the formula for January's Total Income in our budget worksheet. The formula adds the values in cells B5 and B6.

1. Move to cell B7 and type **=B5+B6**, then click the **Enter** box to complete the cell entry while keeping B7 as the active cell.

   If you originally entered the values in B5 and B6 as specified (and I know that you did), cell B7 now displays the value <u>264000</u>, while the formula bar displays the formula, <u>=B5+B6</u>, as shown in Figure 3.9.

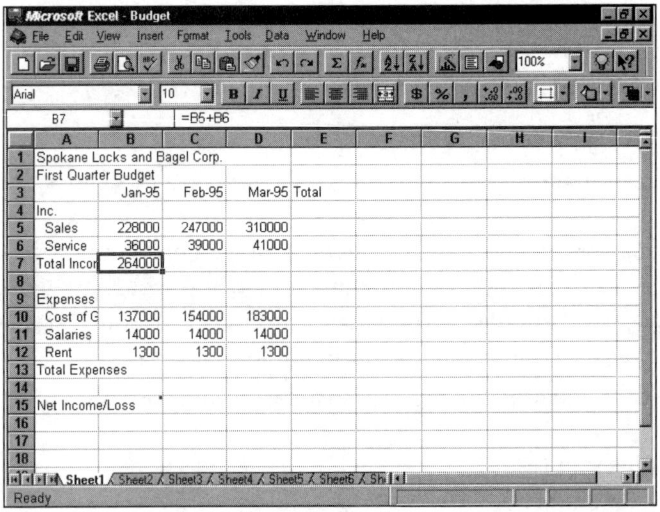

FIGURE 3.9 A FORMULA AND ITS RESULT.

Now, let's try a different method of specifying the cells to be included in a formula. We'll use the pointing method to click on the cells we want to include, thus eliminating any possibility of entering an incorrect cell reference. To create the formula for January's Total Expenses, do the following.

2. Move to cell B13 and start the formula by typing **=**.

3. Click on cell B10 to let Excel know that B10 is the first cell you want to include in the formula.

   The beginning of the formula (=B10) followed by the insertion point appears in the formula cell, and a dashed border appears around B10, as displayed in Figure 3.10.

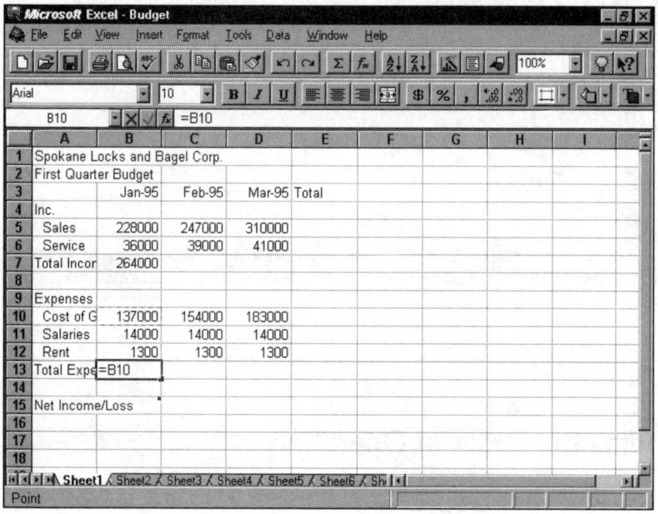

FIGURE 3.10 THE BEGINNING OF A FORMULA USING THE POINTING METHOD.

4. Type **+** then click on cell B11, type **+** again and click on cell B12.

5. Click on the **Enter** box or press the **Enter** key to accept the formula.

   In this example, pointing may not appear more advantageous than just typing in the cell references, but when dealing with more distant cell references or specifying ranges of cells, pointing can make a substantial difference. I think you'll start to see the advantage of pointing as we create the formula for January's Net Income/Loss.

6. Move to cell B15 and type **=**.

7. Click on cell B7 (January's Total Income), then type **−** (the minus sign). Now click on cell B13 (January's Total Expenses) and press **Enter**.

With the three formulas entered, your screen should now look like Figure 3.11.

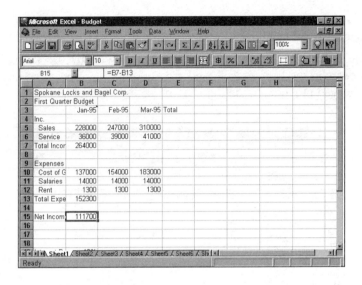

FIGURE 3.11 THE BUDGET WORKSHEET.

Understanding the Order of Operation

When using more than one operator in a single formula, it's important to understand in which order the operations are performed to achieve the desired result. Table 3.3 shows Excel's default order of operation.

TABLE 3.3 ORDER OF OPERATION

Operator	Description
-	Negative (as in -34)
%	Percent
^	Exponentiation
* and /	Multiplication and division
+ and -	Addition and subtraction
&	Text joining/concatenation
= < > <= >= <>	Comparison or relations

The order of an operation can be changed by using parenthesis and creating expressions. All expressions inside parenthesis are performed first. Look at the different results based on the order of operation of the following formula entered with and without parentheses:

=4+8*10	produces the value of	84
=(4+8)*10	produces the value of	120

UNDERSTANDING AND USING FUNCTIONS

Think of *functions* as predefined formulas. Using just the four mathematical operators, you could duplicate just about any of the supplied Excel functions. It might take a long time to re-create a function with the math operators, particularly for some of the more complicated functions. Just as importantly, you'd have to go through the same process every time you wanted to use the formula.

Perhaps the most common function is the *SUM* function, which adds the values in a range of cells. Most functions require *arguments*, contained within parentheses, which are just pieces of information the function needs to complete the calculation. Only one argument is required for the SUM function—the range of cells to be added.

One advantage of using the SUM function (versus specifying plus signs between each cell reference) is that it's just plain easier. Using the plus signs between each cell reference can become very unwieldy for a large range of cells. For example, don't you think that

    =C2+C3+C4+C5+C6+C7+C8+C9+C10+C11+C12

is much more cumbersome and error-prone than

    =SUM(C2:C12).

The colon between the two cell references in the argument is the *separator*. It means through, as in C2 through C12.

Also, using the range argument makes it easier to insert or delete cells in the range without having to modify the function's argument. Let's say you needed to add a row for a new category within the range of C2 through C12. If you had used the SUM function, the new row would automatically be included in the range.

Let's use the SUM function to calculate February's Total Income.

1. Move to cell C7 and type **=SUM(**

    You are now ready to enter the range of cells to be totaled. Of course we'll use the pointing method to enter the range, and we can do it in one fell swoop.

2. Point to cell C5, drag down to cell C6, and release the mouse button. A dashed border surrounds the range of cells, C5 through C6, and the cell references have been entered after the left parenthesis, as shown in Figure 3.12.

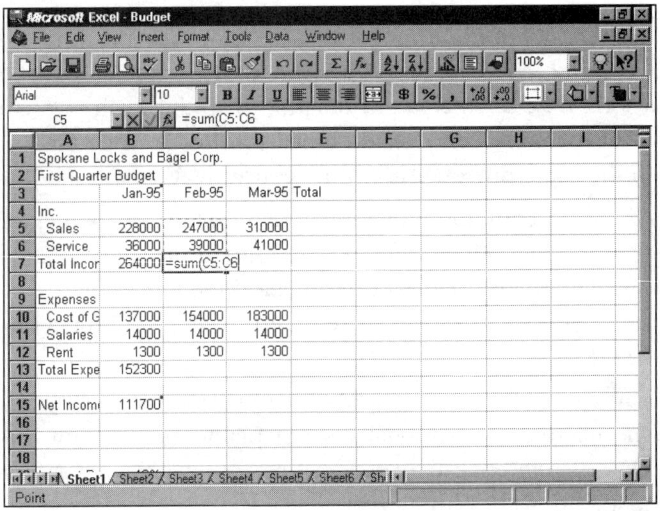

FIGURE 3.12 THE BEGINNING OF THE SUM FUNCTION WITH ITS ARGUMENT.

I know you think the next step is to enter the right parenthesis. Not so fast. Excel is so smart that it usually knows when a closing parenthesis is required and enters it for you when you complete the cell entry. Let's try it.

3. Press **Enter** to complete the cell entry.

    The result of the function's calculation appears in cell C7 (286000), and the function with its argument and both parentheses appears in the formula bar.

Now get ready for some Excel magic. Most of the time, when you want to SUM a range of numbers, you don't even need to enter the function or specify the range. You can put Excel's brains to work and let it figure out the proper range to sum. Let's try to SUM the March Total Income.

1. Click in cell D7.

2. Click on the **AutoSum** button on the toolbar. The SUM function is automatically entered and the closest contiguous range (D5 through D6) is specified as the argument, as shown in Figure 3.13.

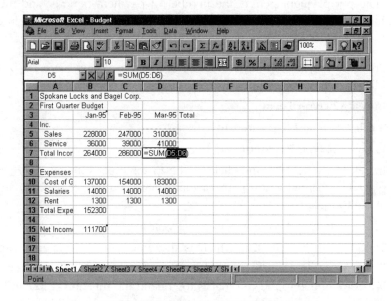

FIGURE 3.13 USING THE **AUTOSUM** BUTTON.

3. Press the **Enter** key to complete the entry.

SHORTCUT If you are sure that Excel will select the correct range for the argument, you can double-click on the **AutoSum** button, and the entry is completed for you. This isn't too dangerous, even if the wrong range is selected. You can always delete and start over.

Okay, that was pretty easy, but what about all those other functions that are hidden away somewhere in Excel? Don't worry, they aren't too hidden. In the following steps, I'll show you how easy it is to find just the function you need.

Let's use one of the more complex functions—one that requires several arguments to see what the monthly payments would be for a new piece of equipment the Spokane Locks and Bagel Corporation is thinking of purchasing. It's one of those fancy new combination key-duplicator-and-cream-cheese-spreading machines.

The function we'll use is the *PMT* function which calculates the payments if we simply supply a few arguments. The information we need to supply is the interest rate per payment period, the number of payment periods, and the present value (the amount of the loan). We'll enter those three pieces of information onto the budget worksheet now.

1. Press the **PageDown** key if needed to move to a new screenful of rows. Click in cell A19 and type **Interest Rate**.

2. In cell A20 type **Term**.

3. n cell A21 type **Loan Amount**.

4. In cell A22 type **Payment**.

5. In cell B19 type **10%** and click on the **Enter** box. Notice that 10% is displayed in the cell and 0.1 (the actual value used in calculations) appears in the formula bar.

6. In cell B20, type **5** to represent a five-year loan period.

7. Type **28500** in cell B21, which is the amount the company wants to finance over the five-year period.

   We could move to the cell that is to contain the function (B22) and enter the function name and the appropriate arguments, but with three arguments required, it can be difficult to remember what goes where. Never fear! Excel Function Wizard to the rescue. Excel includes several *wizards*—specialized help systems that take you by the hand and step you through some of the more mysterious procedures. Wizards are covered later in the book, in Chapter 4, and the Function Wizard is one of the most useful.

   You can invoke the Function Wizard in a variety of ways. Choosing **Insert: Function** will do it, or you can click on the **Function Wizard** toolbar button, which is what we'll do now.

8. Click in cell B22 and then click on the **Function Wizard** button on the toolbar.

   If the Function Wizard dialog box obscures the values in column B, point to its title bar, drag to the right about an inch, and release the mouse button.

If the function you want is visible in the Function Name list on the right side of the dialog box (see Figure 3.14), you can click on it. Otherwise, click on the category of functions you think your function might be in and then use the scroll bar to find it.

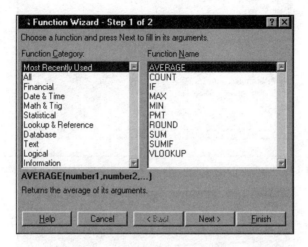

FIGURE 3.14 THE FUNCTION WIZARD DIALOG BOX.

We'll go through the steps to find the PMT as if it weren't visible and we didn't know what category to choose.

9. Click on **All** in the Function Category list to display all the available functions in every category.

10. Click on any of the functions in the Function Name list.

11. Use the scrollbar to scroll down the list until PMT is visible, and click on it.

You can type the first letter of the function name, and the highlighter jumps to it. Then you only have to search through the functions that start with that letter.

SHORTCUT

With **PMT** selected, the Function Wizard dialog box displays the proper syntax for the function and, below that, a brief explanation of what the function does, as displayed in Figure 3.15.

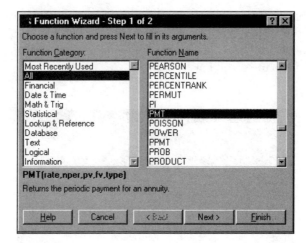

FIGURE 3.15 THE FUNCTION WIZARD DIALOG BOX WITH THE **PMT** FUNCTION SELECTED.

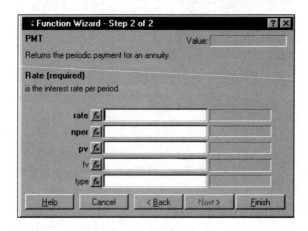

FIGURE 3.16 THE FUNCTION WIZARD DIALOG BOX FOR ENTERING ARGUMENTS.

If you want to enter the arguments manually, you can click on the **Finish** button, but it's much easier to let the Wizard step you through the argument entry process.

12. Click on the **Next** button to proceed to the Function Wizard dialog box that lets you enter the arguments, as shown in Figure 3.16.

The insertion point is in the rate text box. Just above and to the left of the text box, the dialog box lets you know that you are ready to enter the rate per period and that this entry is a required argument.

You could type the cell reference for the rate, but it's easier to point and click.

13. Click on cell B19 (the interest rate). <u>B19</u> is entered in the rate text box and <u>0.1</u> is entered in the box to the right of the text box. We need to make an adjustment here. Remember that the rate the function needs is the rate per period. Since we want to determine the monthly payment and 10% is an annual rate, we need to divide it by 12.

14. Type **/12**. The rate in the box to the right now displays the monthly interest rate, <u>0.0083333333</u>.

15. Press the **Tab** key to move to the nper (number of payment periods) text box and click on cell B20. Again we need to modify the entry. Cell B20 contains the number of years for the loan and we want the number of months, so we need to multiply by 12.

16. Type ***12**. The value to the right of the text box now displays the value <u>60</u>, which is the correct number of months.

17. Press the **Tab** key to move to the pv (present value) text box and click on cell B21. This entry doesn't need to be altered, and the dialog box should now look like Figure 3.17. The fv (future value) and type arguments are optional, and we won't use them. With all the required arguments entered, the dialog box displays the value <u>$605.54</u> in the upper-right corner. This is the result of the calculation that appears in cell B22 when we are finished.

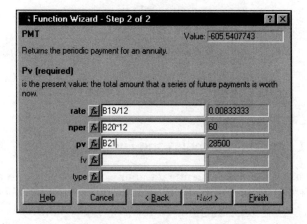

FIGURE 3.17 The filled-in dialog box.

18. Click on the **Finish** button to complete the Function Wizard procedure. Figure 3.18 shows the result.

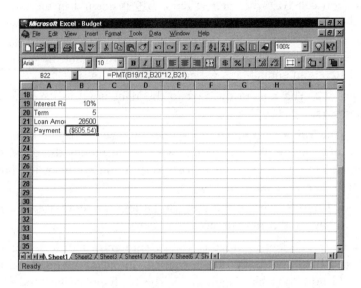

FIGURE 3.18 THE RESULT OF THE PMT FUNCTION.

The value in cell B22 is in parentheses and in red (if you have a color monitor) to let you know that this is a negative value. The monthly payment is negative because it results in an outflow from the business. If this were money being received, it would be positive.

You may have to make your column width wider to display the full column.

N O T E

Editing and Correcting Formulas and Functions

Suppose you made a mistake entering a formula or function. Go to an empty cell and type **=a3+** and press **Enter**. Excel 95 will display an error message stating: <u>Error in formula: missing operand</u> and then will highlight the existing operand. The most common mistakes made in formulas are missing equal signs at the beginning of the formula, extra or missing parenthesis, or missing arguments.

Some formula entries will *not* display an error message. Instead, Excel 95 may produce an error value inside the cell itself. The error value is a message that tells you why the formula doesn't work. See Table 3.4 for an explanation of these error values.

TABLE 3.4 ERROR VALUES AND EXPLANATIONS

Error Value	Explanation
#DIV/0!	Attempting to divide by zero
#NAME?	Cell or range name not known
#VALUE!	Value unknown or uses argument or operand incorrectly.
#NUM!	Invalid number or number is used incorrectly.
#REF!	Refers to an invalid cell
#####	The result produce is too long to fit inside of cell.

SAVING YOUR WORK

Perhaps the most important habit to learn and use is to *save your work on a regular basis.* Until you save, the data you enter or edit is in your computer's temporary memory, called *RAM* (*random access memory*). Okay, so what's the definition of regular basis? Often enough that, if you lost all the work you had done since the last time you saved, you wouldn't be too upset.

Excel stores worksheets in files called *workbooks.* Within a single workbook, you can have many worksheets, all of which are saved to your computer's disk when you save. You don't need to specify which sheet or portions of a sheet you want to save.

The first time you save a workbook, you are presented with several questions. You need to assign a filename and, if you like, fill in a Summary dialog box with more detailed information about the workbook. Let's save the workbook that contains the worksheet we've been working on with the name BUDGET. Excel automatically assigns the name BOOK1.XLS to its first blank unnamed workbook, so that's likely the name you see on your title bar now.

1.   Choose **File: Save As**. The Save As dialog box appears, as displayed in Figure 3.19.

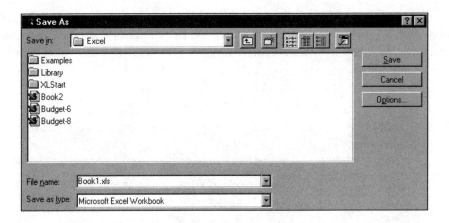

FIGURE 3.19 THE SAVE AS DIALOG BOX.

2. In the File Name text box, type **budget**. The Directories list box tells you which directory your workbook will be saved in. A *directory* is like a file folder on your disk that allows you to organize your files, just as you would in a file cabinet. If you want to save in a directory other than the one specified, double-click on the top-level file folder in the list (usually **C:**), then scroll to the directory you want to use and double-click on it.

If you want to save to a drive other than the one specified in the Drives drop-down list box, as would be the case if you wanted to save to a floppy disk in drive A or B, click on the list box arrow and then click on the appropriate drive letter from the list.

3. Click on the **Save** button.

The Budget Properties Info dialog box appears, as shown in Figure 3.20, with the author's name already filled in. The *author* is the name of the registered user of the program. You can fill in additional information that might help you locate the workbook when you're looking for it later. You can enter any combination of title, subject, or comments. Also, the Keywords entry box lets you type special words that will help you identify the document for later use. These extra pieces of information are useful if you plan to save dozens of files in the same folder—you can then use the **Advanced** options of the Open dialog box to search for a file using any of these pieces of information.

4. Click on the **OK** button to finish saving your workbook.

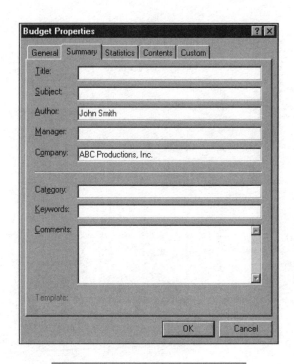

FIGURE 3.20 THE SUMMARY INFO DIALOG BOX.

As you work in Excel, entering and editing data, you'll want to save often, perhaps every ten or twenty minutes. The fastest way to do this is to click on the **Save** toolbar button. The saved file on your disk is automatically replaced with the updated version, and you won't even have to confirm that you want to replace it.

5. Double-click on the document's control menu box to close the document, and then exit Excel if you aren't continuing on to the next chapter immediately.

A FINAL THOUGHT

With what you have learned in this chapter, you already know as much as 80% of the spreadsheet users out there, and you are ready to put Excel to productive use. Give yourself a pat on the back.

In the next chapter, you will learn to make some modifications to your worksheet, including inserting and deleting data, and copying formulas.

EXPLORING MORE EXCEL FUNCTIONS

- ♦ More about functions
- ♦ Exploring additional functions
- ♦ Working with dates and times

MORE ABOUT FUNCTIONS

Functions are the workhorse of Excel. In Excel you'll find a function for practically every need. There may be times when you'll have to devise your own formulas from scratch, but it won't be very often. In this chapter, you'll learn the different categories of functions, how to find help using a function, and have some hands-on experience of using various functions. This chapter cannot explain everything there is to know about functions—entire books have been written on the subject. But we hope to cover enough ground so that you will understand the concepts for putting more complex functions to work.

N O T E Several of the functions are presented in the context of our example business, the Spokane Locks and Bagel Corporation. However, each is used in a separate worksheet rather than using them to build one huge sheet. You are instructed to move to a new worksheet in a workbook for each function.

Function Categories

Although you can recreate the capabilities of most of the functions by using the operators discussed in the previous chapter, you save time and reduce errors if you track down the function that does the job for you. To better help you find the function that will work best for you, Excel functions are divided into separate categories. Table 4.1 lists the categories in which the functions are classified by and gives a brief description of each.

TABLE 4.1 FUNCTION CATEGORIES

Function	Categories
Database	Functions used to process data.
Date and Time	Functions used to do mathematical calculations on date and time.
Engineering	Functions used to do calculations on engineering values.

Function	Categories
Financial	Functions used to determine values as they relate to such things as loans and depreciations.
Information	Functions that help you determine the type of data in a cell, or if any data exist in a cell.
Logical	Functions that perform logical and conditional tests.
Lookup and Reference	Functions that will analyze tables to help you locate various values utilizing search features.
Mathematical	Functions that perform simple and complex mathematical calculations.
Statistical	Functions that perform statistical analysis on data.
Text	Functions that alter text as oppose to numbers.

If you are not sure which function to use for a particular task, look through the categories for a logical choice. Then do some browsing. Click on the **Function Wizard** button and look through the functions in the category that seems to match your needs. You will see a brief description of the function at the bottom of the Function Wizard dialog box.

Parts of a Function

Every function must have four parts. They are:

♦ An equal sign
♦ Function name
♦ Parentheses (open and close)
♦ Arguments

The most common error in entering functions manually is the omission of the equal sign. Take a look at the following example of a function and see if you can identify all four parts:

```
= SUM ( F8:F10 )
```

The equal sign and parentheses are easy to locate. "SUM" is the function name while "F8:F10" is the argument.

The rest of this chapter will provide you with step-by-step instructions in using and understanding certain functions. With other functions, we will simply explain their use and you can experiment with them on your own. The function categories are in parentheses.

Using the NPER Function (Financial)

The NPER (number of payment periods) function lets you calculate how many payment periods are required to amortize a loan. Suppose the Spokane Locks and Bagel Corporation is thinking about purchasing that nifty piece of equipment discussed in the previous chapter, but they determine they can only afford monthly payments of, say, $575.00. They can figure out how long they'll be in hock for this purchase by using the NPER function.

1. Start Excel if it is not running.
2. If a workbook containing data is on the screen, click on the **New Workbook** button on the Standard toolbar to display a blank workbook.

   The title bar of a new workbook displays the name **Book** followed by the number of the workbook. If you were working on the BUDGET workbook, and that was the first workbook you used in the current Excel session, clicking on the **New Workbook** button causes the title bar to display Microsoft Excel-Book2.
3. In cell A1, type **Interest Rate**.
4. Move to cell A2 and type **Payment**.
5. Move to cell A3 and type **Loan Amount**.
6. Move to cell A4 and type **Number of Payments**.

 We have increased the width of column A to accommodate the longest entries. It is not necessary to do this for your practice sheets. If you can not wait to learn how to change column widths, it is covered

N O T E   in the section entitled *Using the NOW Function*, later in the chapter.

---

7. In cell B1, type **10%**.
8. In cell B2, type **–575**.

The minus sign is important because this is an expense (money going out) rather than income.

9. In cell B3, type **28500**.

10. Move to cell B4, where the result of the function's calculation appears, and click on the **Function Wizard** button on the Standard toolbar.

   The first Function Wizard dialog box appears.

11. In the Function Category list of the Function Wizard dialog box, click on **Financial**.

12. In the Function Name list, click on **NPER**, then click on the **Next** button.

   The second Function Wizard dialog box appears, with the argument text boxes for the NPER function, as shown in Figure 4.1. If the dialog box obscures the entries you made on the worksheet, move it out of the way by dragging it by its title bar.

   You can get more detailed information about the use and proper syntax for a function by clicking on the **Help** button in the Function Wizard.

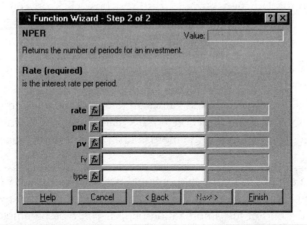

FIGURE 4.1 THE FUNCTION WIZARD DIALOG BOX STEP 2 OF 2 FOR THE NPER FUNCTION.

13. Click on the **Help** button.

   The help screen appears, as shown in Figure 4.2. Remember, you can click on the **Maximize** button on the far right side of the help screen's title bar to enlarge it.

14. After you finish perusing the Help screen, double-click on the **Control** menu box on the left side of the Help screen's title bar.

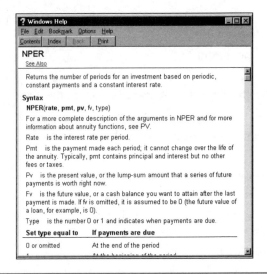

FIGURE 4.2 THE MICROSOFT EXCEL HELP SCREEN FOR THE NPER FUNCTION.

15. Click in the Function Wizard's **rate** text box, click on cell **B1**, then type **/12** to convert the annual interest rate to a monthly rate.

16. Press the **Tab** key to move the insertion point to the pmt text box, then click on cell **B2**.

17. Press the Tab key, then click on cell **B3**.

    Now that the three required values are entered, the answer appears in the Value portion of the Function Wizard dialog box. It is going to take a little more than 64 months to amortize this piece of equipment.

We are not using the two optional parameters—future value and type. You can use *future value* to enter a dollar amount you want to reach at the end of the amortization period. The *type* parameter determines

N O T E whether the payments are made at the beginning or end of each payment period.

18. Click on the **Finish** button to accept the entries you have made in the Function Wizard.

    Before moving to the next worksheet to explore another function, we name the sheet. Each sheet in a workbook can have its own name, replacing the default Sheet1, Sheet2, and Sheet3 that appear on the sheet tabs.

19. Move the mouse pointer to the sheet tab for this worksheet and right-click (click the right mouse button).

    The sheet shortcut menu pops up, as shown in Figure 4.3.

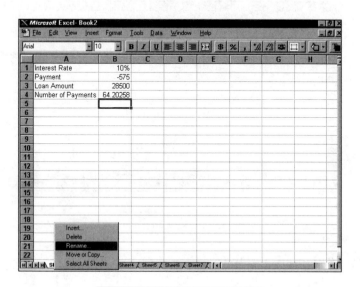

FIGURE 4.3 THE SHEET SHORTCUT MENU.

20. Click on the **Rename** button in the shortcut menu.

    The Rename Sheet dialog box appears, as shown in Figure 4.4.

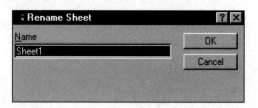

FIGURE 4.4 THE RENAME SHEET DIALOG BOX.

21. Type **Loan Length**, then click **OK.**

    The sheet tab now displays the new sheet name, as shown in Figure 4.5.

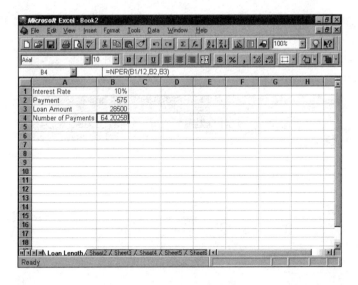

FIGURE 4.5 THE RENAMED SHEET TAB.

Using the PV Function (Financial)

The PV (Present Value) function helps you determine what future cash flows are worth in today's dollars. Suppose Spokane Locks and Bagels is considering investing $10,000 of its cash reserves in a fixed rate annuity that returns three annual payments of $4,000.

Sounds good. After all, $4,000 times 3 is $12,000. That's a two thousand dollar profit. There's an opportunity cost. If you figure that Spokane Locks and Bagel Corp. could get 8% by just parking the money in CDs, then how do the two investments compare? The PV function tells us.

1. Click on the **Sheet2** tab to bring a blank worksheet into view.

2. In cell A1, type **Initial Investment**.

   The initial investment is not used as one of the arguments in the PV function. We are just putting it on the worksheet for reference.

3. In cell A2, type **Interest Rate**.

4. In cell A3, type **Number of Payments**.

5. In cell A4, type **Payment**.

6. In cell A5, type **Present Value**.

7. In cell B1, type **$10,000**.

8. In cell B2, type **8%**.

9. In cell B3, type **3**.

10. In cell B4, type **4000**.

11. Move to cell B5, where the result of the function's calculation appears, and click the **Function Wizard** button on the Standard toolbar.

12. Be sure Financial is highlighted in the Function Category list, then click on **PV** in the Function Name list, then click the **Next** button.

13. Click in cell **B2**, the cell containing the interest rate.

14. Press the Tab key, then click in cell **B3**, the cell containing the number of payments.

    Notice the name of the argument for the number of payments is nper (for number of periods), just like the NPER function discussed in the previous section.

15. Press the **Tab** key again and click in cell **B4**, the cell containing the annual payment amount.

16. Click the **Finish** button.

N O T E   As in the previous examples, if you use the default column widths, some of the text in column A are truncated. Even worse, the result of the formula in cell B5 is too wide to fit and is therefore represented by number signs (#####). You can adjust the column width by positioning the mouse pointer on the right column heading border and then dragging. For more information about adjusting column widths, take a look at the next chapter.

---

17. Name the worksheet **Present Value**.

    Ah ha! The investment appears to be a good one, as you can see in Figure 4.6.

    If you need a reminder of how to rename a sheet, look at steps 19 through 21 in the previous section.

18. Save the workbook by clicking the **Save** button on the Standard toolbar. Enter **FUNCPRAC** (for function practice) in the File Name text box and then click **OK**.

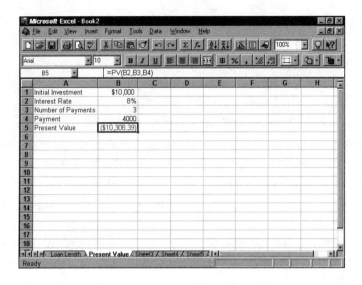

FIGURE 4.6 THE PRESENT VALUE WORKSHEET.

Using the MIN and MAX Functions (Statistical)

In the group of statistical functions, two of the more common functions are MIN and MAX. These functions return the smallest or largest number in a range. The only argument for these functions is the range or ranges.

Spokane Locks and Bagel Corp. could use these functions to determine which is the lowest or highest priced item in a list of products, or which customer spent the least or the most.

1. Click on the **Sheet3** tab to bring another blank worksheet into view.

2. Name the worksheet **MinMax**.

3. Enter the data in columns A and B on the new worksheet, as shown in Figure 4.7.

4. Click in cell **B8**, where the result of the MIN function appears.

5. Click the **Function Wizard** button.

6. In the Function Wizard dialog box, click on **Statistical** in the Function Category.

7. Scroll down the Function Name list until MIN is visible.

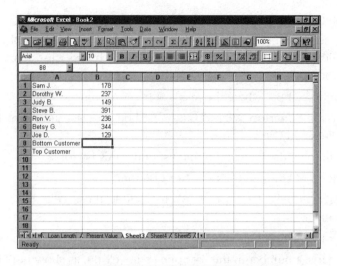

FIGURE 4.7 THE DATA FOR THE MINMAX WORKSHEET.

8. Click on **MIN** and then click the **Next** button.

9. Drag over cells **B1** through **B7** to include those cells in the function's argument.

A dashed line appears around B1 through B7, as shown in Figure 4.8.

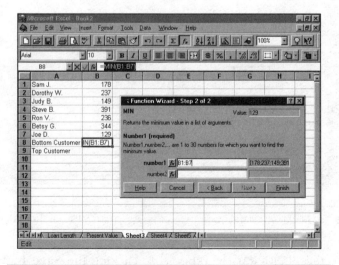

FIGURE 4.8 THE FUNCTION WIZARD DIALOG BOX STEP 2 OF 2 MIN FUNCTION.

10. Click the **Finish** button.

    The smallest number in the list is displayed in cell B8. Obviously this would be a more useful function with a much larger list, but you can see how it works.

11. Move to cell B9, where the result of the MAX function appears.

12. Click the **Function Wizard** button and be sure Statistical is highlighted in the Function Category list.

13. Scroll down the Function Name list until MAX is visible.

14. Click on **MAX**, then click the **Next** button.

15. Drag over cells **B1** through **B7** to include those cells in the function's argument.

16. Click the **Finish** button.

    The largest number in the list appears in cell B9, as shown in Figure 4.9.

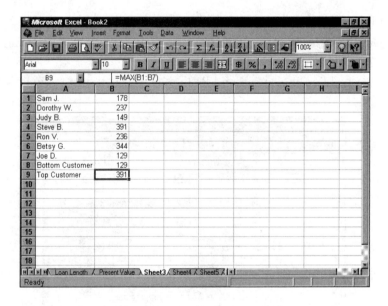

FIGURE 4.9 THE MINMAX WORKSHEET WITH THE RESULTS OF BOTH THE MIN AND THE MAX FUNCTIONS.

17. Save the FUNCPRAC workbook by clicking the **Save** button on the Standard toolbar.

Using the NOW Function (Date and Time)

Excel employs a variety of functions to facilitate date and time calculations. One of the common uses for date calculations is for aging an accounts receivable report. For example, Spokane Locks and Bagel Corp. might use an aged receivable report to determine how long its credit customers are taking to pay their bills. This can be important information, because it is generally true that the longer a past due account remains past due, the less likely it will ever be collected. Calculating the length of time an account is past due could also allow Spokane Locks and Bagel Corp. to tack on late fees.

When you enter dates and times in Excel, they are displayed as dates and times. Makes sense. In fact, you can change the way they are displayed (Chapter 7 covers cell formatting).

As you may remember from Chapter 3, Excel keeps track of dates and times using a systems of numbers. Dates are tracked as serial numbers based on the year 1900, and times are stored as decimal fractions.

1. Click on the **Sheet4** tab to bring another blank worksheet into view.

2. In cell A1, type **=now( )**.

   At this point you are probably looking at (########). The reason the values are not showing is because of the narrow column width. The values need a larger column width in order to be displayed. In the next chapter, you'll learn all about column width adjustments. But for now, in order to see the value of your NOW function, perform the following steps.

3. Make cell A1 the active cell.

4. Select **Column** from the Format menu.

5. Select **AutoFit**.

   You should now be able to see the date and time value from the NOW function.

The NOW function uses the date from your computer's clock/calendar. The parentheses are required, although no argument is entered between them. Of course, you could use the Function Wizard to apply the NOW function, as well as numerous other date and time functions. However, since NOW does not require any arguments, it is just as easy to enter it manually.

NOTE If the incorrect date appears when you move to the next cell, you need to reset your computer's time and date. Many computers use a special method for setting the time and date, so you should check your computer's documentation for instructions.

Now we let Excel calculate what the date is 45 days from now.

♦ In cell A2, type **=now( )+45** and press **Enter**.

The date displayed in A2 is 45 days later than the date displayed in A1. The date and time entries as they should appear on your worksheet are displayed in Figure 4.10. Of course, some of your dates and times may differ, depending on the time and date that is set on your computer.

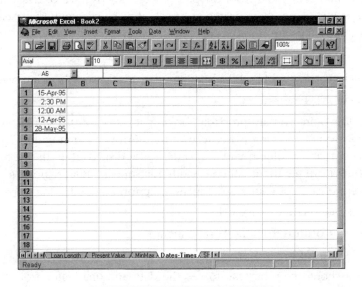

FIGURE 4.10 THE DATES-TIMES WORKSHEET.

Using the IF Function (Logical)

Of all the functions in Excel, the IF function rates triple-A for power. In fact, it's the IF statements in most software programs that really give computers logic and power. We can also use this powerful tool with Excel's IF function. The IF function performs tests to determine if a condition is true or false. If true, then it returns a certain value or takes a certain action, and if false it returns a different value or takes a different action. The following is the syntax for the IF function

IF(condition,value_if_true,value_if_false)

condition	a mathematical expression as a test condition (for example *A1=C2*).
value_if_true	the value of the tested condition if it is true.
value_if_false	the value of the tested condition if it is false.

As seen in the *condition* explanation above, in order for a condition to be true or false it must use certain logical operators. In the above example (A1=C2), the equal sign was the logical operator used to compare the two values. You can use any of the following logical operators to perform comparisons in your IF functions:

>	Greater than
<	Less than
=	Equal to
> =	Greater than or equal to
< =	Less than or equal to
< >	Not equal to

In order to get a sense of how the IF function work, let's create a matrix. At this point, we do not want to create an elaborate IF scenario. We simply want you to have a sense of how the IF function works so that you can use it later with more complex applications. But for now, click on a new sheet, and enter the data shown in Figure 4.11.

A	B	C	D
34	35	183	354
31	883	125	82
68	73	34	64
44	38	35	54

FIGURE 4.11 THE DATA FOR THE IF WORKSHEET.

We will be using this matrix to test certain IF conditions and to see how the IF function returns a value depending upon the tested results. Following the steps below will give you some hands-on experience with the IF function.

1. Make cell A5 the active cell where we'll place our IF function.
2. Click the **Function Wizard** button on the Standard toolbar.
3. Click on **Logical** in the Function Category box.
4. Click on **IF** in the Function Name box and then select **Next**.
5. Click cell **A1** which is automatically entered into the logical_test window.
6. Type **=**.
7. Click cell **C3** which again will be entered in the formula automatically. You have just entered the condition for your IF function using the equal sign as your logical operator.
8. Type: **,"Good","Bad")**. You have just entered the value you want returned if the condition is true or false. Notice the value box in the upper right hand corner reads: GOOD.
9. Click **Finish**.

Cell A5 now reads Good. This is because the IF function you entered tested to see if the value in cell A1 was equal to the value of cell C3. Notice the values in both cells are 34. Therefore, 34 does equal 34. We had our IF formula written so that if the value in cell A1 was equal to the value in cell C3, then return Good which it did. If the value in cell A1 did not equal the value in cell C3, then return Bad.

Let's change the value in cell C3 to make it unequal to the value in cell A1 and see what happens.

1. Click cell **C3**.
2. Type **45**.

What happened? If the word <u>Bad</u> replaced the word <u>Good</u> in cell A5 then your IF function works properly. Now, the value in cell A1 does not equal the value in cell C3. 34 does not equal 45. Therefore, the IF function returned <u>Bad</u> because the tested condition is false. Are you getting a sense of the IF function?

Let's illustrate another example using the IF function.

1. Change cell C3 back to **34** and the word <u>Good</u> reappears in cell A5.
2. Make cell A5 the active cell.
3. Press the right mouse button to bring up the short-cut menu. Click **Copy**.
4. Click into cell **B5**. Click **Paste**.
5. Press your **Esc** key.

Notice the word <u>Bad</u> in cell B5 where you just copied your function. Look in the formula bar and you'll see that the formula for that cell is comparing the values in cells B1 and D3. Since they are not equal and the test result is false, the function returns <u>Bad</u>. Let's try one more technique.

1. Click the formula bar.
2. Delete the equal sign and replace it with the less than operator (<).
3. Press **Enter**.

You have just used the less than logical operator to compare the two values in both cells. The value in cell B1 is less than the value in cell D3 and therefore your function is true and returns <u>Good</u>. In other words, 35 is less than 64.

Continue practicing with your matrix; but don't delete it. You'll use it with the IFBLANK function discussed next. Try out other logical operators and see the results you'll get. The IF function is worth understanding because it is one of Excel's most powerful functions and can be used in conjunction with several other functions.

Using the ISBLANK Function (Informational)

It is probably obvious what this function does. If you said it tests for blank cells, you're absolutely right. Sometimes in a moderate or large worksheet (or sometimes even small worksheets), you'll need to identify cells that have no data in them. The ISBLANK function accomplishes this for you.

The ISBLANK function uses the following simple syntax:

ISBLANK(*cell*)

The ISBLANK function is usually used in conjunction with the IF function as a condition. For example, you could write an IF function that says if the value in cell B3 is blank, then type "missing data" and if the value in cell B3 is not blank, then do nothing.

Let's test the ISBLANK function. Use the same matrix you developed with the IF function. Some of your numbers in the matrix may have changed but that's okay. We're going to test for blank cells as opposed to a certain value. Let's look at how you might combine the ISBLANK function with the IF function. Follow the steps below in creating your ISBLANK function.

1. Use the same matrix developed for the IF function.
2. In cell E1 type **Message =**.
3. In cell F1 type the following IF function using ISBLANK:

    =IF(ISBLANK(B3)=FALSE,"","Missing Data")

Your worksheet should be similar to Figure 4.12 except maybe for some of the values.

The IF function tests to see if the result of the ISBLANK test is true or false for cell B3. If it is false, it should return a blank string (note the two quotation marks), but if it is true, then our <u>Missing Data</u> message appears. Since we have data in cell B3, a blank test string is returned. Let's remove the data and see what happens.

1. Click cell **B3**.
2. Press **Delete** on you keyboard then **Return** or **Enter**.

Notice what happened? Your missing data message appears. This is because the ISBLANK test is now true. Cell B3 has no data and is blank.

As your expertise with Excel improves, you will be able to use both the IF and ISBLANK functions in macros. Using macros with IF and ISBLANK, you can do a complete search of your database for blank cells. You'll see more on macros later in the book.

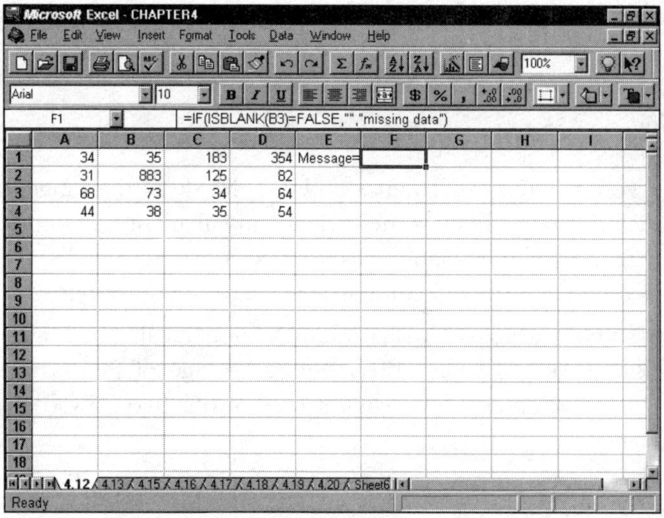

FIGURE 4.12 USING THE ISBLANK FUNCTION.

Using the AVERAGE Function (Statistical)

The AVERAGE function calculates the average, also known as the mean, of a series of numbers by totaling their values and then dividing this total by the number of values. For example, if you wanted to know the bowling average or mean of a person that bowls three games, you would total the scores of the three games and then divide this total by 3, the number of games played. You can use the AVERAGE function to achieve the same result.

The correct syntax of the AVERAGE function is simply:

```
=AVERAGE(numbers)
```

One of the best reasons to use the AVERAGE function is to avoid having to type in long formulas that are prone to error. For example, if you were to create a formula to calculate the average value of a range of 13 cells, without using the AVERAGE function, it would look something like this:

```
=(C1+C2+C3+C4+C5+C6+C7+C8+C9+C10+C11+C12+C13)/13.
```

The chances of having errors in formulas similar to this one is very high.

Another reason to use the AVERAGE function is that if the range of the cells you want to average changes, you will have to manually change your formula each time to incorporate the change. With the above example, it is simply easier to enter:

```
=AVERAGE(C1:C13)
```

Therefore, if you inserted more values and cells inside of the range, the function will automatically incorporate the new values in calculating the correct average. Also, if your range includes blank cells, text cells or logical cells, they are completely ignored and will not effect the true average of your range.

Let's do some averaging of our own. Do you recall the bowling example mentioned above? Let's calculate the bowling average of five bowlers. Go to a clean worksheet and enter the bowling scores of our five bowlers, as shown in Figure 4.13.

Follow these steps to accurately calculate the average bowling scores for our five bowlers.

1. Duplicate Figure 4.13 on a clean worksheet.

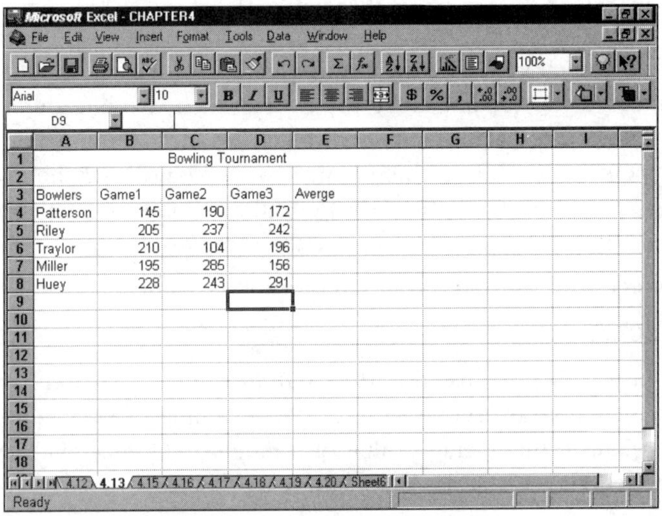

FIGURE 4.13 BOWLING SCORES OF FIVE BOWLERS.

2. Activate cell E4 to compute Patterson's bowling average. This is where we'll enter the AVERAGE function and then copy the formula for the other bowler's averages. The formula is actually short enough to be typed in, but let's use the Function Wizard to gain more experience with it.

3. Click on the **Function Wizard** button on the Standard toolbar. You may have to occasionally move the Function Wizard dialog box out of the way throughout this exercise.

4. Select **Statistical** in the Function Category box, then Average in the Function Name box of the Function Wizard dialog box, then select **Next**.

5. Select the cell range of cells **B4** through **D4** by clicking on cell **B4** and dragging to cell **D4**. The range is entered into the dialog window. Select **Finish**.

   You now see that Patterson's average bowling score has been calculated to 169. Now copy the formula in cell E4 to cells E5 through E8 to calculate the average scores of the remaining bowlers by performing the following step.

6. Make sure cell E4 is active. Using the mouse pointer, point to the small box in the lower right corner of cell E4 until the mouse pointer changes from a thick cross cursor to a thin cross cursor. Hold and drag the mouse pointer to cell E8.

 See Chapter 5 for more on copying formulas.

N O T E

You should now have all the bowling averages of the five bowlers. Figure 4.14 shows the average of each bowler.

We'll be using the data in Figure 4.14 with our next exercise with the AND, OR, and NOT functions. If you don't plan to continue at this point, you should save Figure 4.14 to avoid having to reenter it.

Using the AND, OR, and NOT Functions (Logical)

Let's get a little bit more fancy, using our IF function in conjunction with other functions. The AND, OR, and NOT functions are used to create compound conditional tests. You may remember that the IF function evaluates whether a condition is true or false. Using the AND, OR, and NOT functions, we can evaluate whether compound conditions are true or false. The AND, OR, and NOT functions use the logical operators =, >, <, >=, <=, and <>.

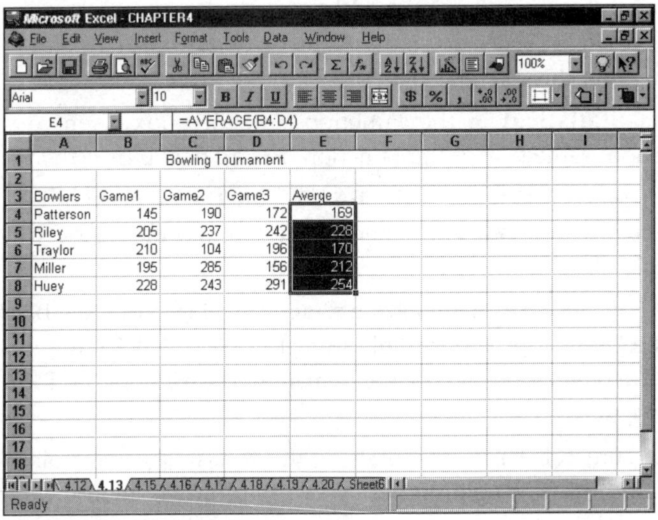

FIGURE 4.14 BOWLING AVERAGES CALCULATED WITH THE AVERAGE FUNCTION.

Suppose there was a senior bowling tour to be held in sunny Florida. The only requirements to be on the senior team is that your bowling average must be equal to or greater than 200 *and* you must be over 50. Suppose further that you wanted Excel to return the text value <u>Tour</u> only if you meet both conditions and <u>No Tour</u> if you do not meet these conditions.

Recreate Figure 4.15. Figure 4.15 is the same as Figure 4.14 which you created with the AVERAGE function, but we have added two new columns; one for the bowler's age, and the other to indicate whether or not they go on tour. Therefore, you can simply add the two new columns to your worksheet used with the AVERAGE function exercise.

Follow the steps below to create the compound conditional test using the AND function. We'll use the Function Wizard to gain more experience, but if you get confused, you can simply type the formula from Step 13 below into cell G4. After using the AND function for the first bowler, we'll then copy the formula to the remaining bowlers.

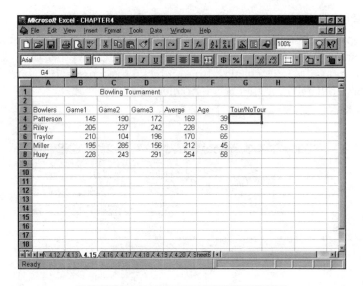

FIGURE 4.15 BOWLER'S AGE AND AVERAGE SCORES.

1. Activate cell G4 to house our function.

2. Click the **Function Wizard** button on the Standard toolbar.

3. Select **Logical** from the Function Category and **IF** from the Function Name window of the Function Wizard dialog box, then click **Next**.

4. Select the function button in the Logical_Test window.

5. **Logical** should be highlighted in the Function Category box; **AND** should be highlighted in the Function Name box. Select **Next**.

6. Click on cell **F4** of the worksheet to enter the bowler's age into the formula. (You may have to move your dialog box.)

7. Type **>50**.

8. Click on cell **E4** of the worksheet to enter the bowler's average into the formula.

9. Type **>=200** and select **OK**.

10. Press the **Tab** key. In the Value_if_true box type **Tour**

11. Press **Tab**. In the Value_if_false box type **No Tour**.

12. Click **Finish**.

13. If you made a mistake along the way you can redo the steps or manually type the following formula into cell G4:

=IF(AND(F4>50,E4>=200),"Tour","No Tour")

14. Copy the formula in cell G4 to cells G5 through G8 by using the mouse pointer. Point to the small box in the lower-right corner of cell G4 until the mouse pointer changes from a thick cross cursor to a thin cross cursor. Hold and drag the mouse pointer to cell G8.

Your worksheet should look like Figure 4.16.

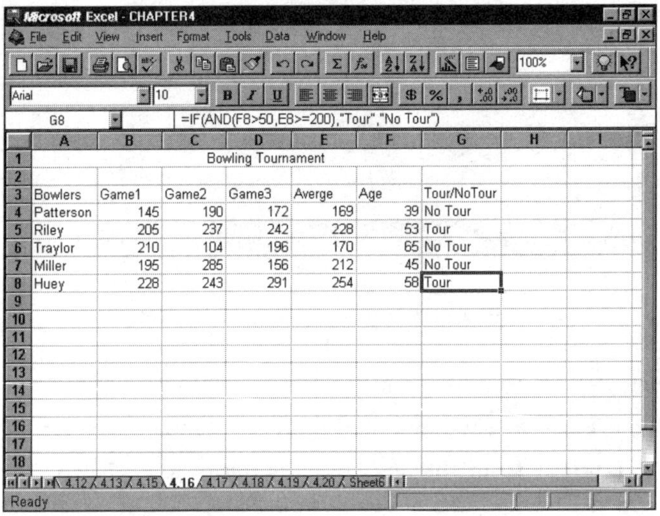

FIGURE 4.16 EXCEL CONDITIONAL TEST OF WHICH BOWLERS SHOULD TOUR AND WHICH SHOULD NOT TOUR USING THE AND FUNCTION.

Look at the formula in the formula bar. The formula simply states that if the bowlers age is greater than 50 *and* the bowler's average is equal to or greater than 200, then the condition is true and return the text value <u>Tour</u>. However, if the bowler's age is not greater than 50 *and* the bowler's average is not equal to or greater than 200, then the condition is false and return the text value <u>No Tour</u>. Pretty neat wouldn't you say?

The OR function takes the same arguments as the AND function. But the results are drastically different. Let's add one more column to our table.

1. In cell H3 type the following column heading: **Avg or Age**.

2. In cell H4 type the following formula. It's the same formula used in Column G but we're changing AND to OR:

=IF(OR(F4>50,E4>=200),"Tour","No Tour").

3. Using select-hold-drag, copy the formula down to the other bowlers in column H.

Your worksheet should look like Figure 4.17.

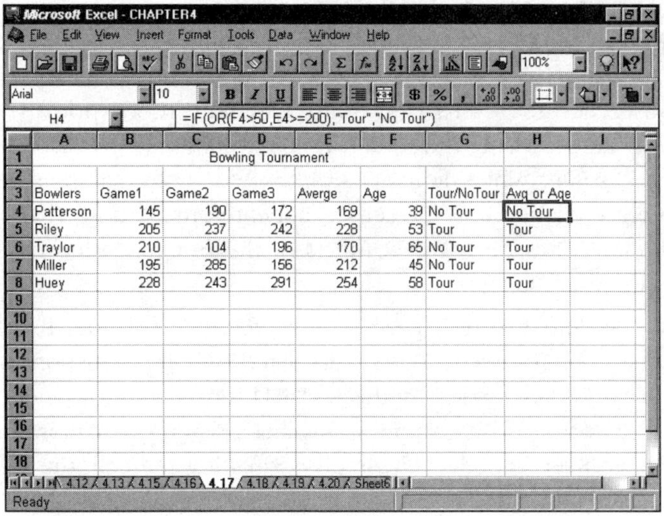

FIGURE 4.17 COMPARISON OF THE AND AND OR FUNCTIONS.

Compare the drastic results returned by the OR function conditions in comparison with the AND function. Notice that bowlers Traylor and Miller could not tour with the AND function conditions because they didn't pass the average score *and* age tests. But with the OR function conditions, they only needed to pass either the average score test (equal to or higher than 200) *or* the age test (more than 50). They didn't need to pass both test. As a result, they can tour with the OR function conditions because they passed one of the two tests.

The NOT function makes a condition not true and therefore it is used in conjunction with other functions. If an argument is false, the NOT function returns a logical value of TRUE and if an argument is true, the NOT function returns a logical value of FALSE. Look at the following formula:

```
=IF(NOT(C1=5),"Pass","Skip")
```

This formula instructs Excel to return a text value of <u>Pass</u> if the value in cell C1 does not equal 5. If it does equal 5, then the NOT function will return the text value <u>Skip</u> instead.

Using the ROUND Function (Mathematical)

Guess what this function does. If you said rounding, you're very smart! The ROUND function rounds a value to a chosen number of digits. Of course, you could also format a cell to cause a number to be rounded to a specific number of digits. However, the ROUND function is different in one primary way. When numbers are rounded using the Round function, they are permanently changed to the rounded value. When numbers are rounded via formatting a cell, they are not permanently changed. Their cells can be reformatted so that the original value reappears. With the ROUND function, the original value is permanently replaced by the rounding action.

Since the Round function permanently changes a value, this has consequences on how the rounded value is calculated. When calculations are done on values that have been rounded by the ROUND function, the rounded value will be calculated, not the original value. Conversely, when calculations are done on values that have been rounded by simply formatting the cell, the original value will be calculated and not the rounded value.

For example, if cell A1 housed the value 1.5432, and then was rounded by the ROUND function to a whole number, the result would be 2. If we were to multiply the result of 2, say by 3, we would have a product of 6. On the other hand, if we rounded the same value, 1.5432, by simply formatting the cell to display whole numbers, then the result would also be 2. But, when we multiplied this result of 2 by 3, we would have a product of 4.6296 and not 6. This is because the original value (1.5432) was not permanently changed when it was rounded and used in the multiplication calculation.

Here's the correct syntax for using the ROUND function:

=ROUND(*value, precision*)	
value	is the number to be rounded
precision	is the number of places the number is to be rounded

You should now try some hands-on experience with the Round function. We're going to take the value 1.5432 and round it as a whole number using the cell formatting method first. Then we will use the same value and round it to a whole number using the Round function. Afterwards, we'll perform a simple multiplication calculation on both rounded values to see the different results. Let's get started.

1. Click on a new worksheet.

2. Set up your worksheet to look like Figure 4.18. Here are the steps we took to create Figure 4.18:

   ◆ Type in cell A1 **Original Number**

   ◆ Type in cell A3 Rounded by Formatting

   ◆ Type in cell A5 Rounded by Function

   ◆ Type in cell D1 1.5432

   ◆ Type in cell D3 1.5432

   ◆ Type in cell F3 Multiplied by 3 =

   ◆ Type in cell F5 **Multiplied by 3 =**

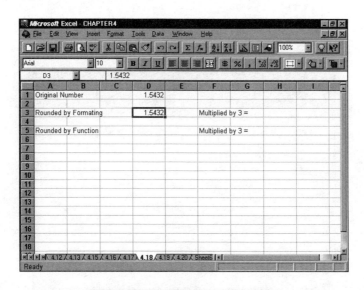

FIGURE 4.18 ROUNDING VS. CELL FORMATTING.

3. Let's format the value in cell D3 so that it is rounded to a whole number:
   ♦ Click on **D3**.
   ♦ Press the right mouse button to bring up the shortcut menu.
   ♦ Click on **Format Cell**.
   ♦ Click on the Number tab if it's not showing.
   ♦ Click **Number** in the Category box.
   ♦ Change the Decimal Places value from 2 to 0.
   ♦ Click **OK**.

   Notice that 1.5432 has been rounded to a whole number, 2.

4. Place the mouse pointer in cell H3. Type **=3*D3**.

5. Place the mouse pointer in cell D5. Type **=ROUND(D1,0)**. The zero in our formula indicates to round to a whole number. If we wanted to round to one decimal place, we would type =ROUND(D1,1).

   You have just used the Round function on the value in cell D1 and placed the result in cell D5. Note that the rounding result appears to be identical to the rounding result achieved by formatting cell D3. But don't let looks along fool you.

6. In cell H5, we want to enter the same basic formula we entered in cell H3. Type **=3*D5**.

   Your worksheet should look like Figure 4.19, showing the results of the multiplication.

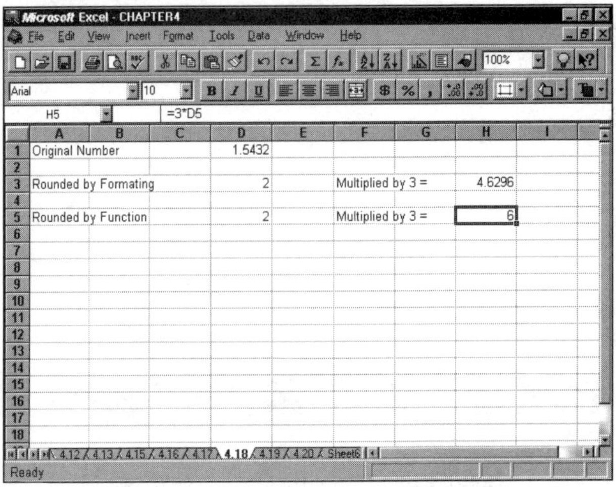

FIGURE 4.19 RESULTS OF ROUNDING VS. CELL FORMATTING.

You can now see that looks sometimes are deceiving. The two multiplication results, although apparently the same, are different. This is because when using the Round function, the value is permanently changed to the rounded amount. But when rounding a value by formatting a cell, although you do not see the original number, it still exists and is the original number that Excel uses in mathematical calculations.

There will likely be occasions when you may want your original values to permanently change to their rounded value. Moreover, you may want mathematical calculations done on the rounded values and not on the original values. This is where the ROUND function will be of great use to you.

Using the ABS Function (Mathematical)

The ABS function returns the absolute value of a number, formula, or cell reference. The correct syntax of the ABS function is:

    ABS(*value*)

The value can be any expression that results in a value. Here's a few examples of types of values that can be used with the ABS function:

◆ ABS(-45)

◆ ABS(C1)

◆ ABS(Range_Name)

◆ ABS(Range_Name+(G3*8))

The ABS value of a number is the number without a positive or negative connection. For example, if -45 was in cell C1, the formula =ABS(C1) return 45.

If the number, however, was a positive number, it would return the same number.

Using the COUNTIF and SUMIF Functions (Database)

A discussion on functions wouldn't be complete without referring to a couple of functions in the database category. The COUNTIF and SUMIF functions are two fairly easy functions to use and understand with databases. Although a step-by-step procedure will not be given, we will, however, be referring to Figure 4.20 which lists employee information such as age, salary, and gender. I suggest you first create the database table in Figure 4.20 (A1 through D13) and then create the analysis by producing the functions and formulas as we come to them.

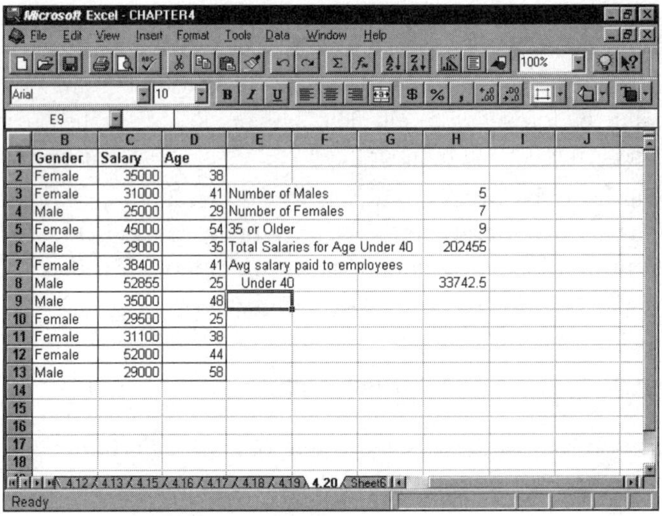

FIGURE 4.20 EMPLOYEE DATA.

The COUNTIF syntax is as follows:

=COUNTIF(range,criteria)

range   the range of values to be counted

critieria   a text value identifying the criteria.

Suppose we want to count the number of male employees in our employee list from Figure 4.20. We would use a formula similar to:

=COUNTIF(B2:B13,"Male").

This formula instructs Excel to look at ranges B2 through B13 and count the number of cells that contain the text value <u>Male</u>. This formula returns 5 as the number of males counted. We can instruct Excel to count the number of female employees using a similar formula:

=COUNTIF(B2:B13,"Female")

This formula returns 7 for the number of <u>Female</u> employees.

N O T E

The COUNTIF is not case sensitive. This means that if we entered "MALE" all uppercase in our formula, it would still count all the "Male" or "male" entries in the database range.

To count the number of employees who are 35 year of age or older, we would use the following formula:

    =COUNTIF(D2:D13,">=35").

The formula returns 9 as the number of employees 35 years of age or older.

The SUMIF function does not count, but instead it totals or sums values in a designated range. The syntax for the SUMIF function is as follows:

> **=SUMIF(*range,criteria,sum_range*)**
>
> *criteria*   an argument applied to a range
>
> *sum_range*   the range of data whose value will be added

Referring again to Figure 4.20, if we want to calculate the total salaries of employees less than age 40, we would use the formula:

    =SUMIF(D2:D13,"<40",C2:C13)

The formula returns $202,455 as the amount of salaries paid to employees less than age 40.

We discussed the AVERAGE function earlier. You may recall that an average is a total sum divided by a count. In this case, we can use a combination of SUMIF (total sum) and COUNTIF (count) to calculate averages. Suppose we wanted to know the average salary paid to our employees less than the age of 40. The following formula will calculate the average:

    =SUMIF(D2:D13,"<40",C2:C13)/COUNTIF(D2:D13,"<40")

This formula returns $33,742.50. Try using these formulas in conjunction with Figure 4.20 to gain hands-on experience in using database functions.

A FINAL THOUGHT

In this chapter, you learned to put several of the more common functions to work, and learned how Excel handles dates and times.

In the next chapter, you'll learn to make some modifications to your worksheet, including inserting and deleting data. You'll also learn more about copying formulas and formatting cells.

CHAPTER 5

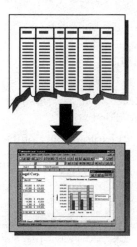

MODIFYING A WORKSHEET

- ♦ Finding and opening an existing document
- ♦ Copying formulas
- ♦ Moving data
- ♦ Selecting ranges
- ♦ Defining and using names
- ♦ Clearing a cell's contents
- ♦ Inserting and deleting rows and columns
- ♦ Changing column widths
- ♦ Getting around in your workbook

FINDING AND OPENING AN EXISTING WORKSHEET

One of the biggest fears of new computer users is that they'll put a lot of time and energy into creating a spreadsheet, dutifully save it to the disk, close the spreadsheet, and then they'll never be able to find it again. It will be lost forever, as though sucked into a black hole.

Relax! Your spreadsheet is there and Excel makes it easy to find. You did save it, didn't you?

Let's explore some of the ways to open a spreadsheet.

1. Start Excel, if it isn't running.

    Unless you've been doing some work with Excel behind my back, the last workbook you had on your screen was BUDGET.XLS. Even if you were working on a few other documents since working with BUDGET, Excel displays BUDGET along with the three other recently opened files at the bottom of the File menu.

2. Choose **File**.

    Notice the group of four file names at the bottom of the menu, just above the Exit command, in Figure 5.1. Your File menu may only display one or two file names, if those are the only files you've worked with.

FIGURE 5.1 THE FILE MENU WITH THE FOUR MOST RECENTLY OPENED FILES DISPLAYED.

You could open the BUDGET workbook by clicking on it or pressing the underlined number in front of its name. Instead, let's examine some other methods for finding and opening the file.

3. Click on any cell outside the menu to clear the menu, or press the **Esc** key twice.

4. Click on the **Open** toolbar button.

Choosing the Open toolbar button is the same as choosing File, Open, and calls up the Open dialog box, as displayed in Figure 5.2.

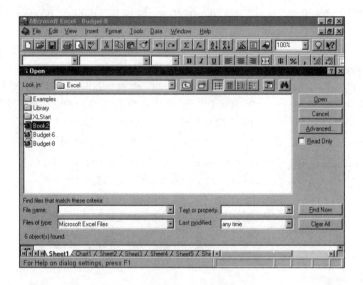

FIGURE 5.2 THE OPEN DIALOG BOX.

5. If BUDGET.XLS isn't displayed in the list of files and directories, use the Look In drop down list to locate the appropriate directory (folder) that contains the file. See the "Saving Your Work" section of Chapter 3, to move to the folder that contains the file. Once you find the folder that contains the file you're seeking, you can use the various options at the bottom of the Open dialog box to locate the file within the folder. This is useful when your folder contains too many files to sort through quickly. You can enter a name into the File Name box to locate the specific file. You can also narrow the list to files of a specific type (naturally, this is automatically set to look for Excel files), or files that contain specific data within their names. Finally, you can narrow the list by selecting just those

files that were modified within the last day, week, month, or year. The more selections you establish, the fewer files will appear in the listing. You should be able to locate any file in the active folder using just one of these criteria. Use the **Clear All** button to reset these options if desired.

I know you're anxious to open the file, but there's one more method we're going to take a look at first. Bear with me for just a few more minutes.

So far, the methods we've explored for opening a file are fine if the file you want to open is one of the last four you worked with, or if you know its name and the directory where it is located. But suppose you haven't worked on the file recently. In fact, it's been so long that you've forgotten its name and even the directory where you saved it. Hey, it happens to the best of us.

It's still easy to find the file using Excel's advanced Find File facilities. As long as you know something about the file, such as the approximate date when it was saved last, some information you entered into the Summary Info dialog box, or even some unique text that is contained anywhere in the file, Excel does the legwork and finds the long lost file for you.

6. With the Open dialog box in view, click the **Advanced** button.

The first time you use Advanced Find File options, the Search dialog box appears on the screen, as displayed in Figure 5.3.

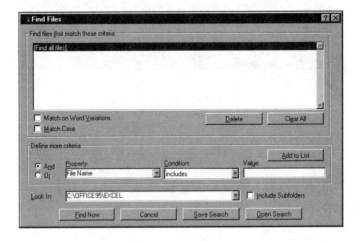

FIGURE 5.3 THE SEARCH DIALOG BOX.

This dialog box lets us search for files based on their file name, location, or other information including data stored in the summary information on the file (information you enter about the file when you first saved it). You use the Define More Criteria options to establish criteria that appears at the top of the dialog box.

7. Click on the Property drop-down list and choose **Author** from the list.

8. Click on the Condition drop-down list and highlight the word **Includes** (it may already be highlighted).

9. Click inside the Value box and type your name.

10. Click the **Add to List** button. The criteria is added to the list at the top of the dialog box, as Figure 5.4 shows.

11. Select the directory in which you want to search for this file. If you are not sure where the file is located, choose **Desktop**, or a specific disk drive, then click the **Include Subdirectories** option. This tells Excel to look in all subdirectories within the disk you specified. Of course, the more you narrow down the search, the faster Excel will be able to find the file.

    At this point, you can add more criteria to the list by repeating steps 7 through 10 after clicking the **And** or the **Or** option to indicate whether you're adding additional conditions (and) or expanding the search to more possibilities (or). Now you can begin the search by clicking the **Find Now** button, but first let's save this search criteria for future searches.

12. Click the **Save Search** button, then enter a name for the search, such as: **Files created by [your name]**.

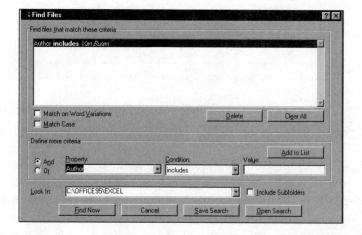

FIGURE 5.4 THE ADVANCED SEARCH DIALOG BOX WITH AUTHOR INFORMATION IDENTIFIED.

13. Click **Find Now** to begin the search. The desired file, if found, will appear in the Open file listing, where you can select it for opening. If you are still in any doubt, you can click the **Preview** button in the Open dialog box to see a preview of the file before opening it. Figure 5.5 shows this option.

Since you saved this search, the same search can be made again without your having to retype all the criteria. Just use the File Open command and click the **Saved Searched** button to view the searches you have saved from the Advanced Find File options. Figure 5.6 shows our example.

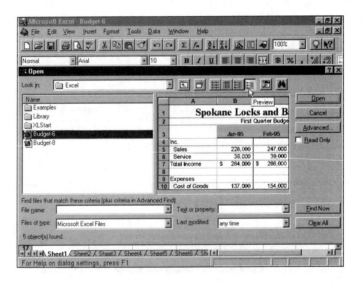

FIGURE 5.5 SHOWING A PREVIEW OF THE FILE YOU ARE ABOUT TO OPEN.

You can only search one drive at a time. If you have more than one hard drive and you don't know which drive contains the file you're looking for, you may need to perform separate searches on each drive.

Using the Include Subdirectories option can dramatically increase the amount of time required for your computer to complete the search. The amount of time depends on the size and speed of the hard disk, the number of files it contains, and the overall speed of your computer. If you know where your file is located, you save time by specifying a directory in the Location portion of the Advanced Search dialog box.

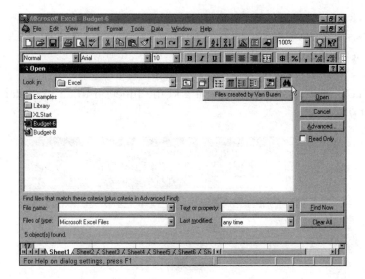

FIGURE 5.6 ACCESSING A SAVED SEARCH.

SELECTING RANGES

So far, we've been manipulating one cell at a time. However, Excel lets you select more than one cell, or a *range* of cells, on which you may want to perform some action. For example, when a range of cells is selected, you can copy it to another area of your worksheet. Or you can move an entire range from one place to another. We'll be talking more about copying and moving later in the chapter. Selecting ranges will be quite helpful to you as you begin creating and revising your worksheets.

Let's take a look at some of the ways you can select a range of cells.

Selecting a Range by Dragging

The easiest way to select cells is to simply drag the mouse over the cells you want to select. Let's select E5 through E7 and use the AutoSum function to calculate the quarter total income in each of the cells simultaneously.

1. Position the mouse pointer in E5.
2. Press and hold the left mouse button, and drag down to E7.

3. Release the mouse button.

   The selected range is highlighted as you drag the mouse and when you release the mouse button. The cell you started with, E5, is the active cell as shown in Figure 5.7.

4. Click on **AutoSum** which will add the function to all the selected cells at once.

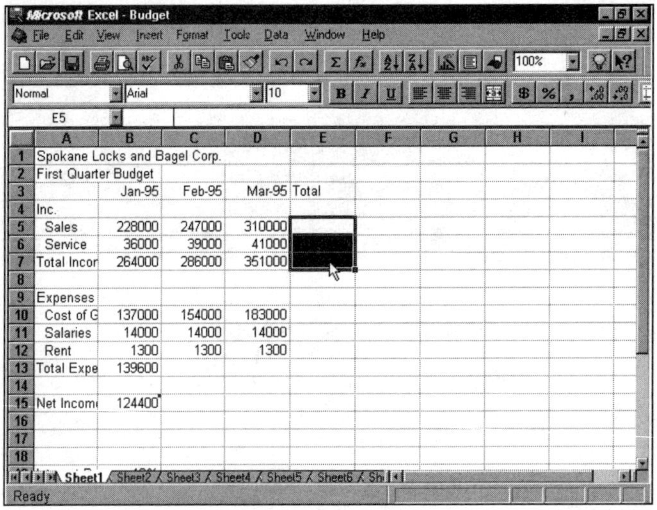

FIGURE 5.7 SELECTING A RANGE OF CELLS.

Selecting Non-Contiguous Ranges

There may be times when you want to select non-contiguous ranges of cells—which is like selecting several ranges at once. For example, suppose you wanted the sum for the quarter totals of the expenses and the net income/loss at the same time. No problem. Just use the **Ctrl** key to add to a selection.

1. Position the mouse pointer in cell E10.

2. Press and hold the left mouse button, and drag down to E13.

3. Release the mouse button.

4. Hold down the **Ctrl** key and click on cell E15.

   E10 through E13 and cell E15 are selected, as displayed in Figure 5.8. The last cell, E15, is the active cell.

5. Click on **AutoSum** to add the function to all the selected cells.

T I P

If you need to select a rectangular range, the Shift key can make the task more efficient. Just click on one corner of the range you want to select, then hold down the **Shift** key and click on the opposite corner of the range. You can also use the Go To dialog box to select a range. Instead of typing a single cell address in the Reference text box, you can enter two cell addresses separated by a colon. When you click on **OK**, the range is selected.

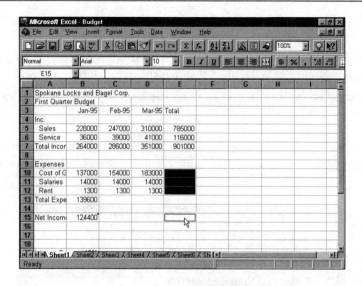

FIGURE 5.8 TWO NON-CONTIGUOUS SELECTED RANGES.

MOVING DATA

Now that you know how to select a range of data, you can perform operations on the data such as moving it from one location to another. There are two basic methods of moving data: drag-and-drop, and cut and paste. Let's take a look at both methods.

Moving with Drag-and-Drop

The simplest way of moving data from one location to another is by the drag-and-drop method. You first select and highlight the range of cells you want to move, and then drag the edge of the selected range to the new location. An outline of the range of cells selected will move as you move the mouse. Once you have the outline in the correct position, simply releasing the mouse button will complete the move.

1. Click on cell A1 and hold the left mouse button down.

2. Holding down the left mouse button, highlight a range of cells by dragging the mouse to E15.

3. Release the mouse button to select the range.

4. Place the mouse pointer at the edge of the selected range until the mouse pointer changes to an arrow.

5. Click and drag the selected range until the top left corner of the range outline is in cell C3. Figure 5.9 shows this procedure.

6. Release the mouse button to complete the move to the new location of the worksheet.

When you are finished moving the range of cells, try moving them back again. This will leave the worksheet in the same condition it was in before we started.

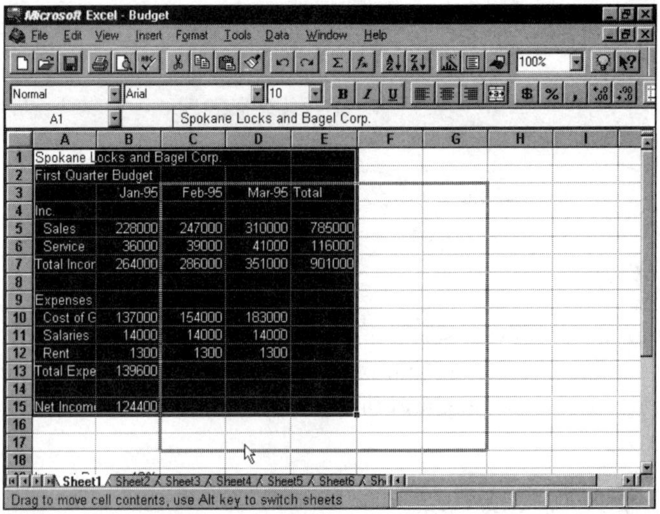

FIGURE 5.9 MOVING A CELL BY DRAGGING ITS BORDER.

Moving Data with Cut and Paste

When using the combination Cut and Paste commands of Excel, you accomplish the same results as moving data by the drag and drop method. You first select the range of cells you want to move. Select the **Cut** command from the Edit menu or press the **Cut** command on the button bar. Place the cursor at the location where the move is to be accomplished. Finally, select the **Paste** command from the Edit menu or press the **Paste** command on the button bar.

Use the following steps to accomplish moving your data using the cut and paste methods.

1. Select the range of cells you want to move.
2. Press the **Cut** command on the Toolbar.
3. Move the cell pointer to the first cell of the new location where you want to move the data.
4. Select the **Paste** command on the button bar, or just press **Enter**.

After selecting the cell range you want to move, you can press the right mouse button inside the range to display the shortcut menu and perform the cut.

T I P

COPYING DATA

To save yourself from having to type and retype the same formulas, functions, or data in more than one area of your worksheet, use Excel's copy feature. Unlike moving data, when you copy data in Excel, you do not alter the original data; you simply duplicate it in another area of your worksheet.

There are three basic ways by which you can copy data. You can copy data using either the drag-and-drop method or copy and paste method. You can also copy certain data by using the AutoFill method. Let's take a brief look at these techniques.

Copying Data with Drag-and-Drop

The same procedures for moving data using the drag-and-drop method are employed when copying data. The only difference is that when you select the highlighted cells to copy, you must hold down the **Shift** key prior to dragging. Try these simple steps to accomplish copying cells:

1. Highlight cell A1.
2. Press and hold the **Control** key.
3. Click on the outer edge of the selected range. The mouse pointer will turn into an arrow with a plus sign above it, indicating copying as oppose to moving.
4. Drag the cells to the new location on the worksheet. Try moving to cell G5.
5. Release the mouse button.

If the destination cell already contains data, Excel will ask if you want to replace the existing data with the data you are copying. You can go through with the copy or cancel the action at this time. Delete the duplicate of cell A1 before proceeding to the next section.

Copying Data with Copy and Paste

When using the combination Copy and Paste commands of Excel, you accomplish the same results as copying data by the drag-and-drop method, but it has one advantage: you can copy one cell and paste it into many cells. You first select the range of cells you want to copy. Select the **Copy** command from the Edit menu or press the **Copy** command on the button bar. Place the cursor at the location where you want the copy. Finally, select the **Paste** command from the Edit menu or press the **Paste** command on the button bar.

1. Select cell E5.
2. Select **Copy** from the Edit menu.
3. Highlight the range E10 through E12.
4. Select the **Paste** command from the Edit menu. Figure 5.10 shows the result.

Notice that when copying formulas, the copied information adjusts to show the results of the appropriate columns. Excel's built-in intelligence knows you want the copied formulas to reflect the appropriate rows or columns of data.

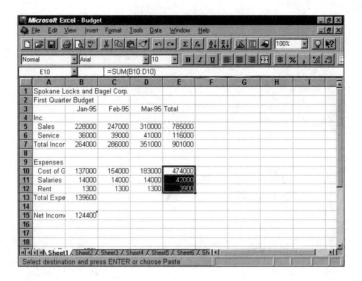

FIGURE 5.10 COPYING ONE CELL TO MANY CELLS USING THE COPY AND PASTE COMMANDS.

Copying Data with AutoFill

On occasions, you will need to copy data from a cell or from a range of cells to adjacent cells. The quickest way to do this is by using the AutoFill feature. Simply highlight the cell or range of cells you want to copy. Then drag the extend box of the selected cells to the new adjacent cells. Excel automatically copies the data from the selected cells into the new adjacent cells. Follow these step-by-step directions for practice:

1. Highlight cell B13.

2. Drag the extend box, located in the lower-right corner of the selected cell, across to cell E13.

3. Release the mouse button. Data in the original cells are now repeated in the adjacent cells of the extended range. See Figure 5.11.

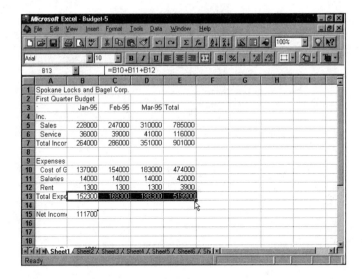

FIGURE 5.11 COPYING FORMULAS WITH AUTOFILL.

Copying Formulas and Functions

With all the Total Income and Total Expenses calculations in place on our spreadsheet, we're ready to add the formulas for calculating the Net Income/Loss for February and March. Instead of creating separate formulas, we'll copy the formula for January's Net Income/Loss to February and March.

1. Move to cell B15.

   If you look in the formula bar, the formula appears to be =B7-B13. Well, appearances can be deceiving. Excel and other spreadsheets employ a type of cell referencing called *relative reference*. By using relative references, cells containing formulas or functions can be copied and they are automatically adjusted to perform properly in their new location.

   Relative reference logic sees the formula in B15 as *subtract the value in the cell that is two rows up from the value in the cell that is eight rows up*. When you copy a formula, the logic of the formula (not the actual formula) is copied, so the formula works in its new location.

   Let's use the fill handle we used in the last chapter to create a series to copy the formula to cells C15 and E15.

2. Position the mouse pointer over the fill handle and drag three cells to the right.

3. Release the mouse button and then press the **Right Arrow** key to make C15 the active cell.

   Take a look at the formula bar to assure yourself that the logic of the formula was correctly copied. You can check out cell D15 for further proof.

Sometimes, when you copy formulas in a cell, you don't want the cell being referenced in your formulas to be relative. Instead, after copying a formula, you want the formula in the cell to reference the exact same reference found in the original cell. This is called *absolute referencing.*

Excel will not adjust cell and range references if the cell in question is set up correctly. When using an absolute reference in a cell, it will never change to a relative reference no matter where you copy the cell to. But you must follow the following format to make a cell reference absolute.

To make a cell reference absolute, place dollar signs in front of both the letter and number address of the cell. For example, if you wanted to make the reference to cell E8 absolute, you would place dollar signs in front of the letter and number, thereby producing E8.

Formulas can also use both absolute and relative references simultaneously. For example, if the formula =SUM(A1:A8)*E8 was copied from one cell to another, the range reference A1:A8 will be relative, while the reference E8 will be absolute.

DEFINING NAMES

So far, we've only referred to cells by their addresses. Naming ranges can make your worksheets much easier to understand. Using names in formulas instead of ranges of cell addresses can make it instantly clear what the formula does. For example, B7-B13 is meaningless until you look at the worksheet and determine what these cell addresses represent. However, if the formula read Total Income-Total Expenses, you'd know exactly what was going on.

You can name individual cells or ranges of cells. You can also specify the name you want to assign, or let Excel do it for you. Generally, an appropriate name is already adjacent to the cell or range of cells you want to name. If this is the case, you can include the name with the range and let Excel use it.

Let's create names for the income and expense categories, including total income and total expenses.

1. Select the ranges A5 through D7 and A10 through D13, as displayed in Figure 5.12. Remember to use the **Ctrl** key to select non-contiguous ranges.

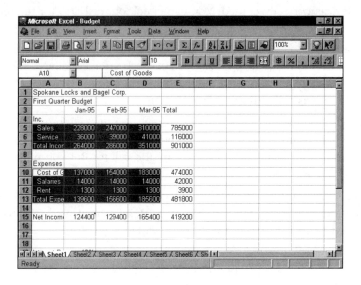

FIGURE 5.12 THE SELECTED RANGES TO BE NAMED.

2. Choose **Insert**, **Name**, **Create**.

The Insert Names dialog box appears, as displayed in Figure 5.13 with the Create Names in Left Column check box checked.

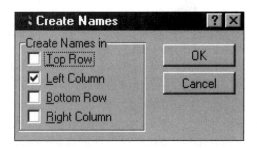

FIGURE 5.13 THE CREATE NAMES DIALOG BOX.

3. Click **OK**.

   Although Excel uses the names in the left column, they aren't included as part of the range. You can use the Define Name dialog box to see which ranges each name is applied to, but the easiest way—and a good shortcut for selecting a named range—is the name list in the cell reference area. Let's use this method to select the Service range.

4. Click on the **Arrow** for the name list, just to the right of the cell reference area.

   The drop-down list, shown in Figure 5.14, displays the names contained in the worksheet.

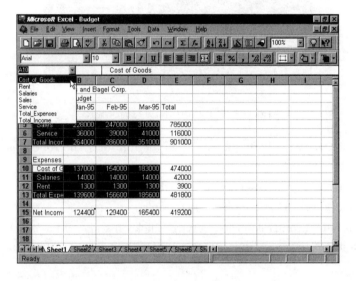

FIGURE 5.14 THE WORKSHEET'S NAMED RANGES.

5. Click on **Service** in the list to select the range B6 through D6.

   Now let's make the formulas in the worksheet more understandable by substituting the range addresses with the range names. To have Excel automatically apply range names, we first need to select the cells that contain formulas or functions. To make sure we don't miss any, we'll select the whole worksheet. A shortcut for selecting the entire worksheet is to click on the **Select All** box (the rectangle in the upper-left corner of the worksheet where the row and column heading intersect).

6. Click on the **Select All** box.

7. Choose **Insert**, **Name**, **Apply**.

The Apply Names dialog box, with all the range names highlighted, is shown in Figure 5.15. If some of the names aren't highlighted, click on each of them.

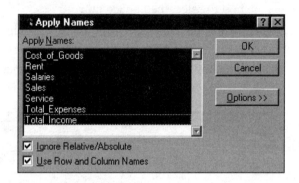

FIGURE 5.15 THE APPLY NAMES DIALOG BOX.

8. Click **OK** to apply the names to all the formulas and functions that refer to those ranges.

The formula in B7 used to read =B5+B6. Let's take a look at how it's changed.

9. Click on cell B7 and look at the formula bar.

The new formula is =Sales+Service. Click on some of the other cells containing formulas or functions to see how the names have been applied.

INSERTING AND DELETING ROWS AND COLUMNS

As you create and edit worksheets, you frequently need to insert or delete rows and columns. Perhaps you want to add or remove categories or time periods.

Let's insert a row to add a new category, *income*, to our budget worksheet, showing interest income for the company's investments.

WARNING

Inserting or deleting rows or columns can be very dangerous. You could inadvertently interfere with some data that you can't see on the screen. You could have data off to the side, or above or below the portion of the worksheet that is currently visible.

When inserting or deleting rows or columns, be sure to take into account the effect these actions could have on all portions of your worksheet.

Even though Excel provides an Undo feature to get you out of sticky situations, it's always a good idea to save your work just before making any sort of change that could wreak havoc on your worksheet.

1. Move to cell A6. Actually, any cell in row 6 will do.

2. Choose **Insert**, **Rows**.

   A new row has been inserted and named ranges have been adjusted to reflect their new locations, as have cells containing formulas and functions.

3. Enter the data for the new row, as shown in Figure 5.16.

	A	B	C	D	E	F	G	H	I
1	Spokane Locks and Bagel Corp.								
2	First Quarter Budget								
3		Jan-95	Feb-95	Mar-95	Total				
4	Inc.								
5	Sales	228000	247000	310000	785000				
6	Interest	1200	1400	1600					
7	Service	36000	39000	41000	116000				
8	Total Incor	264000	287400	352600	904000				
9									
10	Expenses								
11	Cost of G	137000	154000	183000	474000				
12	Salaries	14000	14000	14000	42000				
13	Rent	1300	1300	1300	3900				
14	Total Expe	139600	156600	185600	481800				
15									
16	Net Incom	124400	130800	167000	422200				
17									
18									

FIGURE 5.16 THE BUDGET WORKSHEET WITH THE DATA ENTERED FOR THE NEWLY INSERTED ROW.

Notice that the January Total Income calculation didn't adjust to accommodate the new cell, but February and March did. What happened?

January used a formula that added two specific cells, while February and March used the SUM function to add a range of cells. When we inserted a row, the new row was included in the SUM function's range, but was not automatically added to the formula.

We fix this by replacing the formula with the SUM function. We also use AutoSum to add the calculation for the quarter total interest.

4. Move to cell B8 and double-click on the **AutoSum** toolbar button.

5. Move to cell E6 and double-click on the **AutoSum** button.

One way to reduce expenses would be to get rid of the rent. Let's delete row 13 to improve the company's profit picture.

6. Move to any cell in row 13 and choose **Edit**, **Delete**.

The Delete dialog box appears as displayed in Figure 5.17.

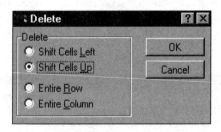

FIGURE 5.17 THE DELETE DIALOG BOX.

Because only a single cell is selected, Excel suggests shifting the cells below the active cell. This is not what we had in mind. We want to get rid of the entire row.

7. Click the **Entire Row** option button and click **OK**.

If you see a dialog box telling you that Excel can't resolve the circular reference, click on **OK**. A circular reference usually means that the formula in the formula cell refers to itself. For example, the formula =B4+B5+B6 in cell B6 would be a circular reference.

Okay, that got rid of our rent, but wait a minute. Maybe we need to pay rent after all, so we'll have a place to operate our business. We'll use the Excel's Undo feature to reverse the deletion.

8. Choose **Edit**, **Undo** or click the **Undo** toolbar button to restore the rent row.

CHANGING COLUMN WIDTHS

Finally, what you've been waiting for. When text entries are too long and are truncated or numbers show up as pound signs (#), your column is probably too narrow and needs to be adjusted.

I'll bet you've been anxiously looking at column A since we first entered the numbers and lost part of the text. Well, the time has come to fix the problem and adjust the column.

You can change the column width by entering a new value in the Column Width dialog box by choosing **Format**, **Column**, **Width**, but there's an even easier, more visual way. You can position the mouse pointer over the right border of the column heading and drag it to the left to reduce the width, or to the right to increase the width. Let's use the dragging method to increase the width of column A.

1. Position the mouse pointer over the right border of the column heading, and drag to the right about half an inch, as shown in Figure 5.18.

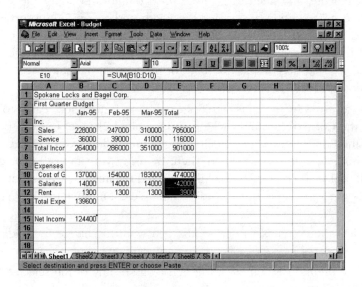

FIGURE 5.18 THE COLUMN WIDTH BEING ADJUSTED.

2. Release the mouse button to complete the adjustment.

The column is now wide enough to display all the text in most of the cells. The disadvantage of the dragging method is that you may need to make several stabs at the proper adjustment before you get it right. Also, if there are long cell entries below what you can see, you won't know if you have it right until you scroll down or print the worksheet—and then it's too late.

There is an even better way. When you double-click on the right border of the column heading, Excel adjusts the column so it is wide enough to accommodate the longest cell entry.

But wait a minute. If the column is adjusted for the longest entry, it will be wide enough for the title in cell A1, which would make the column much too wide for the remaining entries.

3. Select the range A4 through A16 and choose **Format**, **Column**, **AutoFit Selection**. Now the column width is adjusted properly.

Changing Multiple Column Widths

Here's a handy little shortcut for changing more than one column's width at a time. It eliminates the need to go from one column and adjust the width, and then to the next column and adjust the width and so on. Suppose Column A, Column C, and Column F were all the same width and they each needed to be widened by the same amount. One method would be to adjust each column individually. That may not be too bad for 3 columns, but suppose it was 10 or 20 columns with the same situation.

The easiest way to adjust multiple columns is to select each column by pressing the **Control** key and clicking on the column header (e.g., A, B, C, etc.). Holding the Control key while clicking on columns allows you to select columns that are not adjacent to each other. Then, by using your mouse, you can adjust one of the selected columns and all the selected columns, will adjust at the same time. Follow these simple steps to adjust multiple column widths.

1. Select the columns whose widths you want to change by holding down the **Control** key and selecting the appropriate column headers.

2. Place the mouse pointer at the right edge of any of the selected columns in the column header area. The mouse pointer will change from a heavy cross to a double-arrowed column width changing pointer.

3. Press and hold the mouse button down as you move the pointer to the right or left, to either narrow or expand the columns.

4. Release the mouse button. Note that each selected column width has been modified to reflect the change made by the mouse.

Column widths can also be changed by selecting **Column Width** from the Format menu. Enter a number (integer or decimal fraction) for the number of characters the column should contain, based on the current font selected.

Changing Row Heights

Although it's less often required, you can also change the heights of rows in an Excel worksheet. Like changing column widths, you can change row heights by dragging on the bottom border in the heading area of the desired row number. You can also double-click on the border to automatically adjust row heights. Try increasing the height of row 3 to make more room between the title and the column headings. Figure 5.19 shows this example.

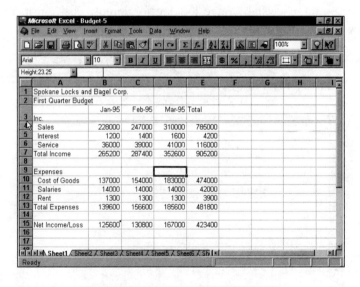

FIGURE 5.19 CHANGING THE HEIGHT OF A ROW.

GETTING AROUND IN YOUR WORKBOOK

Knowing how to move easily about your workbook is an important tool in using Excel. One of the chief benefits of using Excel 95 is that you don't have to open 2, 5, 10, 30, or more worksheets at one time. Opening one workbook in Excel

95 gives you access to 16 worksheets—and you can still add more. This section will teach you how to move between your worksheets, name your worksheets, rearrange your worksheets, and insert and delete worksheets.

Moving Between Worksheets with Page Tabs

When you decide you want to go from one worksheet to another, the easiest way to accomplish this is to simply click on the page tab located at the bottom of the worksheet. For example, if you are working with Sheet1 and wanted to move to **Sheet3**, simply click on tab Sheet3. Clicking on the sheet tabs will give you all the mobility you need to move around.

Normally, you can see only 5 tabs at a time. Suppose you wanted to click to, lets say, tab 7, but you can only see tabs 1 through 5. Excel has several easy solutions to this situation. One solution is to slide the horizontal scroll bar to the right. This will shorten the scroll bar but allow more sheet tabs to be displayed. When you see the sheet tab you're looking for, simply click on it. Figure 5.20 shows how to reduce the size of the scroll bar.

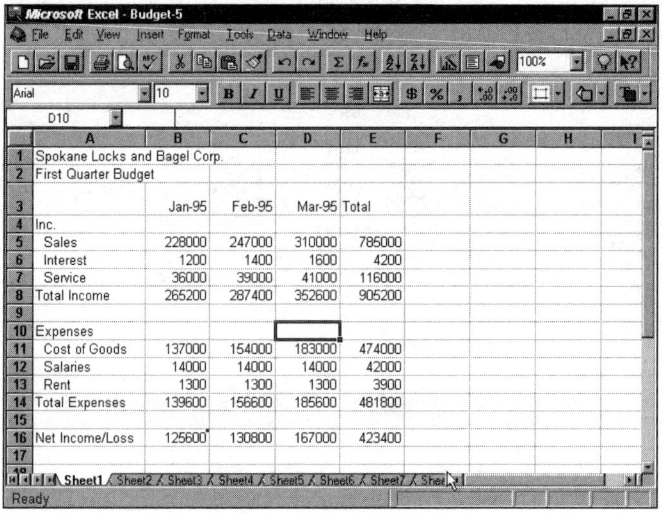

FIGURE 5.20 ADJUSTING THE SCROLL BAR TO DISPLAY MORE PAGE TABS.

Another solution for selecting sheet tabs hidden from sight is to use the page tab buttons, located on the far left bottom scroll bar of the worksheet. If your worksheets were entitled Sheet1 through Sheet16, clicking the far right arrow (pointing right) will take you to the last tab sheet or Sheet16 of your workbook. Clicking the far left arrow (pointing left) will take you to the first tab sheet or Sheet1 of your workbook. Clicking the two middle left and right arrows will allow you to move forward and backward through your workbook one sheet at a time, as shown in Figure 5.21.

FIGURE 5.21 THE PAGE TAB BUTTONS LET YOU MOVE BETWEEN TAB SHEETS.

Moving Between Worksheets Using the GoTo Command

Another way to move between worksheets is by using the GoTo command. You can activate the GoTo command by either pressing the **F5** key or selecting **GoTo** from the Edit menu. Both actions cause the GoTo dialog box to appear. If you were in Sheet1, for example, and wanted to go to Sheet12 using the GoTo dialog box, you would follow these simple steps.

1. Select **GoTo** from the Edit menu.
2. In the reference box of the GoTo dialog box, type: **Sheet12!A1**. *Sheet12* tells the GoTo command which sheet to go to, and *A1* tells the GoTo command which cell to go to. Notice the exclamation mark (!) between the worksheet name, (Sheet2), and the cell address, (A1). Without the exclamation mark the GoTo command will not operate. Also, without the cell address, the GoTo command will not perform.
3. Click **OK** and you are moved to the new worksheet location.

Naming Your Worksheets

If you use several worksheets in your Excel workbook, then the generic names (Sheet1, Sheet2, Sheet3, etc.) may not be descriptive enough for you. You can rename the worksheets to a name that is more meaningful and useful to you. To rename your worksheets, perform the following few steps.

1. Double-click on the worksheet tab you want to rename.
2. In the Rename Sheet dialog box, type in the new name and click **OK**.

Another way to rename your worksheet is by using the tab shortcut menu, as follows:

1. With the mouse pointer on the sheet name tab you want to change, press the right mouse button. The sheet tab short menu appears.
2. Click on **Rename**.
3. In the rename sheet dialog box, type in the new name and click **OK**.

Moving Your Worksheets

As you begin working with several worksheets in a single workbook, you may decide that the current arrangement of the worksheets does not work well. Fear not. Excel provides you with several methods by which worksheets can be rearranged to better suit your needs. Let's briefly discuss them.

The easiest way to rearrange your worksheets is the drag-and-drop method. Follow these steps to move your worksheets.

1. Click and hold the page tab you want to move.
2. Drag your mouse either left or right across the bottom of your screen to where you want the page to move to. A triangular arrow will appear as you move the mouse.
3. When the triangular arrow is at the location where you want your page, simply release the mouse button.

Of course, Excel gives you additional options for moving your worksheets.

1. With the mouse pointer on the sheet name tab you want to move, press the right mouse button. The sheet tab short menu appears.
2. Click on **Move or Copy**.
3. In the Before Sheet window of the move or copy dialog box, click on the worksheet you want to move your worksheet in front of.
4. Click **OK**.

Copying Your Worksheet

At times you may want to copy one worksheet to another worksheet. The procedures are almost identical to the steps of moving your worksheets using the sheet tab short menu.

1. With the mouse pointer on the worksheet tab you want to copy, press the right mouse button. The sheet tab short menu appears.

2. Click on **Move or Copy**.

3. Select the **Create a Copy** box.

4. In the Before Sheet window of the Move or Copy dialog box, click on the worksheet you want to copy your worksheet in front of.

5. Click **OK**.

Inserting Worksheets

You may decide you want to create a new worksheet between two existing worksheets. Excel offers two easy methods to achieve this.

1. Select the worksheet tab you want to insert you new worksheet in front of.

2. Select **Worksheet** from the Insert menu. Your new worksheet is inserted and the sheet name given to it is the next numerical sheet number of your workbook.

That was pretty simple, wasn't it? The following method uses the tab short menu.

1. Select the worksheet tab that you want to insert your new worksheet in front of.

2. Bring up the tab short menu by pressing the left mouse button.

3. Select **Insert**. The Insert dialog box appears as Figure 5.22 shows.

4. Double-click the **Worksheet** icon. Your new worksheet is entered.

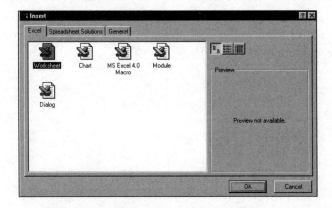

FIGURE 5.22 INSERTING A WORKSHEET INTO THE WORKBOOK.

Deleting Worksheets

You may decide you want to delete a worksheet you no longer need. Again, Excel offers two methods to achieve this. These are the steps for the first method.

1. Select the worksheet tab that you want to delete.
2. Select **Delete Sheet** from the Edit menu.
3. Click **OK** to confirm deleting the selected worksheet.

Of course, we could have used the tab short menu method:

1. Select the worksheet tab you want to delete.
2. Bring up the tab short menu by pressing the left mouse button.
3. Select **Delete**.
4. Click **OK** to confirm deleting the selected worksheet.

Save your work and exit Excel if you're not continuing on to the next chapter at this time.

A FINAL THOUGHT

Now you know that you will always be able to find your worksheets, and this worksheet is starting to shape up nicely. The columns are finally adjusted to accommodate the cell entries, and the range names make the worksheet clearer.

In the next chapter, you learn some ways to make the worksheet look snazzier. You also learn how to add notes to further clarify the worksheet, and how to protect portions of the worksheet.

CHAPTER 6

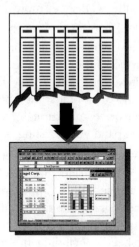

ENHANCING AND ANNOTATING YOUR WORKSHEET

- ◆ Aligning cell contents
- ◆ Formatting numbers
- ◆ Displaying and hiding zero vValues
- ◆ Changing fonts and selecting a standard font
- ◆ Adding borders and shading
- ◆ Using AutoFormat
- ◆ Removing worksheet gridlines
- ◆ Adding notes
- ◆ Protecting data
- ◆ Using styles
- ◆ Using templates
- ◆ Design tips

This chapter concentrates on aesthetics, adding those nice little touches that make the worksheet more attractive, readable and, perhaps most importantly, persuasive.

Most worksheets are prepared to persuade someone else to come to a particular conclusion. In the case of a budget or forecast, perhaps you're trying to convince your boss, or the board of directors, to go along with your assumptions. If you're preparing a business plan, maybe you need to sell your plan so a banker or venture capitalist will provide the needed funds for your new startup or to expand your existing business.

Whatever your worksheet's purpose, the way it looks and how well it's documented does matter and should be given as much consideration as the underlying data. Enhancing the appearance of your worksheet can be as simple as adding number signs to the dollar values or displaying important information in an attractive, bold font. You'll find that Excel has numerous formatting features for your worksheets—including the ability to draw right on the page. Because of the importance of worksheet formatting, you'll probably find that you spend as much time enhancing the appearance of your worksheets as you do creating them.

Don't worry if you think you don't have a good eye for design. This chapter includes some basic tips on making your worksheets attractive. Plus, Excel even has the ability to format your worksheet for you, with predesigned styles, formats, and worksheet templates.

ALIGNING CELL CONTENTS

Choosing the appropriate alignment for the contents of your cells can have an immediate impact on the look of the worksheet. You have seen that, by default, numbers are right-aligned and text is aligned on the left. A variety of alignment options can be applied to a single cell or a range of cells. This includes "pushing" the data to the far left, far right, or center of the cell. Many other content alignment options are available, as the following sections explain.

Left, Right, Center

Let's align the column headings so they are centered over the numbers. Aligning cells falls in the general category of cell formatting. You can reach the cell formatting options through the **Format Cells** command with the Alignment tab, but there is a shortcut.

1. Select cells B3 through E3.

2. Right-click (click the right mouse button) anywhere inside the selected range to display the Shortcut menu, as displayed in Figure 6.1.

SHORTCUT

There are Shortcut menus for almost every screen or worksheet element. You can display the shortcut menu by right-clicking on the object you want to manipulate. If you aren't sure what sort of manipulation you can perform on an object, the Shortcut menu lets you know. We'll be using shortcut menus for many tasks as the book proceeds.

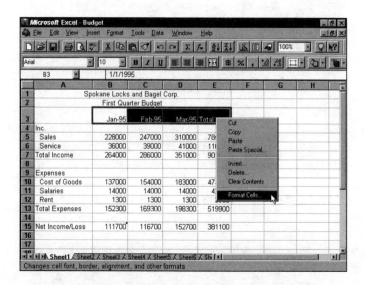

FIGURE 6.1 THE SHORTCUT MENU FOR THE SELECTED CELLS.

3. Choose **Format Cells** in the Shortcut menu.

    The Format Cells dialog box appears, as shown in Figure 6.2.

    The tabs in the dialog box let you specify what sort of formatting you want to do. We want to get to the Alignment portion of the dialog box.

4. If it isn't already highlighted, click on the **Alignment** tab to display the Alignment portion of the dialog box.

    This dialog box lets you specify the type of horizontal and vertical alignment you want, the orientation of the text in the cells, and if you want long text entries wrapped (split into several lines). These options are shown in Figure 6.3.

The two alignment types that might need a bit of explanation are Justify and Fill. If the Wrap check box is checked, the Justify option forces the cell entry to spread out so the left and right edges are even, like the text in this book. The Fill option repeats the cell entry until the cell is filled. These two options are explained in more detail later in this chapter.

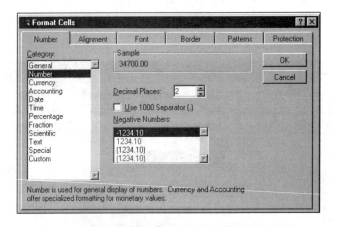

FIGURE 6.2 THE FORMAT CELLS DIALOG BOX NUMBER PORTION.

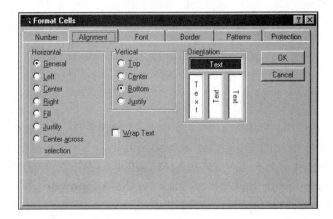

FIGURE 6.3 THE FORMAT CELLS DIALOG BOX ALIGNMENT PORTION.

5. Click on the **Center** option button in the Horizontal portion of the dialog box and click **OK**.

SHORTCUT

The toolbar has buttons for some of the more common cell formatting options, including these alignment options. Instead of using the dialog box, you can simply click on the appropriate toolbar button. In the previous step, you would click on the **Center** button on the Formatting toolbar.

Each column heading is now centered over its column, as displayed in Figure 6.4.

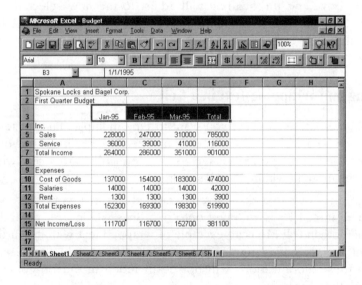

FIGURE 6.4 THE CENTER-ALIGNED COLUMN HEADINGS.

Centering Headings Across Columns

The title in cell A1 would look better if it were centered over all the columns in the worksheet. We can't just center it in the cell. It's already longer than the column width of column A. What can we do? One of the alignment options is to center across a selection. That's the option we'll use for the title.

1. Select cells A1 through E2.

   You are highlighting the information you want to center, plus the area in which you want to center it.

2. Click on the **Center Across Columns** toolbar button.

The title is now centered between columns A and E. Note that the toolbar button is a shortcut method of centering a title. You can also access the Center Across Selection option from the Alignment tab in the Format Cells dialog box, as shown in Figure 6.3.

You can adjust the width of any of the columns A through E and the headings will automatically adjust to fit your changes. If you add columns to your table and want to center the heading across a new set of columns, just repeat the steps above and the heading will adjust to the new selected columns. Remember, even though the headings now appear to be centered, the headings actually still exist in cells A1 and A2 where you typed them.

Justifying and Wrapping Text in a Cell

There may be occasions when you want to type multiples lines of text into a cell. This can be useful for entering notes or extended headings into your worksheet. Excel lets you type 255 characters of information into a cell, which you can then "wrap" to fit within the cell's width.

Figure 6.5 shows two examples of wrapped text in a worksheet. Note that the heading in cell E3 is wrapped onto two lines within the cell and is centered. The note in cell F16 is an example of wrapped text with the Justification alignment option. Following are the general steps to achieve these results, although these modifications will not be included in our on-going sample throughout this chapter.

1. Type the information you want wrapped onto multiple lines, then select the cell containing this data.

2. Select the **Format Cells** command and click on the **Alignment** page tab. Figure 6.3 shows the Alignment options.

3. Click the **Wrap Text** option, then choose any of the Horizontal alignment options to apply. Justify will create the results shown in cell F16 of Figure 6.5; left will create the results in cell A16.

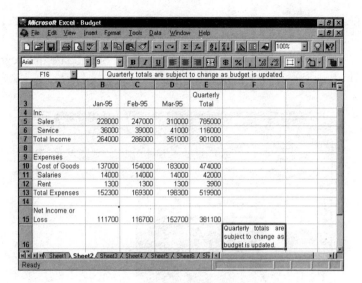

FIGURE 6.5 USING THE WRAP TEXT OPTION.

You can change the column width associated with any wrapped text and Excel will automatically adjust the wrapped data to fit the new column width. You may also adjust the corresponding row height for best results. Refer to Chapter 5 for more information on adjusting column widths and row heights.

FORMATTING NUMBERS

In addition to changing cell alignment, you may also choose to alter the format of the numbers in your worksheet. All of the numbers have been entered using Excel's default formatting. The numbers would look better if they were formatted with commas separating thousands and a decimal point with two decimal places.

1. Select B5 through E16 and click on the **Comma Style** button on the Formatting toolbar.

    The number format has been changed as shown in Figure 6.6, but some of the numbers have been replaced by pound signs. Uh oh! What does this mean? It means some of the numbers, with their new commas and decimal places, are now too wide for the column width. Don't worry, we can fix that.

2. Choose **Format, Column, AutoFit Selection**—or double-click on the right column border as described in Chapter 5.

The column widths have been adjusted to accommodate the new number format, as shown in Figure 6.7.

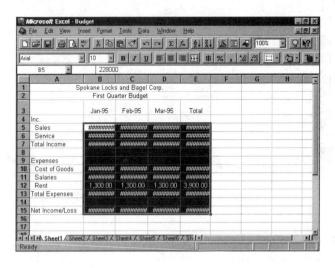

FIGURE 6.6 THE NUMBERS WITH THE COMMA FORMAT.

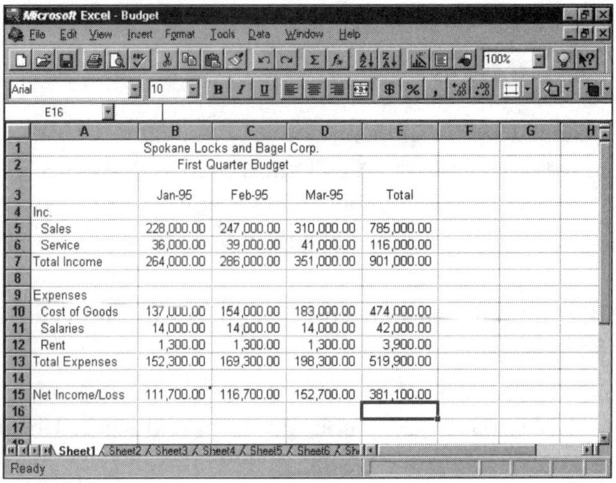

FIGURE 6.7 THE ADJUSTED COLUMN WIDTHS.

The totals might look better if they were formatted with dollar signs, so let's take care of that little detail now.

3. Select the ranges B8 through E8, E5 through E7, B16 through E16, and E11 through E14. Remember to press the **Ctrl** key as you highlight the ranges to select multiple ranges.

4. Click on the **Currency Style** button on the Formatting toolbar.

5. Once again choose **Format**, **Column**, **AutoFit Selection** to adjust the column widths to accommodate the dollar signs.

Your screen should now look like Figure 6.8.

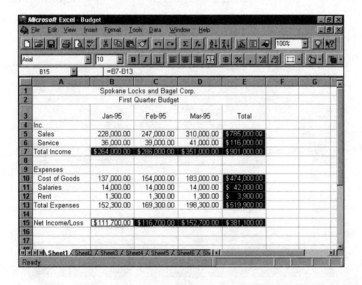

FIGURE 6.8 THE TOTALS ARE FORMATTED WITH THE CURRENCY STYLE.

There are many other number formatting options available through the Cell Formatting dialog box, which can be displayed through the Shortcut menu or the Format menu.

NOTE

Since the toolbar buttons offer only a limited selection of number formatting options, let's take a look at all the possibilities through the Format Cells command. In this case, we'll create a special numeric format that includes the dollar signs for the totals, but leaves out the two decimal places. We'll do the same with the values formatted with the comma style.

1. Select the ranges B8 through E8, E5 through E7, B16 through E16, and E11 through E14. Remember to press the **Ctrl** key as you highlight the ranges to select multiple ranges.

2. Select the **Cells** command from the Format menu and click the **Number** tab to see the number formatting options. The screen should look like Figure 6.9.

   Notice that the number format box shows that the current format of the selected cells is an Accounting format using a dollar sign and two decimal places. We can add or remove the dollar sign, change the number of decimal places, or even select a completely different format from here.

3. Click on the number wheel controlling the decimal places until it reads 0. When finished, click **OK**.

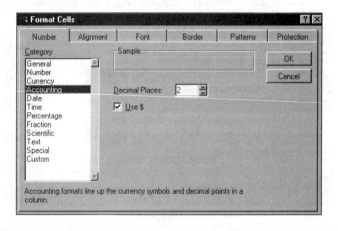

FIGURE 6.9 THE NUMBER FORMATTING OPTIONS IN THE FORMAT CELLS DIALOG BOX.

Using the above steps 2 and 3, change the ranges B5:D6 and B10:D13 to the Accounting format with no dollar sign and no decimal places.

DISPLAYING AND HIDING ZERO VALUES

Although the worksheet example we are using does not contain any zero values in its cells, eventually you will create a worksheet that does. Frequently, these zeros are not input by you on the keyboard, but calculated by formulas. However, your worksheet may look better if the cells with zero values are blank. Excel lets you choose whether to display or hide the zero value cells. Experiment with the following steps to see how this works; you can delete the added cells when finished.

◆ Choose **Tools**, **Options**, **View Selection**.

◆ If you check the **Zero Values** option, Excel displays all zero value cells, whether you enter the zeros yourself on the keyboard or they are calculated by a formula.

◆ Click on the **Zero Values** box to uncheck the box. Now you will have a worksheet with blank cells where there are zero values.

FONTS

A *font* is a particular typeface. Windows 95 includes several typefaces from which you can choose to add impact to your documents. You can also purchase additional fonts that work with almost any Windows program. Choosing the correct font for the situation can do more to help or hinder your cause than just about any other type of formatting, so choose carefully.

NOTE   There are many good books available to help you choose and use fonts well. If one of your goals is to produce the most professional looking and persuasive worksheets possible, learning more about fonts is a worthwhile investment of your time and money.

In addition to changing the font, you can change the style (bold, italic, underline) and the size of the font. Font sizes are specified in points because most fonts these days are proportional fonts.

The fonts used on a typewriter (and even some that are still used on computers) were fixed-width or monospaced, where each character took up the same amount of horizontal space. In proportional fonts, some characters are wider or narrower than others. For this reason, using the old method of measurement, based on the number of characters per inch (pitch) no longer works. Points measure the font's height. One point is roughly 1/72nd of an inch.

Typical font sizes for the main body of the worksheet are between 9 and 12 points. Anything smaller than 9-point type is considered fine print. Larger than 12-point type is considered large type.

NOTE With the introduction of Windows 3.1, a new font technology called *TrueType fonts* became available. TrueType fonts have several advantages over other font technologies. They are scalable to just about any point size you choose and have corresponding screen fonts so they display very accurately. They work with just about every Windows program in existence. Unless you are a real font connoisseur, you'll likely find the quality of TrueType fonts more than adequate. Keep in mind that TrueType is not a brand of fonts, but rather a *type* of font technology. You can buy TrueType fonts from a variety of manufacturers and the quality can vary.

Changing Fonts

Let's change the font, style and size of the title so that it really stands out. We'll do this using the Font list in the Excel toolbar at the top of the screen.

1. Click on cell A1.
2. Click on the **Arrow** for the font drop-down list on the Formatting toolbar to display the list of available fonts, as shown in Figure 6.10.

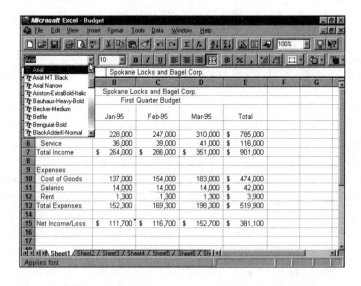

FIGURE 6.10 THE FORMATTING TOOLBAR'S DROP-DOWN FONT LIST.

The fonts in your list may differ from those in the figure. Only those fonts that are installed and available on your system appear on your list. Also, notice that some of the fonts have *TT* in front of them, signifying that they are TrueType fonts.

Let's use a slightly more ornate font called Times New Roman, which is currently out of view near the bottom of the list.

3. Use the scroll bar to scroll down until **Times New Roman** comes into view and then click on Times New Roman.

Notice that the typeface of the title has changed. Since this is a title, it should also be larger, so we'll change the size. The current size, as you can see from the Font Size box on the Formatting toolbar, is 10 points. Let's change it to 18 points.

4. Click on the **Font Size** arrow on the Formatting toolbar to reveal the list of font sizes, as shown in Figure 6.11.

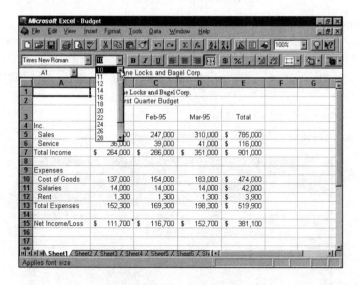

FIGURE 6.11 THE FONT SIZE DROP-DOWN LIST.

Unlike the list of fonts, the Font Size list only displays the more common sizes. However, you are not limited to these sizes. You can type in the size you wanted, say 19 points, and the font would change to that size.

5. Click on **18** to enlarge the title, as displayed in Figure 6.12.

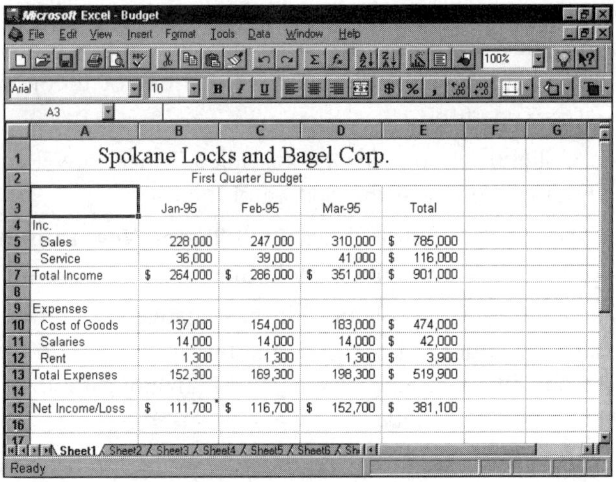

Figure 6.12 18-POINT TYPE.

Notice that the row height automatically adjusted for the larger size. If your font changes ever cause the heading to exceed the total width of the columns over which it is centered, you may have to use the Left alignment option to fix the problem. On the other hand, it's bad formatting to have a heading that exceeds its columns.

6. Click on the **Bold** toolbar button.

Your worksheet should look like Figure 6.13.

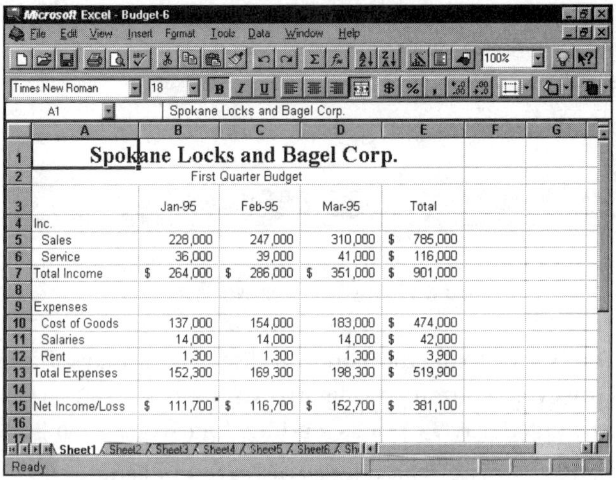

FIGURE 6.13 THE BOLD TITLE, COMPLETELY VISIBLE.

Although the fastest way to change fonts is from the toolbar, it may be advantageous to use the Font portion of the Format Cells dialog box, particularly if you aren't familiar with the way the different fonts look. The dialog box provides a preview of the font, including size and style, so you can see what the font looks like before you apply it.

Selecting a Standard Font

You can save time on fonts by selecting a standard font for your worksheet, which applies your font choice to the entire worksheet. This is useful if you want all the fonts on the worksheet to be the same. Of course, you can change individual cells at any time—even if you have changed the standard font. You can change the standard font in the Format Cells dialog box.

1. Select **Font** from the Format Cells dialog box.
2. In the **Font** box, select the font you like. In the **Font Style** box, select the font style (regular, italic, bold), and in the **Size** box, select the font size.
3. Click to place an X in the Normal Font box. You've now set the standard font on your worksheet. Click **OK** when finished.

Once you've found a font that you prefer, you may want to use it for all your worksheets. You can make your favorite font appear automatically on all your worksheets.

1. From the Tools menu Choose **Options**. Then click the **General** tab.
2. In the Standard Font box, select the font you prefer.
3. In the Size box, select the font size you prefer.
4. Click **OK** when finished.

Now your favorite font will automatically appear on all workbooks you open in Excel.

Adding Borders and Shading

To further embellish your worksheet, you can surround cells with borders and fill them with shading. As with fonts, you need to use appropriate borders and shading or these elements can detract from the look of the worksheet.

Let's add a border and some shading to the column headings.

1. Select B3 through E3.

2. Click on the **Arrow** for the Border drop-down box on the Formatting toolbar.

   The Border drop-down box is displayed, as shown in Figure 6.14.

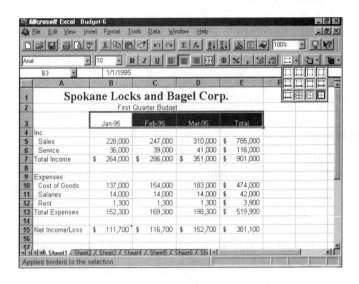

FIGURE 6.14 THE BORDER DROP-DOWN LIST.

3. Click on the border style of your choice. In our example, we're using the thick underline border (the one in the second row, second from the left).

4. Click outside the selection so you can see the border below the column headings, as shown in Figure 6.15.

   Now let's add some shading to the titles.

5. Select B3 through E3 again and right-click in the selection area to display the shortcut menu.

6. Click on the Shades drop-down list, as shown in Figure 6.16.

7. Click on the desired shade to fill the highlighted cells. Figure 6.17 shows the changes on the example worksheet.

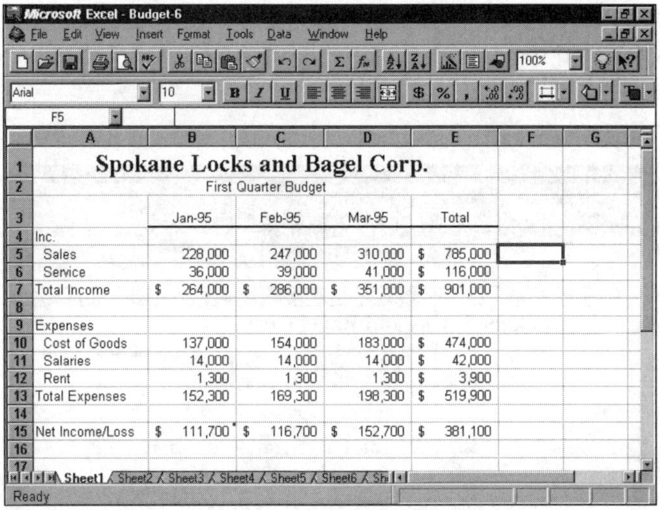

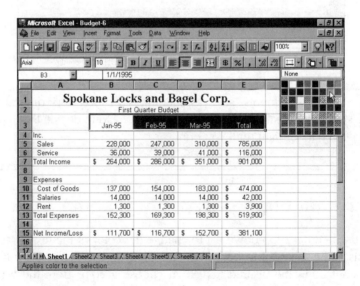

FIGURE 6.15 THE COLUMN HEADINGS WITH A BORDER BENEATH THEM.

FIGURE 6.16 THE CELL SHADES AVAILABLE.

8. Click on the fourth pattern from the left on the top row (it's the one the mouse pointer is pointing at in the figure).

The sample area in the dialog box displays the pattern you have chosen.

9. Click **OK** and then click outside the selected area so you can see the pattern's effect.

		Microsoft Excel - Budget-6				

Spokane Locks and Bagel Corp.

First Quarter Budget

	A	B	C	D	E	F	G
1							
2							
3		Jan-95	Feb-95	Mar-95	Total		
4	Inc.						
5	Sales	228,000	247,000	310,000	$ 785,000		
6	Service	36,000	39,000	41,000	$ 116,000		
7	Total Income	$ 264,000	$ 286,000	$ 351,000	$ 901,000		
8							
9	Expenses						
10	Cost of Goods	137,000	154,000	183,000	$ 474,000		
11	Salaries	14,000	14,000	14,000	$ 42,000		
12	Rent	1,300	1,300	1,300	$ 3,900		
13	Total Expenses	152,300	169,300	198,300	$ 519,900		
14							
15	Net Income/Loss	$ 111,700	$ 116,700	$ 152,700	$ 381,100		
16							
17							

FIGURE 6.17 THE COLUMN HEADINGS WITH A BORDER AND SHADING.

Graphic elements, such as shading, can look very different on the printed page than they do on the screen. Don't decide that a pattern is too dark or light until you print.

SHORTCUT

CHANGING THE COLOR OF TEXT

You can use another drop-down list to change the color of the text on the worksheet. This is the Text Color drop-down list, as shown in Figure 6.18. Just select the cells containing the desired text, then choose a color from the list. This is useful for showing certain values in red or blue. Remember that you'll need a color printer to see these enhancements on the printed version of your worksheet. A black-and-white printer will either print the worksheet without the colors or it will convert the colors to shades of gray. See Chapter 7 for more information about printing in color and gray shades.

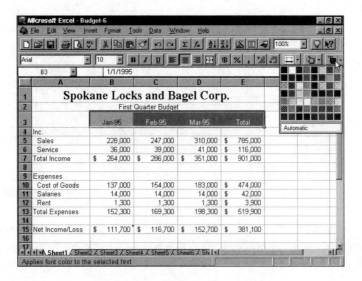

FIGURE 6.18 THE TEXT COLOR DROP-DOWN LIST.

SHORTCUT The Borders, Shades, and Text Color drop-down lists have a special shortcut feature available. The face of the button changes to the last selected border or shade. This indicates that you can simply click on the button's face to re-select the same choice again.

USING AUTOFORMAT

Suppose you have as little design sense as I have. Excel's AutoFormat feature turns your shabby old unformatted worksheet into a work of art.

All you have to do is select the portion of the worksheet you want automatically formatted and choose the most pleasing format style from the list in the AutoFormat dialog box. Let's try it out.

1. Select the range A3 through E16 and choose **Format**, **AutoFormat** to display the AutoFormat dialog box, as shown in Figure 6.19.

   The Simple Table Format is highlighted and you can see what that style looks like in the Sample area. The easiest way to check out the various options is with the down arrow key. Each time you press the **Down Arrow** key, you see another format style in the sample area.

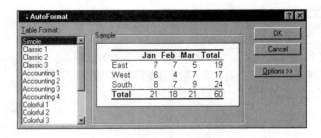

Figure 6.19 THE AUTOFORMAT DIALOG BOX.

We'll use the Classic 1 style. It's simple, yet elegant. We don't want to use anything too overpowering, do we?

2. Click on **Classic 1**, then **OK**, and then click outside the selected area so you can behold the beauty of the newly formatted worksheet, as displayed in Figure 6.20.

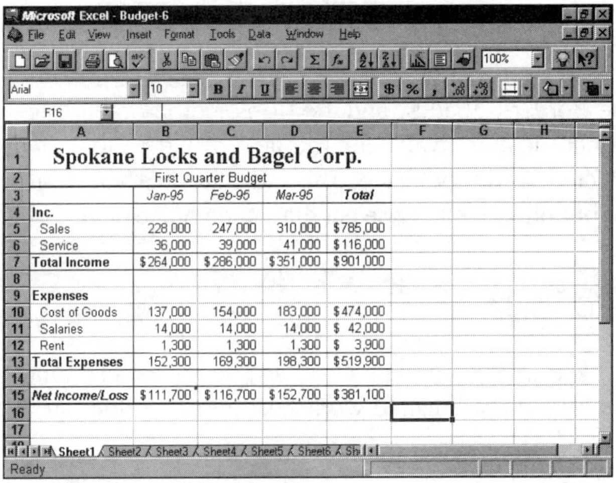

FIGURE 6.20 THE WORKSHEET FORMATTED WITH THE CLASSIC 1 STYLE.

REMOVING WORKSHEET GRIDLINES

As your worksheets begin to fill up with data, you might find the gridlines distracting rather than helpful. Removing the worksheet gridlines helps you see the worksheet formatting more clearly. Like removing zero values from cells, you can remove gridlines in the Tools menu.

1. From the Tools menu, select **Options**, then click the **View** tab.

2. Click on the **Gridlines** box, then click **OK**. Now you can view your worksheet without all those distracting lines. Figure 6.21 shows the results.

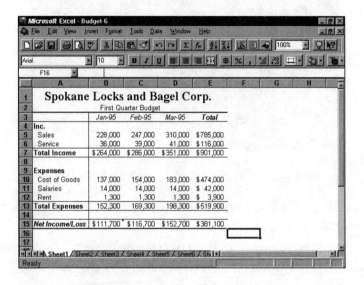

FIGURE 6.21 THE WORKSHEET WITH GRIDLINES REMOVED.

PROTECTING DATA

If you want to ensure that certain cells in the worksheet can't be accidentally altered (or even seen at all) you can lock or hide them. It's often a good idea to lock cells containing formulas so someone cannot accidentally delete them or enter something over them.

If your worksheet contains confidential information, you may want to hide portions of it. You can also require that a password be used to remove the protection you've specified.

Let's protect the formulas in column E.

1. Select cells E5 through E16 and right-click in the selected area to display the shortcut menu.

2. Choose **Format Cells** and click on the **Protection** tab to display the Protection portion of the Format Cells dialog box, as displayed in Figure 6.22.

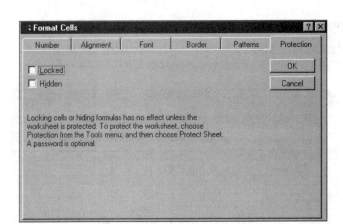

FIGURE 6.22 THE FORMAT CELLS DIALOG BOX PROTECTION PORTION.

3. Click in the **Locked** check box (unless it is already checked), and then click **OK**.

   Before the protection takes effect, you must turn on the protection facility.

4. Choose **Tools**, **Protection**, **Protect Sheet** to display the Protect Sheet dialog box, as displayed in Figure 6.23.

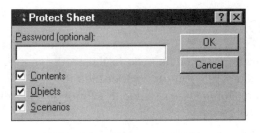

FIGURE 6.23 THE PROTECT SHEET DIALOG BOX.

5. After making sure all three check boxes are checked, click **OK**. (We won't add a password.)

   Now, let's see if the protection is really working.

6. Press the **Delete** key to try to delete the contents of the selected cells.

   The message dialog box, as shown in Figure 6.24, lets you know that you cannot mess with locked cells. It works!

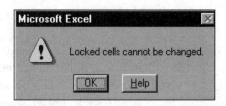

FIGURE 6.24 THE MESSAGE DIALOG BOX SHOWING THAT A CELL IS LOCKED.

7. Click **OK** to clear the dialog box.
8. Choose **Tools**, **Protection**, **Unprotect Sheet** to remove protection from this sheet.

COPYING FORMATS

If you spend time creating the desired fonts, sizes, styles, colors, borders and protection status in the cells of your worksheet, you might want to duplicate your efforts rather than repeat them. You can easily copy the formatting from one cell and apply it to another cell containing different data.

1. Move to cell E3.
2. Select the **Copy** command from the Edit menu.
3. Highlight cells B3 through D3.
4. Choose the **Paste Special** command from the Edit menu, then click the **Formats** option from the Paste options provided. Click **OK** when finished.

The formatting of the cell you copy is applied to the other cells. A shortcut to perform this task is by using the Format Painter button on the toolbar. Just click on the cell you want to copy, then click the **Format Painter** button. Next, click on the cell on you want to apply the formats (see Figure 6.25).

FIGURE 6.25 THE FORMAT PAINTER

USING STYLES

Now that you've made your worksheet look just the way you want it, you may want to create other worksheets that look just like it. Rather than going through all the steps in this chapter, you can save a lot of time by setting it up as a style in the Styles list. The Styles list contains some preset styles, but you can also save your own formatting masterpieces in the Styles list.

Accessing the Style Tool

To use the Styles list, first you have to add the Style button to your toolbar. Creating custom toolbars is explained in detail in Chapter 15. Here we'll just quickly move through the steps.

1. Choose **View**, **Toolbars**, **Customize**.
2. Click on **Text Formatting**.
3. Drag the Style tool to your toolbar.
4. Click **Close**.

Now you're ready to start working with Styles. Figure 6.26 shows a toolbar with the Styles list added next to the Fonts list.

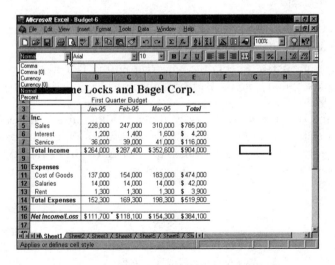

FIGURE 6.26 THE STYLES LIST ADDED TO THE TOOLBAR.

Applying Styles

You can automatically format all or a portion of your worksheet using the Styles list. The following steps can be applied to any cell or range on any worksheet.

1. Select the cells on your worksheet you want formatted.
2. Click the **Styles** button and choose the style you want from the list.
3. Excel asks if you want to change the current style to match the cells you selected. Choose **No**.

   Excel changes the worksheet to match the style you selected.

Creating Styles

If you want to re-use the formatting on the worksheet you just finished, you can use the formatting as an example to create your own style. This is called *creating a style by example.*

1. When you've finished formatting a cell the way you want it (from the Format Cells menu), place the cell pointer on that cell.
2. Click in the box where the style name is displayed (don't click on the down arrow next to it). This should cause the style name to become highlighted.
3. Think up a short, descriptive, and catchy name for your style, and type it in the style name box. Your typing will replace the current style name in the box.
4. Press **Enter**.

You've now added your very own style to the styles list, and it will appear every time you choose the Styles list. To reuse the style (which includes all of the formatting options: fonts, colors, shading, and so on) simply choose it from the list.

 As you become a more advanced Excel user, you may know exactly how you want to format cells without seeing the formatting first. Then you can create a style from the **Style Name** command in the Format menu, which brings up the Format Cells dialog box. Create your style using the options in the Format Cells dialog box. This is called *creating a style by definition.*

Changing Existing Styles

If you have a change of heart about something in a style that you've already used in your worksheet, Excel allows you to change it and automatically applies the changes to all cells that use that style. You can change a style either by example, or by definition. Let's look at how to change a style by example.

1. Select a cell that has been formatted with the style you want to change.

2. Select **Format, Cells** and make the changes you want to the cell format.

3. Pull down the Styles list and choose the name of the style that is already applied to the cell.

4. Excel asks if you want to change the current style to match the cells you selected. Choose **OK** to change the style. (If you choose **No**, Excel reapplies the old style and all your formatting changes are lost.)

   All the cells with that style are automatically changed.

To change a style by definition, you access the **Style** command from the Format menu and select the style you want to change. Click on the **Modify** button and make the changes you want.

As you can see, using styles can be a real time saver. But the benefits only occur when you format using styles. For this reason, you should use styles to format all your worksheets.

Using Templates

Once you begin creating lots of worksheets, you may notice that many of them contain the same elements over and over again. These repeated elements may include formatting (including styles, display settings, and outline settings) and actual data and calculations. You can create a master worksheet (called a *template*) based on these repeated elements, so that you don't have to re-create them with every new worksheet.

A template is actually a certain type of file format in Excel that you use as a starting point for new files. When you create a worksheet using a template, saving the file does not change the template you used to start it.

Creating a Template

You can create a template by making a worksheet that contains all the elements you want to repeat in your worksheets and then saving it as a template.

1. Make the master worksheet you want to use as a template.
2. Choose **Save As** from the File menu.
3. Choose **Template** from the **Save As Type** list.
4. Think up a name for your master worksheet and type it in.

   Excel saves your master worksheet as a template, which you can use over and over again.

DESIGN TIPS

Although you have an almost unlimited choice of fonts, font sizes and font styles, try to avoid cluttering your worksheet with too many different fonts. Stick to two or three fonts, and establish a system that you use throughout your worksheet. For example, you can use one font for headings (with two or three levels identified by size, bold or italics) and another font for text.

A FINAL THOUGHT

You now know how to put together a worksheet so that it is presentable, fully documented, and protected. In the next chapter you learn how to transfer your masterpiece to the printed page.

CHAPTER 7

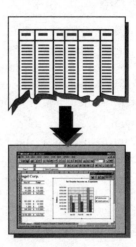

PRINTING WORKSHEETS

- ♦ Choosing a printer
- ♦ Setting up pages

Because the printed page is ultimately how the information in most worksheets is communicated, printing may be the most important task you can learn in Excel. The options for what portion of your workbook (or worksheets) you want to print, and how you want them printed, are almost limitless.

CHOOSING A PRINTER

Windows makes life easy by allowing all your Windows programs to share the same printer files without having to install your printer for each program, as you do with non-Windows programs. If you already have one or more printers installed in Windows, they are automatically available to Excel. If you don't have a printer installed, refer to your Windows documentation for instructions.

If you have more than one printer installed, you need to choose the printer you want to use from the Printer Setup dialog box to be sure Excel uses the right one.

1. Start Excel and open the Budget workbook if it isn't already on your screen.

2. Choose **File, Print**.

   The Print dialog box appears, as shown in Figure 7.1.

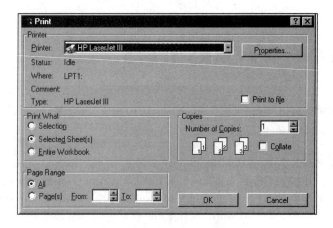

FIGURE 7.1 THE PRINT DIALOG BOX.

When we are ready to print the worksheet in a little while, we'll take a look at the various options in the Print dialog box.

3. Click on the **Printer** drop-down list to display the Printer list, as shown in Figure 7.2.

   You can choose any printer from this list as a destination for your document. Depending on how you installed Windows 95, you may have a fax listed and one or more printers.

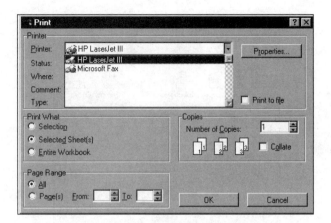

FIGURE 7.2 THE PRINTER DROP-DOWN LIST.

4. Click on the printer you want to use from the list of available printers, then click **OK**.

   If your chosen printer is already selected, click **OK**. Notice that under the Printer selection list is a summary of details about the printer. Also included is a Properties button to set up different aspects of your printer. Each type of printer has different setup information. Let's take a look.

The list of printers you see in the Printer Setup dialog box most likely differs from the list in the figure. Your list reflects the printers that have been installed in Windows. If only one printer is connected to your computer, your list probably only has that one printer's name in the list.

N O T E

5. Choose the **Properties** button to see the setup screen. Figure 7.3 shows an example for the HP LaserJet III printer. Your printer setup information might look different.

6. Click **Cancel** to return to the Print dialog box.

You could click **OK** to print the active worksheet according to default settings, but we're going to explore some of the other printing options before sending the worksheet to the printer.

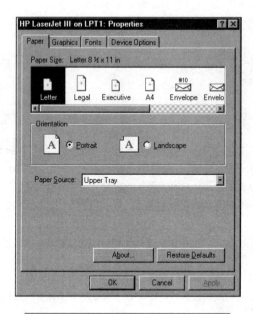

FIGURE 7.3 THE PRINTER PROPERTIES DIALOG BOX.

SETTING UP PAGES

Excel needs some information about how you want your pages printed before you start printing. If you don't provide this information, Excel prints using its current settings, which may not be what you want to use.

Let's take a look at the settings in the Print dialog box on your screen (refer to Figure 7.1). The Print dialog box lets you opt to print the selection (if you've selected a portion of your worksheet), the selected sheet(s), or the entire workbook. You'll see how to specify specific ranges to print in a little while.

You can also choose how many copies you want to print and whether you want to print all the pages or, if not, which specific pages. Let's call up the Page Setup dialog box now to start giving Excel some more details.

1. Click **Cancel** to remove the Print dialog box if it's still on the screen, then choose the **Page Setup** command from the File menu to display the Page Setup dialog box, as shown in Figure 7.4. If the Sheet portion of the dialog box isn't visible, click on the **Sheet** tab.

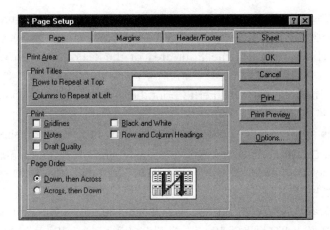

FIGURE 7.4 THE PAGE SETUP DIALOG BOX SHEET PORTION.

In the Print Area text box, you can specify a range of cells to print. Let's specify the range A1 through G16.

2. Click in the **Print Area** text box and type **A1:G16**.

The reason we need to go all the way over to column G is to make sure the entire title is printed. Even though the title is actually in cell A1, the print area specifies an actual rectangular area on the worksheet. If we only printed over to column E, for example, we'd end up cutting off the last word and a half of the title.

SHORTCUT

You can use the pointing method to specify a print area. Simply point to one corner of the rectangular area you want to print and then drag to the opposite corner and release the mouse button. The range automatically is entered in the Print Area text box.

This method can be a little tricky because the Page Setup dialog box usually obscures the range you want to print. You can drag over the dialog box, but that's kind of like flying blind, so, whether typing the range or pointing and dragging, it's a good idea to know what range you want to print before you display the Page Setup dialog box. The Rows to Repeat at Top and the Columns to Repeat at Left text boxes let you specify one or more rows and columns to repeat on each page of multiple-page printouts. This can be useful for keeping track of which column and row headings a particular cell entry belongs to. We don't have a multiple-page worksheet to print, so we won't use these options.

The check boxes in the Print area of the dialog box provide several options for customizing the way your pages print.

◆ **Gridlines** chooses whether to print the lines you see on your worksheet separating rows and columns.

◆ **Notes** prints any cell notes you have attached to your worksheet.

◆ **Draft Quality** causes Excel to omit any charts or other graphic objects, as well as gridlines, from your printout. Draft Quality often causes your pages to print faster.

◆ **Black and White** is chosen if you have used any colors for text or graphics on your worksheet and are printing on a black and white printer. This option may also cause your pages to print faster on a color printer, since color printers often print slower in color than black and white.

◆ **Row and Column Heading** causes the row numbers and the column letters to print. This can make it easier to determine which cell a particular entry is in, but it can also detract from the look of the page.

◆ **Print Order** specifies how multiple pages print. This won't affect our single-page printout.

3. With the Print Area text box filled in and only the Gridlines check box checked, click on the **Page** tab to display the Page portion of the Page Setup dialog box, as shown in Figure 7.5.

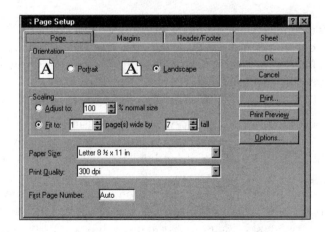

FIGURE 7.5 THE PAGE SETUP DIALOG BOX PAGE PORTION.

♦ **Orientation** determines whether you want the information printed on the page in the normal upright (portrait) orientation, or sideways (landscape). Portrait orientation allows you to print more rows but fewer columns on a page. Landscape accommodates more columns but fewer rows. We'll keep portrait as our orientation option.

♦ **Scaling** adjusts the size of the document you are about to print. The Adjust to option button lets you print at 100% (normal size) or a smaller or larger percentage. For example, if you adjust to 200%, all the data, including text, numbers, and graphics prints at twice their normal size. This means that each page only holds half as much data. You can scale pages up to 400% and down to 10%.

♦ **Fit to** lets you force the information you want to print to fit on a specified number of pages. This can be useful for shoehorning your data into fewer pages than it might otherwise require. This option does not enlarge the data on the worksheet to fit on the specified pages.

WARNING

Be careful with this option. You could end up with such small print that you cannot read it. Actually, come to think of it, for some worksheets, that might be an advantage!

♦ **Paper Size** lets you choose the paper size you are using in your printer. Some printers are only able to use one or two sizes of paper and the list reflects your printer's capabilities.

♦ **Print Quality** selects the quality of print for your document. The tradeoff here is that choosing a higher quality generally results in slower print speeds. You may want to print with a lower print quality for drafts and a higher quality of final prints.

N O T E

Some printers don't have print quality options. For others, a change in print quality only affects graphics. The latter is true of laser printers. On a laser printer, the worksheet's text and numbers print at the same quality regardless of your print quality choice in Excel.

♦ **First Page Number** specifies the starting number that is printed on the first page of a worksheet. For example, if you enter 3 as the First Page Number for a three-page worksheet you are about to print, the pages are numbered 3, 4, and 5. This option has no effect if you choose not to have page numbers printed on your pages.

We won't be changing any of the options on the Page portion of the dialog box, so let's take a look at the Margins portion of the dialog box.

4. Click on the **Margins** tab to display the Margins portion of the dialog box, as displayed in Figure 7.6.

Changing the margin setting lets you determine where your document appears on the printed page. The default top, bottom, left, and right margins are generally adequate. You may wish to reduce the margins so you can fit more data on a page, or you may want to increase the margins so you have more breathing room (white space) around your data.

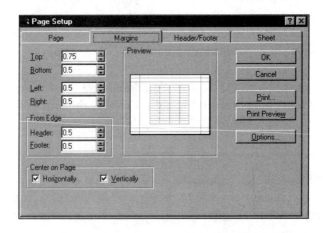

FIGURE 7.6 THE PAGE SETUP DIALOG BOX MARGINS PORTION.

You can also specify how far from the edge of the page your headers and footers appear. You'll learn more about headers and footers in just a bit.

We use a couple of the options on this dialog box to center the data both vertically and horizontally on the printed page.

5. Click both the **Horizontally** and **Vertically** check boxes in the Center on Page area of the dialog box.

Notice that the Preview area now shows a representation of the data as centered on the page.

Before we finish setting up the pages, let's take a look at headers and footers.

6. Click on the **Header/Footer** tab to display the Header/Footer portion of the Page Setup dialog box, as shown in Figure 7.7.

    Headers and footers are text elements that appear at the top and bottom of your printed documents. There is no difference between a header and a footer except that a header appears at the top of the printed page and a footer appears at the bottom.

    Excel prints default headers and footers unless you specify different ones, or specify none at all. The default header simply prints the sheet name. The sheet name is Sheet1, Sheet2, and so forth, unless you've changed the name to something else. The default footer is Page 1 for the first page, Page 2 for the second page, and so on.

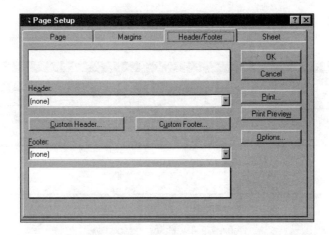

FIGURE 7.7 THE PAGE SETUP DIALOG BOX HEADER/FOOTER PORTION.

Excel also provides a variety of predefined headers and footers that you can use. Figure 7.8 displays some of the predefined headers (the predefined footers are the same) that can be seen by clicking on the **Arrow** for the Header drop-down list.

Instead of using one of the predefined headers, let's create a custom header.

7. Click on the **Custom Header** button to display the Header dialog box, as shown in Figure 7.9.

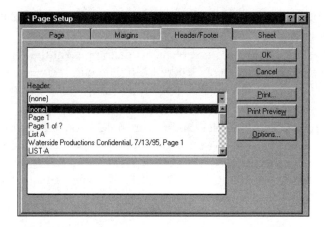

FIGURE 7.8 THE HEADER DROP-DOWN LIST.

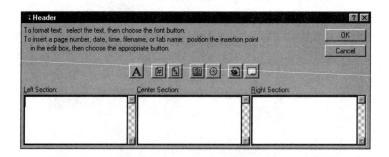

FIGURE 7.9 THE HEADER DIALOG BOX.

The dialog box displays the current header. But wait a minute. That thing in the middle box doesn't look like the header we saw in the previous dialog box. The default header is the sheet name centered between the left and right margins. What you see in the Header dialog box is the code for the sheet name. In addition to the sheet name, when creating a custom header (or footer) you can insert codes for the page number, the total number of pages, the date and time, and the filename by clicking on the appropriate icon. There's even an icon to allow you to change the font you're using for the header or footer.

Let's type some text in the Left Section.

8.	Click in the **Left Section** box and type **Prepared by Saul Salmon**.

9. Click in the **Center Section** box and press **Backspace** until all the text is deleted, then click on the **Date** icon. (Refer to Figure 7.9)

10. Click in the **Right Section** box and then click on the file name icon.

Your screen should now look like Figure 7.10.

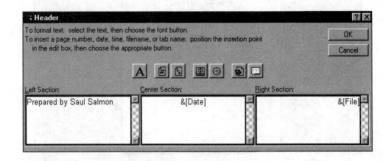

FIGURE 7.10 THE HEADER DIALOG BOX WITH THE CUSTOM HEADER FILLED IN.

11. Click **OK** to accept the custom header and return to the Header/Footer section of the Page Setup dialog box, where you see what your new header actually looks like.

12. Click **OK** to accept the header and footer and return to the Print dialog box.

We're just about ready to print, but first we'll preview the page. It's almost always a good idea to preview before sending a document to the printer. It can save time and paper by letting you ensure that everything is just the way you want it.

13. Click **OK** to complete the Page Setup settings you've established, then choose the **Print Preview** command from the File menu to display a reasonable facsimile of what your printed pages will look like when they emerge from the printer.

Because you're looking at a full page, it's hard to see the detail of the worksheet (unless you have a very large screen). Notice that as you move the mouse pointer over the representation of the page, the pointer turns into a magnifying glass. By clicking on a portion of the page, you can zoom in on that portion.

Let's zoom in on the January column heading (where the mouse pointer is in Figure 7.11).

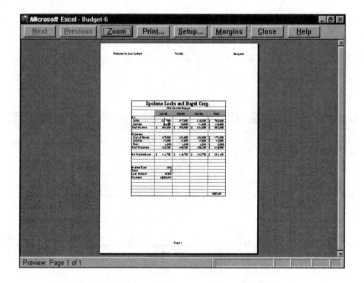

FIGURE 7.11 THE PRINT PREVIEW SCREEN.

14. Point to **Jan** and click. See Figure 7.12 for results.

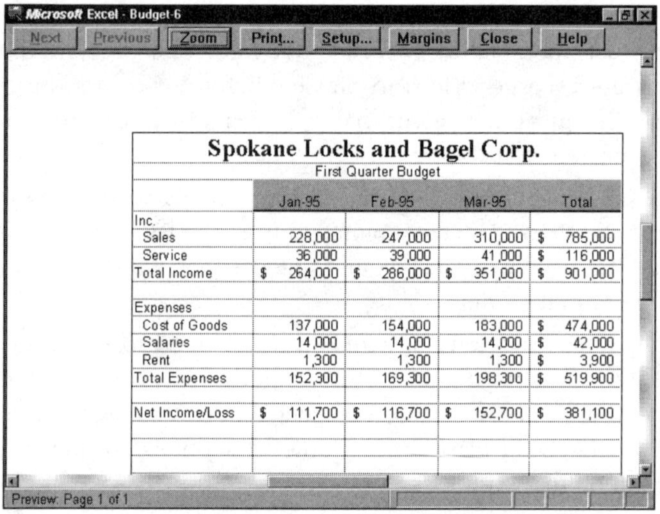

FIGURE 7.12 THE ZOOMED PREVIEW.

You can zoom out by clicking anywhere on the page or clicking on the **Zoom** button at the top of the Preview screen. The Next and Previous buttons let you preview the next and previous pages in multipage documents. The Setup button takes you back to the Page Setup dialog box.

The one button in preview that does something a bit unique is the Margins button. I know, we already looked at the Margins portion of the Page Setup dialog box. But clicking on the Margins button in Print Preview lets you change margins by dragging margin and column markers so you can see the result prior to printing.

15. Click on the **Margins** button.

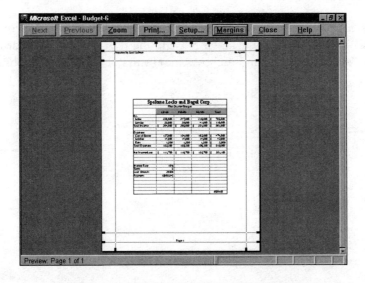

FIGURE 7.13 THE MARGIN MARKERS DISPLAYED IN PRINT PREVIEW.

By moving the mouse pointer over one of the markers until it turns into crosshairs, as shown in Figure 7.13, you can reposition any of the margins or columns by dragging. The status bar displays information about which margin you are changing and its position as you drag.

We won't change any of the margins here. It's time to print. Be sure your printer is properly connected, has paper, is turned on, on line, and ready to print.

16. Click on the **Print** button to send the worksheet to the printer.

You see a message dialog box informing you that you are printing to the printer you have selected. In a few seconds, your printed worksheet should appear.

The next time you want to print using the same settings, simply click on the **Print** button on the toolbar.

To go directly to Print Preview, click on **Print Preview** on the toolbar.

17. Save your work so the print setting is retained for the next time you want to print and exit Excel if you are not moving on to the next chapter.

A FINAL THOUGHT

The process of setting up your pages for printing and sending them to your printer should be a piece of cake by now. In the next chapter you learn how to turn your worksheet's text and numbers into beautiful charts and graphs.

CHAPTER 8

CREATING A CHART

- ♦ Chart fundamentals
- ♦ Understanding chart types
- ♦ Creating charts
- ♦ Changing chart data
- ♦ Changing chart types
- ♦ Editing charts
- ♦ Adding a data series
- ♦ Creating charts in chart sheets
- ♦ Printing charts

As the saying goes, a picture is worth a thousand words. If you have ever thought of a chart as a nice little extra, or even a waste of time and energy, think again!

If the purpose of your worksheet is to increase your readers' understanding of the numerical data and to persuade them to accept your point of view, then adding a chart is much more than a frill. It is an integral part of the information package. A chart can enhance clarity and add strength to your message.

Until now we have been working strictly with numerical data. I won't deny the importance of numbers—just try sending a bunch of pictures to the IRS and see how far you get! But often, numeric data is just a means to an end. A chart can enable you to direct your reader's focus and make your points with pizzazz.

CHART FUNDAMENTALS

Before we start creating charts, we need to understand some fundamental chart concepts and terminology. After all, the world of charts is very different from the worksheet world we have been working with until now. We are really charting new territory here. (Sorry about that—I just couldn't help myself.)

If some of the terminology we are about to cover seems a bit murky and arcane, don't worry. As we progress through the steps in this chapter, the fog lifts. Excel makes preparing charts automatic enough that you do not need to master all the details to be able to create good looking charts. However, an understanding of charting basics increases your comfort level and allows you to prepare even more powerful charts.

Chart Elements

A *chart* is a graphical representation of the numeric data in a worksheet. Each cell (piece of data) represented in the chart is called a *data point*. Data points are represented on the chart by bars, columns, lines or some other graphical device. A group of related data points is called a *data series*. For example, if we were charting the quarter's monthly income compared with expenses, each month's income or expense figure would be a data point. The January, February, and March income figures are one data series and the January, February, and March expense figures are another data series.

Typically, values are plotted along the vertical plane (y-axis) and categories are plotted along the horizontal plane (x-axis). Labels that run horizontally under the various data series and display the categories represented are *x-axis labels*. Labels running vertically and listing the value increments are *y-axis labels*. Tick marks on the axes are the small lines that indicate different data categories or increments of value. The plot area of the chart is the area that includes the axes lines and all the data series.

Chart text is a label that identifies items in the chart. If you attach it to an object (like a data point) in the chart, it is unmovable. If the chart text is not attached to an object, it can be moved. You can also add gridlines to your chart to help identify the values. Notice that the chart consists of data series, which are the two sets of bars in Figure 8.1. In a line chart, the data series would be the lines. Data series are made up of a number of data points, which are the individual bars or points on a line.

Most charts include a title, a legend to help clarify what each data series represents, a y-axis title and an x-axis title. Many other elements can be added to a chart and all of the chart elements can be customized to suit your requirements, but these are the most common elements you find in a chart.

Figure 8.1 shows a typical chart with the data series represented by columns. This is called a *column chart.*

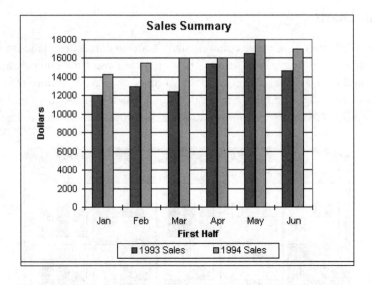

FIGURE 8.1 A TYPICAL COLUMN CHART WITH THE BASIC CHART ELEMENTS.

Use Excel's Chart Wizard to step through the chart creation process. You can create charts that are embedded in the worksheet or place charts on their own chart sheets. It makes sense to place charts on their own chart sheets if you want to print charts on separate pages from the worksheet data to use for handouts. You might want to incorporate chart files in a presentation graphics program such as Microsoft PowerPoint. Embedded charts are placed on the same worksheet as the data they represent. Using an embedded chart, you can see the chart and numerical data at the same time.

Whether a chart is embedded or on a chart sheet, it is linked to the data it represents. This means if the numbers change, the chart changes to reflect the new numbers.

UNDERSTANDING CHART TYPES

Excel lets you choose from a dizzying array of chart types. To add to your decision-making burden, you can also choose from a variety of formats for each of the chart types. So how do you decide which chart type to use for a particular situation? There are no hard and fast rules. However, if you understand the primary intended uses for each of Excel's chart types, the choice is easier.

Column Charts

Excel's default chart type is the column chart. *Column charts* are made up of vertical columns representing data series. They are often used for comparing two or more related data series at a specific point in time, or a small amount of data over time. Excel provides options for several column chart formats, including side-by-side columns, overlapping columns, and stacked columns, as shown in Figure 8.2.

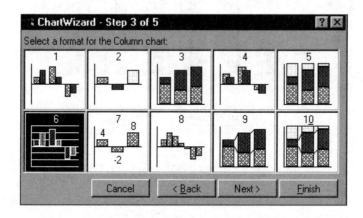

FIGURE 8.2 THE VARIOUS COLUMN CHART FORMATS.

The stacked column chart formats (options 3, 5, 9, and 10) are useful for displaying how much a piece of data contributes to the aggregate. Option 2 is the best choice for column charts representing only one data series, since each column in the series uses a different color or pattern.

In addition to the array of two-dimensional column charts, there are also several three-dimensional (3-D) column chart formats. Choosing a three-dimensional versus a two-dimensional chart is mostly a matter of aesthetics. However, the third dimension gives an additional axis—the Z (value) axis.

Figure 8.3 shows the 3-D column chart formats.

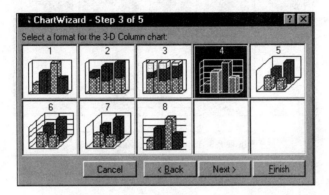

FIGURE **8.3** THE 3-D COLUMN CHART FORMATS.

Bar Charts

Bar charts are column charts turned on their side—the columns are horizontal instead of vertical. Just as with the column charts, options 3, 5, 9, and 10 are stacked bars. Option 2 is the choice for charts with a single data series.

Figure 8.4 shows the bar chart formats.

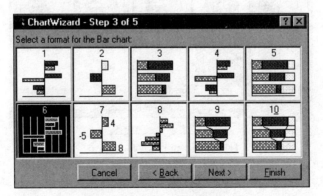

FIGURE **8.4** THE BAR CHART FORMATS.

You can also select from a variety of 3-D bar charts, as shown in Figure 8.5.

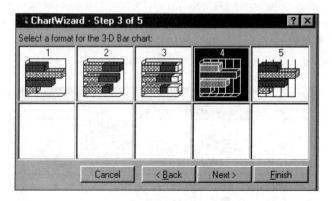

FIGURE 8.5 THE 3-D BAR CHART FORMATS.

Pie Charts

Pie charts are great for displaying proportional relationships between data, such as the share each bagel flavor contributes to the hole, er, whole. The pie chart's primary limitation is that it can only display one data series.

Figure 8.6 shows the pie chart formats.

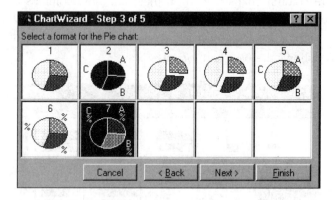

FIGURE 8.6 THE PIE CHART FORMATS.

Pie charts are also available as 3-D charts. Unlike 3-D column and bar charts, 3-D pie charts do not gain an additional axis. Their only advantage is their different appearance. Figure 8.7 shows the 3-D pie chart formats.

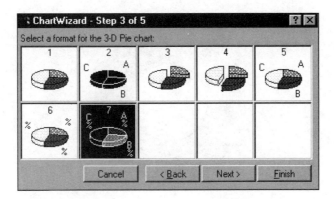

FIGURE 8.7 THE 3-D PIE CHART FORMATS.

Doughnut Charts

Doughnut charts are much like pie charts, and are used for the same purpose. They have one major advantage over pie charts; they can be used to plot more than one data series. A doughnut chart with more than one data series uses a separate ring for each series.

Figure 8.8 shows the doughnut chart formats.

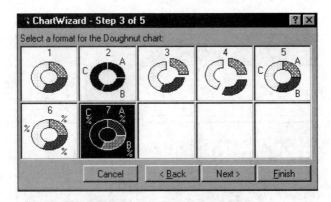

FIGURE 8.8 THE DOUGHNUT CHART FORMATS.

Figure 8.9 is an example of a doughnut chart with three data series.

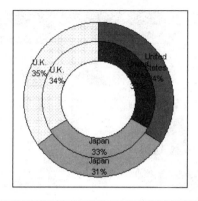

FIGURE 8.9 A DOUGHNUT CHART WITH MULTIPLE DATA SERIES.

Line Charts

Use *line charts* to emphasize the continuity of data over time. They are also a good choice for showing trends. They are especially useful for showing large sets of data, such as the sales of a product over a five-year period. Several of the line chart format options are particularly useful for charting highs and lows, such as snowfall or stocks, and are sometimes referred to as *Hi-Lo* and *Hi-Lo-Close* charts. Options 7, 8, and 9 are of the Hi-Lo variety.

Figure 8.10 shows the line chart formats.

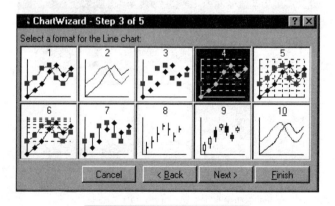

FIGURE 8.10 THE LINE CHART FORMATS.

Figure 8.11 shows the available 3-D line chart formats.

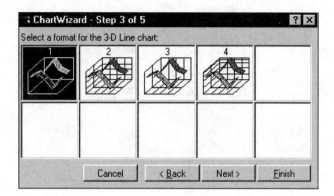

FIGURE 8.11 THE 3-D LINE CHART FORMATS.

Area Charts

Area charts are essentially line charts with the space between the lines filled in. Figure 8.12 shows the area chart formats.

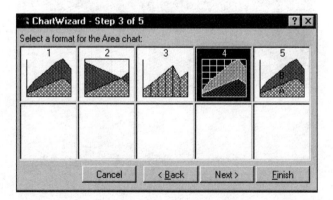

FIGURE 8.12 THE AREA CHART FORMATS.

Figure 8.13 shows the 3-D area chart formats. Like the 3-D column and bar charts, this gives them an additional axis.

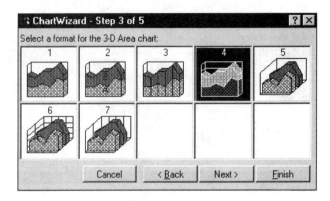

FIGURE 8.13 THE 3-D AREA CHART FORMATS.

3-D Surface Charts

3-D surface charts are similar to 3-D area charts. Figure 8.14 shows the 3-D surface chart formats.

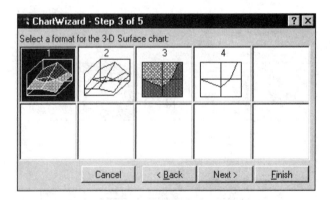

FIGURE 8.14 THE 3-D SURFACE CHART FORMATS.

Radar Charts

Radar charts are similar to line charts, but are often used for comparing the whole value of several data series. Figure 8.15 shows the radar chart formats.

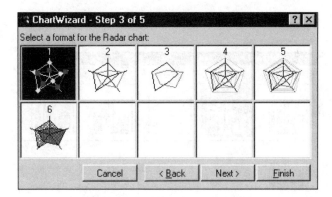

FIGURE 8.15 THE RADAR CHART FORMATS.

XY (Scatter) Charts

Unlike the other chart types discussed so far, *XY (scatter) charts* use both axes for values. This allows you to plot relationships between two data series, such as the effects of temperature on an electronic component's failure rate.

Figure 8.16 shows the XY (scatter) chart formats.

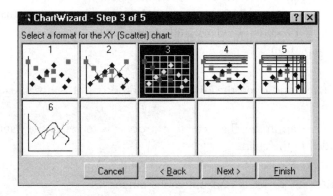

FIGURE 8.16 THE XY (SCATTER) CHART FORMATS.

Combination Charts

Combination charts let you combine two chart types to contrast multiple data series. For example, you might use the column chart portion of a combination chart to plot store sales and use a line chart to show the store's projected sales.

Figure 8.17 shows the combination chart formats.

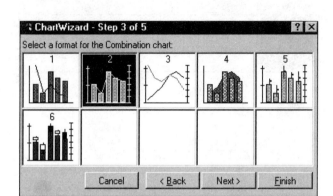

FIGURE 8.17 THE COMBINATION CHART FORMATS.

CREATING CHARTS

Let's start by creating a chart next to the numbers in our Spokane Locks and Bagel Corp. First Quarter Budget numbers. We start with a chart that plots the first quarter's total income. Later we add the total expenses over the three month period for comparison.

1. Start Excel and open the **BUDGET** workbook if it is not already on your screen.

    The first step in the chart creation process is to select the data you want included in the chart.

2. Select the ranges A3 through D3 and A8 through D8. Do not forget to use the **Ctrl** key to select noncontiguous ranges.

    We included the empty cell A3 in the first range because the Chart Wizard understands how to deal with selections if each spans the same number of columns.

    Although this example does not show it, you do not have to select complete elements when creating your chart. You can select any element of your worksheet to include in your chart. For example, you might want to create a chart that compares the Sales Income and Salary Expenses for January and February. You can select an entire block of data to chart if you like; the number of columns and rows you choose determines the number of data series and plot points in your chart. For more information on how your data selection affects the data series in your chart, see "Editing Charts" later in this chapter. One caveat: don't include totals in a chart that also plots the values making up the total. For example, if you create a chart that plots the Income lines in our example worksheet (rows 4 through 7) then don't include the total in row 8.

3. Click on the **Chart Wizard** button on the toolbar and then, without clicking, position the mouse pointer (which now has chart icon attached) in the upper-left corner of cell G3. Figure 8.18 shows the selected range.

You could just click the mouse and let Excel choose the size of the chart for you. Drag the mouse pointer to the lower-right corner of our desired chart size to create a larger chart that is easier to work with. You can, of course, change the size of a chart after it is created, and you learn how to do that later.

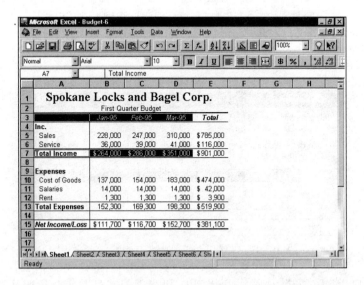

FIGURE 8.18 THE SELECTED RANGES FOR THE CHART AND THE CHART WIZARD MOUSE POINTER.

4. Drag down to row 16 and over to column M, as shown in Figure 8.19. The screen automatically scrolls as you drag the mouse pointer to the right edge of the screen.

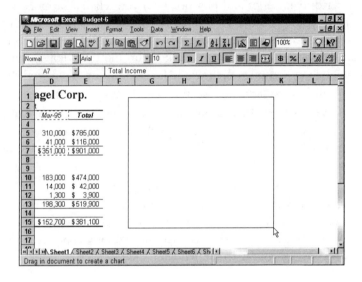

FIGURE 8.19 THE OUTLINE OF THE CHART WE ARE ABOUT TO CREATE.

5. Release the mouse button and the first Chart Wizard dialog box appears, as displayed in Figure 8.20.

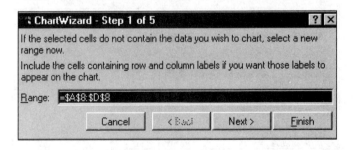

FIGURE 8.20 THE FIRST OF FIVE CHART WIZARD DIALOG BOXES—STEP 1 OF 5.

The Range text box displays the ranges you selected in step two. The dollar sign ($) in front of each column letter and row number indicates that these are absolute references. These references do not change if the data is moved or copied.

Since the ranges are correct, we move on to the next dialog box.

6. Click on the **Next** button to move to the next Chart Wizard dialog box, as displayed in Figure 8.21.

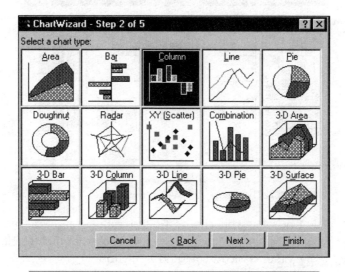

FIGURE 8.21 THE SECOND CHART WIZARD DIALOG BOX—STEP 2 OF 5.

N O T E If you want to go back to the previous Chart Wizard dialog box to make different choices, you can click on the **Back** button. You can click on the **Finish** button to have the Chart Wizard complete your chart based on the defaults for the following Chart Wizard dialog boxes.

This dialog box lets you choose from among fifteen available categories. The default is the Column chart, which is a fine choice for the type of data we are charting. To choose a different chart type, you simply click on the chart type of your choice.

N O T E As discussed earlier in the chapter, there is no one correct choice when choosing chart types. Fortunately, Excel makes it easy to experiment with various chart types, even after you've created the chart, to see how your data is best presented. You may choose to present the same data with more than one chart type to draw attention to different aspects of the data.

7. Click on the **Next** button to move to the third Chart Wizard dialog box, as shown in Figure 8.22.

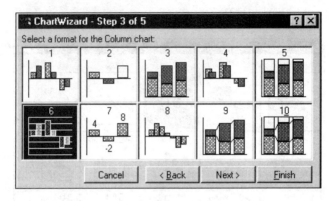

FIGURE 8.22 THE THIRD CHART WIZARD DIALOG BOX—STEP 3 OF 5.

This dialog box lets you choose from a variety of subcategories of the chart type you've chosen. Once again, we stick with the default, although many of the other choices would do nicely too.

Notice that choices 3, 5, 9 and 10 are different from the others. They are called *stacked column charts*, and they are good for displaying how much one piece of data in a series contributes to the overall series. Since this is not what we are doing here, these are not appropriate choices.

8. Click on the **Next** button to display the fourth Chart Wizard dialog box, as portrayed in Figure 8.23.

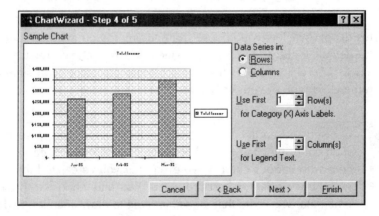

FIGURE 8.23 THE FOURTH CHART WIZARD DIALOG BOX—STEP 4 OF 5.

This is where we get to see a preview of the chart we are creating and to make sure Excel is charting the data the way we intend. On the right side of the dialog box, the first thing the Chart Wizard wants to know is whether the data series are in rows (the default) or columns. Our data series are indeed in rows, so we don't need to change this option.

The next piece of information the Chart Wizard wants to know is which row or rows to use for the Category axis (the horizontal, or x-axis) labels.

The first row we selected to chart was row 3, which included the column headings *Jan*, *Feb*, and *Mar*—our category labels—so we don't have to change anything here. If you squint, you can see Jan, Feb, and Mar under the columns in the sample chart.

The Chart Wizard wants to be sure the first column contains the text for the legend. The label for our data series, *Total Income*, is in column A, which is the first column we selected, so we are all set here as well. The legend (on the right side of the sample chart) displays the text and the color/pattern keys for our chart.

There is nothing in this dialog box to change, so let's move on.

9. Click on the **Next** button to move to the fifth and final Chart Wizard dialog box, as shown in Figure 8.24.

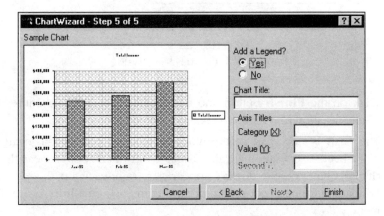

FIGURE 8.24 THE FIFTH CHART WIZARD DIALOG BOX—STEP 5 OF 5.

The first option in this dialog box is to add a legend. Without a legend, it is difficult to tell which columns belong to which data series, so we leave the **Yes** option button selected. Next, we have the option of adding a chart title. Let's add one.

10. Click in the **Chart Title** text box and type **1st Quarter Income vs. Expenses**.

   As you type the title, the Sample Chart portion of the dialog box is updated to display the title. We can also add titles to the category (x) axis and the value (y) axis. Let's add a value axis title to show that the numbers indicate dollars, which are helpful when we remove those distracting dollar signs later.

11. Click in the Value (**Y**) text box and type **Dollars**.

   Before we finish, be sure your dialog box looks like Figure 8.25.

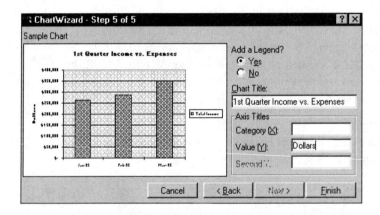

FIGURE 8.25 THE FILLED-IN FINAL DIALOG BOX.

12. Click on the **Finish** button and then scroll right until the entire chart is visible, as shown in Figure 8.26.

   The chart is now part of the worksheet. Upon placing the chart in the worksheet, Excel automatically displays the Chart toolbar near the chart. (If the Chart toolbar doesn't appear, just right-click on the Standard or Formatting toolbar (not on a tool) and then click on **Chart** in the shortcut menu.)

   If the Chart toolbar obstructs the chart elements you want to manipulate, you can position the mouse pointer over its title bar and drag it out of the way. You can also remove the Chart toolbar from the screen by clicking the **Close** box in its upper-left corner. We keep the Chart toolbar around for a while to help us manipulate some of the chart's properties.

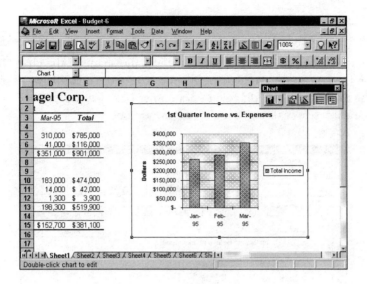

FIGURE 8.26 THE CHART.

Moving and Sizing Charts

After you create your chart, you may want to move it to another area of your worksheet. You can move charts on top of data or to empty areas of the worksheet. Charts actually float on top of the worksheet, so they can cover up worksheet cells.

1. Click once on the chart.

    Small black boxes, called *size boxes*, appear. The chart is selected, or activated, when the size boxes appear.

2. Point to the chart area (not the sides) and hold down the mouse button as you drag it to where you want it.

If you need to move the chart further than you can drag it, use the **Cut** and **Paste** commands from the Edit menu. Just click on the chart to select it, choose **Edit**, **Cut**, then click on a cell to mark the destination area and choose **Edit**, **Paste**. This is also a good way to move a chart to a different worksheet inside the workbook.

You can also change the size and shape of the chart by selecting it and using those little size boxes.

1. Click once on the chart so the size boxes appear.
2. Click and drag on any of the size boxes. Figure 8.27 shows an example.

   Dragging on the side size boxes changes the shape of the chart. Dragging on the corner size boxes changes the size of the chart. If you hold down the **Shift** key while dragging on a corner box, you can reduce or enlarge the chart size without changing its proportions.

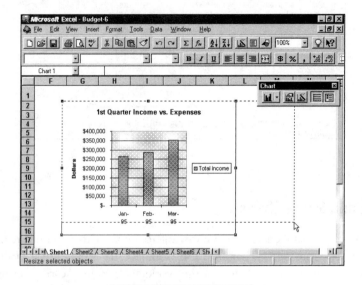

FIGURE 8.27 RESIZING THE CHART.

Deleting Charts

If the chart you've created in your worksheet just isn't what you wanted, you can always delete it and start over. Simply select it as you would to move or size it, and press the **Delete** button. This will have no affect on your worksheet data; it simply removes the chart from the worksheet. You can start the process over again if you like.

Copying Charts

Copying a chart is also accomplished by first selecting it. Then you can either use the **Copy** button on the toolbar or use the **Copy** command from the Edit menu. Move to the destination range by highlighting a cell in any worksheet, then click the **Paste** button or use the **Paste** command in the Edit menu. The copy will chart exactly the same data as the original chart.

CHANGING CHART DATA

Charts are linked to the underlying data in the worksheet. When you change the values in the worksheet, the chart will automatically update to reflect the new numbers. To prove the chart really is linked to the worksheet data, let's change some of the worksheet data and see how the chart is affected.

1. Click on any of the worksheet cells outside the chart area to deactivate it, and scroll left until column A is visible.

> While the chart is active, the scroll bars are hidden. They reappear when the chart is deactivated.

N O T E

The Chart toolbar usually disappears from the screen when the chart isn't selected. Let's change the Sales figure in cell D5 to reflect a more optimistic forecast.

2. Enter **500000** in cell D5 (the March sales figure), then scroll right until the chart is visible again and observe the change in the March Total Income column, as displayed in Figure 8.28.

3. Now change cell D5 in the worksheet back to **352600** and see that the chart returns to its original figures.

You can also change the March Total Income column directly on the chart by activating the chart and changing the data elements in the chart.

1. Double-click the chart frame to select the chart. This brings up the Chart toolbar and changes the Excel menu bar and menus. Now you can select individual elements in the chart.

2. Select the **March Total Income** column by clicking on it two times, very slowly. The selected column has small boxes around its edges. See Figure 8.29.

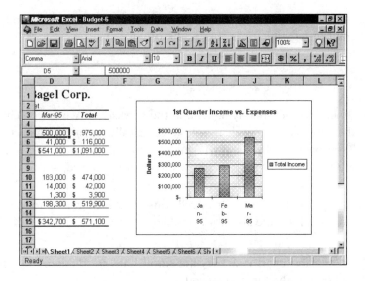

FIGURE 8.28 THE CHART REFLECTS YOUR CHANGES.

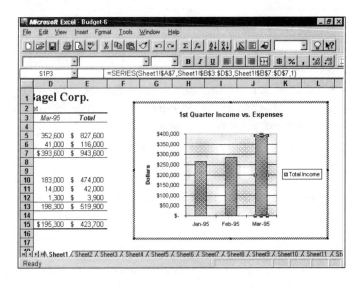

FIGURE 8.29 SELECTING A DATA POINT.

3. Drag on the size box on top of the March Total Income column until you reach approximately 500000.

If you are changing a value on the chart that comes from a cell containing a formula, Excel will ask you how it should modify the resulting value. In other words, which cell do you want to change to make the formula change? Figure 8.30 shows the dialog box requesting this information. In this example, we want to change cell D7 by changing the value in cell D5. Enter **D5** into the appropriate space in the dialog box and press **OK**. Now look at your worksheet, and you will see that your change has been reflected in the appropriate cells.

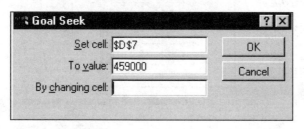

FIGURE 8.30 CHANGING CHART VALUES BY ADJUSTING CHART DATA POINTS.

CHANGING CHART TYPES

Just to see how easy it is to change chart types, let's use the Chart toolbar to display our data as a line chart. First, let's make sure the chart frame is selected and displays the thick outline. Do this by double-clicking on the chart frame.

1. Click on the **Chart Type** toolbar button on the Chart toolbar to display the drop-down chart type list, as shown in Figure 8.31.

2. Click on the **Line Chart** button in the drop-down list of chart types (the one the mouse pointer is pointing to in Figure 8.31).

    This line chart doesn't show the comparison between income and expenses as clearly as the column chart, so let's change it back. But first, let's have some fun and change it to an area chart, just to see how it would look.

3. Click on the **Area Chart** button to see how the display has changed yet again. See Figure 8.32.

4. To change it back to a bar chart, click on the **Column Chart** button.

You can see how your choice of chart type is important to understanding the data presented.

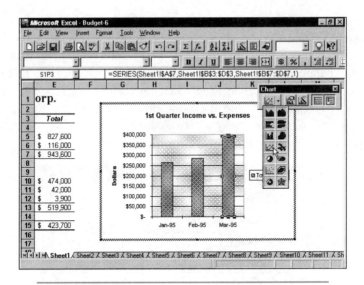

FIGURE 8.31 THE CHART TOOLBAR'S DROP-DOWN LIST OF CHART TYPES.

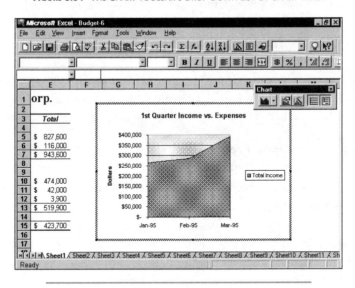

FIGURE 8.32 THE CHART HAS BEEN CHANGED TO AN AREA CHART.

EDITING CHARTS

We've already seen how you can edit a chart by changing the value in a cell of the worksheet—or by changing the value of the data points in the chart itself.

This section shows some other ways to edit the chart's data, such as by adding a new data series to the chart or removing a data series.

Adding a New Data Series

If you want to add a new data series to a chart, you can take advantage of an interesting feature called *drag and plot.* Simply select the new data series in your worksheet, drag it onto the chart and release the mouse button. The new series is automatically added to the chart. Even the data series label is added to the legend if you include the label in the selection.

NOTE Keep in mind that Excel makes a best guess as to how you want the data series applied to the chart. If it guesses incorrectly, you may need to make some modifications manually.

1. Scroll to the left so column A is visible and select cells A14 through D14 (the Total Expenses for the quarter).

2. Position the mouse pointer just below the selection so it is in the shape of an arrow pointer, as shown in Figure 8.33.

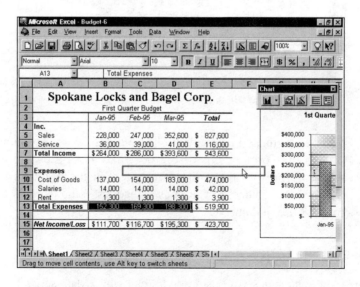

FIGURE 8.33 A NEW DATA SERIES READY TO BE ADDED TO THE CHART.

3. Hold down the left mouse button and drag to the right until the mouse pointer is within the visible chart boundaries, then release the mouse button.

4. When the Paste Special dialog box appears, click **OK** to accept the default settings.

   This dialog box lets you specify whether the highlighted range should be added as a new data series or as individual plot points at the end of the chart. Also, you can tell Excel if the data in the first cell contains the series label for the new series.

5. Scroll to the right so the entire chart is visible, as shown in Figure 8.34.

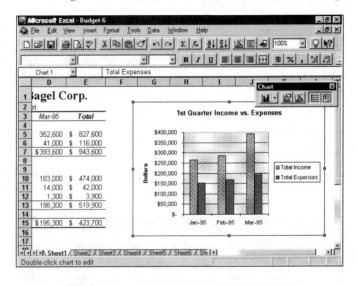

FIGURE 8.34 THE CHART WITH A NEW DATA SERIES ADDED.

WARNING Numbers formatted using the toolbar buttons, or the Accounting category in the Format Cells dialog box, may not be usable as a data series. If you run into a problem, reformat the numbers using the Number, Percentage, or Currency categories in the Number tab of the Format Cells dialog box.

Removing a Data Series

Let's remove the data series you just added. Removing a data series is as simple as a click of the mouse.

1. Double-click on the chart frame to select the chart. The heavy outline should appear around the chart.

2. Select one of the Total Expenses columns by clicking on it once. The selected column has small boxes around its edges. If this does not appear, click again (once) on the column.

    Remember that when you select a bar, line or other plot point, you select the whole data series in which the selected point appears.

3. Press the **Delete** key and all the Total Expenses columns disappear from the chart.

Data Series Orientation

You've previously seen how selecting the chart type affects the impact of the chart. Now let's experiment with how orientation of the chart data affects interpretation of the data. When you select chart data, it is important to keep in mind if you want to use the rows or columns on your worksheet to represent the data series on your chart. This is called *data orientation*. As you found out earlier in the chapter, you can present a data series in a column, line, pie chart, and so on.

Figure 8.34 shows how rows of your worksheet became a data series in a column chart. The data series is from the Total Income row, with columns for the categories of January, February and March. Now let's change the data series orientation so the categories (Jan., Feb., Mar.) become the data series, and the Total Income row becomes the categories.

1. Double-click on the chart to select it (if it's not already selected) and then click on the **Chart Wizard** tool.

2. Step 1 of the Chart Wizard dialog box appears. Click **Next**.

3. Click on **Columns**.

    Now look at your chart and see how the presentation has changed the impact of the chart. Figure 8.35 shows the new chart orientation. Notice that the chart now plots the months as data series within the Total Income axis. You have three bars across one period, rather than one bar across three periods.

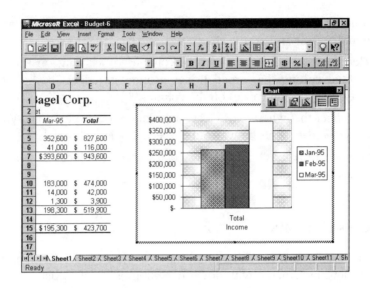

FIGURE 8.35 CHANGING THE ORIENTATION OF THE CHART.

CREATING CHARTS IN CHART SHEETS

The steps for creating a chart in a chart sheet are essentially the same as for creating an embedded chart. The first difference is that you need to start from the Insert menu and not the Chart Wizard button on the toolbar.

You can perform the same manipulations on a chart in a chart sheet as in an embedded chart. The only difference is that you can't see the data the chart is based on while the chart is on screen.

Let's create a chart comparing the company's Net Income/Loss for the quarter.

1. Select the ranges A3 through D3 and A16 through D16 and then choose **Insert**, **Chart**, **As New Sheet** to begin the chart sheet creation process.

    The first Chart Wizard dialog box appears, just as it did when creating an embedded chart.

2. Click the **Next** button to accept the selected ranges and move to the second Chart Wizard dialog box.

    Since this chart only has one data series and we are comparing how much each month contributes to the quarter, a pie chart would work well here.

3. Click on **Pie**, which is the last one on the top row of choices in the dialog box, and then click the **Next** button to proceed.

4. In the third and fourth Chart Wizard dialog boxes, click the **Next** buttons to accept the default options.

5. In the fifth Chart Wizard dialog box, click the **No** button under Add a Legend.

   We don't need a legend here because the pie format the Chart Wizard selected places the month labels next to each wedge of the pie.

6. In the Title text box, type **Pie in the Sky Projection** and click the **Finish** button.

The finished pie chart appears in a chart sheet that is inserted in front of the worksheet containing the data it is based on (as shown in Figure 8.36). If you look at the sheet tabs above the status bar you see the highlighted Chart1 tab to the left of the Sheet1 tab.

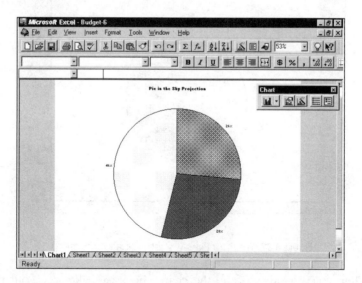

FIGURE 8.36 THE PIE CHART IN ITS CHART SHEET.

Use exactly the same techniques to format any of the chart elements in a chart sheet that you'd use with an embedded chart. The only step you can omit is double-clicking on the chart to activate it. When a chart sheet is visible, the chart is active and you can manipulate the chart elements.

PRINTING CHARTS

You print embedded charts in exactly the same way as the other portions of the worksheet. Just include the embedded chart in the print range and you're all set to go.

Printing a chart on a chart sheet is even easier than printing an embedded chart since there is no range to select. It is, of course, still a good idea to use Print Preview before printing to be sure you are printing what you think you are printing.

1. Click the **Print Preview** toolbar button to display a preview of the printed page, as displayed in Figure 8.37.

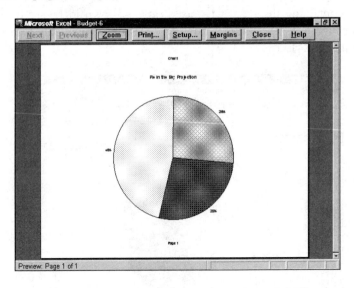

FIGURE 8.37 THE PRINT PREVIEW SCREEN FOR THE CHART SHEET.

2. When you're ready to print the chart, check to make sure your printer is turned on, is on-line, and has paper loaded. Then click on the **Print** button.

3. Click on the **Sheet1** tab to move back to the worksheet containing your data.

4. Save your work and exit Excel if you're not continuing on to the next chapter now.

When you save your work, you are saving the entire workbook, so you don't need to save the chart sheet separately from the worksheet.

N O T E

A FINAL THOUGHT

You have learned to turn numbers into dazzling charts that are sure to add punch to your presentations and help you persuade even the most skeptical person. In the next chapter you'll learn to enhance and customize your charts using Excel's powerful chart formatting features.

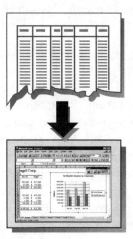

CHAPTER 9

ENHANCING CHARTS AND DRAWING

♦ Selecting chart elements

♦ Customizing chart axes

♦ Customizing chart forms text

♦ Customizing the plot area

♦ Customizing data series

♦ Displaying data labels

♦ Basic drawing techniques

♦ Drawing, moving and sizing objects (ellipse)

♦ Copying objects (ellipse)

♦ Drawing arrows

♦ Creating text boxes

Now that you know how to create a chart, it's time to learn some of Excel's snazzy chart enhancement features. In this chapter, you'll learn about formatting different parts of a chart, such as changing the color of the chart's background. You'll also learn about using Excel's drawing tools to annotate your charts and worksheets. There are many, many ways to enhance and customize your charts;

this chapter will cover some of the main things you can do. Exploration is your greatest teacher in this subject. Have fun.

SELECTING CHART ELEMENTS

Before you can customize the different parts of a chart, you must first know how to select them. The following discussion is to help you understand how to select chart elements so you can manipulate and customize them. You have already experienced clicking on the chart once to display the small size boxes around the chart. Single clicking on a chart allows you to move or size your chart, but does not allow you to alter any of the elements inside of the chart. In order to edit elements in your chart you must double-click the chart frame or inside of the chart itself. Double-clicking the chart or its frame creates a thick border around your chart indicating that individual elements can now be selected. Let's illustrate.

1. Double-click the frame on your chart. Notice the thick border around the chart as shown on Figure 9.1.

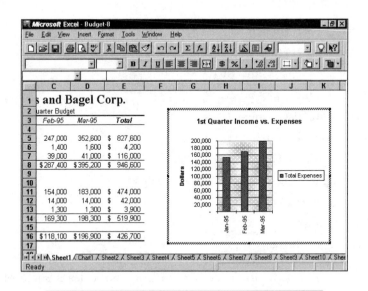

FIGURE 9.1 THICK BORDER AROUND CHART FROM DOUBLE-CLICKING.

2. Click once on the **March** column.

Notice that when you selected the one bar for March, you select the entire data series. Therefore the bars of January and February are also selected, as shown in Figure 9.2.

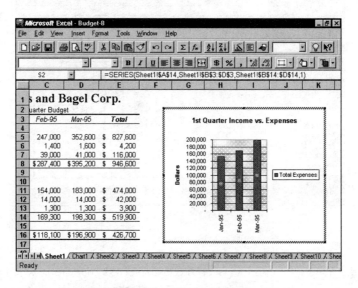

FIGURE 9.2 A DATA SERIES SELECTED IN A CHART.

3. Click once more on **March**.

   Notice that the small black size boxes appear only around the March column indicating that it can be altered and sized if desired.

4. Click on the chart's title. Notice that size boxes now surrounds it indicating it is selected.

5. Click once outside of the chart. The thick border disappears and your chart remains selected as shown by the selection boxes around its edges.

6. Again, click once outside of the chart area to deselect the chart.

   Let's see what happens when you again double-click on your chart.

7. Double-click on the chart or chart frame.

   You will notice that the chart title has the size boxes surround it. This is because the chart title was the last element in the chart that was selected. Figure 9.3 shows the chart title selected.

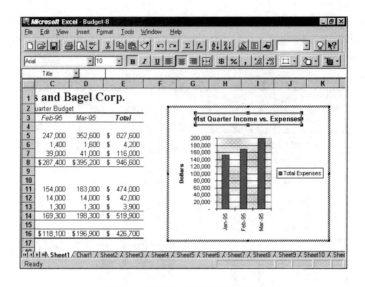

FIGURE 9.3 THE CHART TITLE SELECTED.

If the March column had been the last selected chart item, when you deselected the item by clicking outside the chart area, then it would have been selected when you double-clicked the chart.

Knowing how to select your chart and elements on the chart will make it easier for you to manipulate and edit your charts.

8. Click on the chart frame (the thick border) once to deselect the chart title. We're doing this so that when we double-click back on the chart, the chart title will not be selected.

9. Click outside of the chart area twice to deselect the chart.

CUSTOMIZING CHART AXES

You've already experienced changing the value (y) axis in the section on Changing Chart Data in Chapter 8. We can also change the way the numbers are formatted along the value (y) axis to have it better represent the data of our worksheet.

Let's try changing the values along the value axis and see what happens.

1. Double-click the chart to activate it in order to edit the chart's elements.

2. Double-click on one of the numbers along the value (y) axis to display the Format Axis dialog box, as shown in Figure 9.4. Click on the **Number** tab if it is not highlighted.

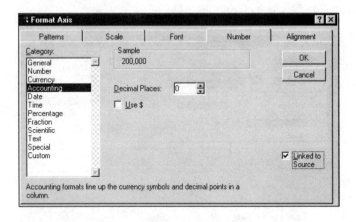

FIGURE 9.4 THE NUMBER TAB OF THE FORMAT AXIS DIALOG BOX.

This dialog box should look familiar to you. It is almost the same as the number portion of the Format Cells dialog box used earlier in the book. The Check Box in the lower-left corner of the dialog box tells you that the formatting for the numbers along the value (y) axis are linked to the source.

This means that whatever formatting was applied to the data series being represented is being used here. While this is often a good assumption, we want to make a change here. We don't need to uncheck the Link to Source check box because, as soon as we chose another number format, Excel understands the formatting is no longer linked to the source and removes the checked mark.

3. In the Category list, scroll down until the Custom Category is visible and click on it.

4. In the box marked Type, enter the custom format **##0,** (include the comma at the end).

This format will display the numbers in thousands. In other words, the number 200,000 will be displayed as 200.

Now let's change the font of the value (y) axis labels to spruce up your chart. We'll simply add italic to your font's style.

5. Click on the **Font** tab of the Format Axis dialog box.

This dialog box (Figure 9.5) should also look familiar to you. It is identical to the Font tab of the Format Cell dialog box. We'll keep Arial as the default font but let's change its style.

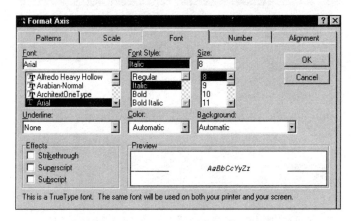

FIGURE 9.5 FONT TAB OF THE FORMAT AXIS DIALOG BOX.

6. Click on **Italic** in the Font style.

Now let's add a few more tick marks, change the color of your value (y) axis and have the value (y) axis labels increment differently.

7. Select the **Pattern** tab from the Format axis dialog box, as shown in Figure 9.6.

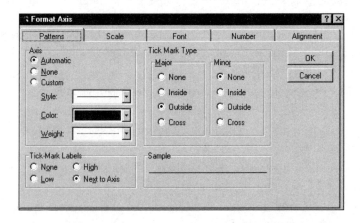

FIGURE 9.6 PATTERN TAB OF THE FORMAT AXIS DIALOG BOX.

If you preferred not to have a value (y) axis (which would be strange indeed) you could click **none** in the axis area of the Pattern tab.

8. Click on the **Color** drop-down menu and select dark blue. This action will change the color of the value (y) axis from black to blue.

9. In the Tick Mark Type area, make sure Outside is selected for both Major and Minor tick marks. Minor tick marks will give you additional hashes on the value (y) axis.

    If you did not want to show the tick mark labels, also referred to as the value (y) axis labels, you would select **None** in the Tick-Mark Labels area. If you want your tick mark labels on the right side of your chart, you would select **High** in the Tick-Mark Labels area.

    Finally, your chart was incremented on a per 100,000 basis. Let's increase the increments so that the chart is not too crowded with numbers.

10. Select the **Scale** tab from the Format Axis dialog box as illustrated in Figure 9.7.

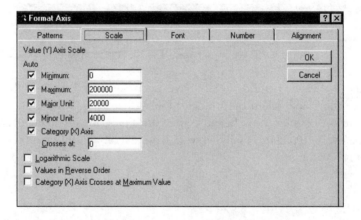

FIGURE **9.7** SCALE TAB OF THE FORMAT AXIS DIALOG BOX.

The Scale tab allows you to change the way values are represented on your value (y) axis. It displays the minimum value of zero and maximum value of 200,000. When the Auto text box is activated, Excel selects these values.

However, we can customize these options to suit our own needs. For instance, let's have our value (y) axis labels increment by 50,000.

11. Type **50000** in the Major Unit text box.

Are you ready to see the changes you've made to your chart?

12. Finally, click **OK**. Your chart should look like Figure 9.8.

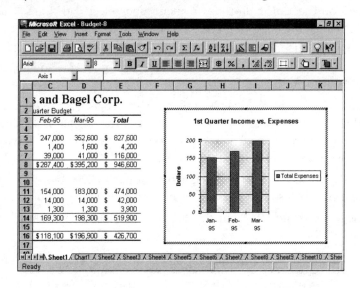

FIGURE 9.8 CHART AFTER FORMAT AXIS DIALOG BOX CHANGES.

Notice that the value (y) axis labels have been simplified to only three digits. Also notice they have taken on a fancier look—that is, an italic look. Moreover, there are fewer of them now because they are being incremented every 50,000 instead of every 100,000. Finally, if you have a color monitor, you'll see that your axis is now blue.

CUSTOMIZING CHART TEXT

Now that we have changed the chart axis values, we should let people know that the dollar values are shown in thousands. We can change the value axis label to add the appropriate information.

1. Click once on the **Dollars** label along the value axis.

   Notice that the text box is highlighted.

2. Click once again on the label. The label changes position and the cursor is inside the label box so you can make changes.

3. Add **(in thousands)** to the end of the label, as shown in Figure 9.9.

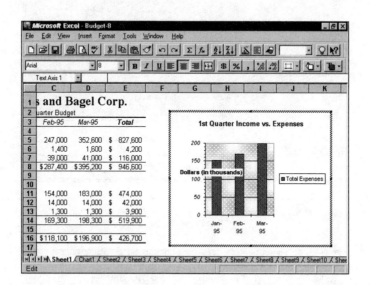

FIGURE 9.9 CHANGING CHART TEXT.

4. Click outside the chart frame (thin border) to see the text changes in place.

CUSTOMIZING CHART FONT

Now let's change the font and size on our chart title to improve its look.

1. Double-click the chart to select it.

2. Double-click on the chart title (**1st Quarter Income vs. Expenses**) to display the Format Chart Title dialog box, as shown in Figure 9.10. Click on the Font tab if it isn't selected.

   This is the same as the Font tab of the Format Cells dialog box used in Chapter 6, so its options should be familiar. The default Font is Arial, its style is bold and its size is 12-point. Let's change to Times New Roman, bold italic, 18-point.

3. Scroll down the Font list and click **Times New Roman**. Click **Bold Italic** in the Font Style list, and then click **18** in the Size list. Finally, click **OK** button to change the title as seen in Figure 9.11.

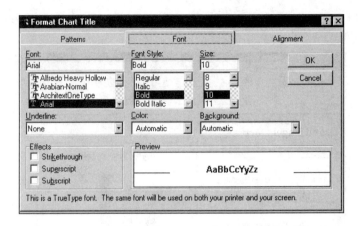

FIGURE 9.10 THE FONT TAB OF THE FORMAT CHART TITLE DIALOG BOX.

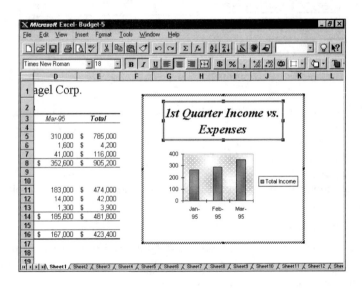

FIGURE 9.11 THE CHART WITH ITS NEWLY FORMATTED TITLE.

Since the title is larger, it takes up too much room. Let's modify the title to be more concise.

4. Click on the title to place the cursor inside the text box. Then double-click on the word Expenses to highlight it. Press the **Backspace** key to remove the word.

5. Double-click on the word **vs.** to highlight it. Then, press the **Backspace** key to remove the word. The title should now look like Figure 9.12.

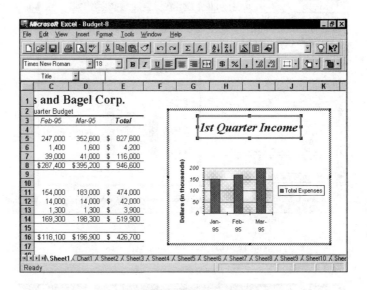

FIGURE 9.12 THE NEW TITLE.

Double-click outside of the chart area to view the change to the title. Notice how well your chart is looking. But let's do more.

CUSTOMIZING THE PLOT AREA

Notice that the changes we made to the main title made the chart too small inside the frame. We want to enlarge the chart's plot area to be more prominent.

1. Click once inside the plot area. Click between two of the horizontal grid lines on the colored background of the chart. The screen should look like Figure 9.13.

2. Move the mouse pointer over the size box in the upper-right corner of the plot area, until the mouse pointer changes shape. It should look like a double-sided arrow.

3. Click the mouse and drag the size box so that the plot area expands, as shown in Figure 9.14.

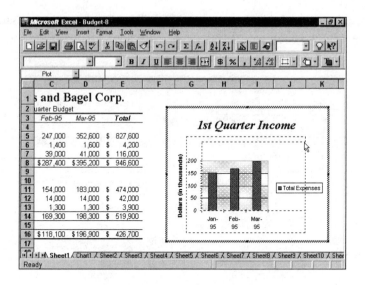

FIGURE 9.13 SELECTING THE PLOT AREA.

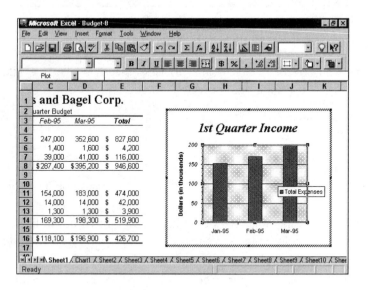

FIGURE 9.14 EXPANDING THE PLOT AREA.

4. Release the mouse to see the new plot area.

CUSTOMIZING DATA SERIES

Excel gives you the ability to change the color and pattern of any data series. This is useful if you are printing to a color printer or if you want to change the visual look on the your screen. Let's change the color of our Total Income data series to yellow with a red border.

1. Double-click inside of the chart area to select the chart (if it's not already selected).

2. Double-click on one of the Total Income columns. The Format Data Series dialog box appears.

3. Click on the **Patterns** tab in the Format Data Series dialog box if it isn't selected. Figure 9.15 shows the Pattern tab.

4. Under Border in the Color section, click on the drop-down menu and select the color red for your border.

5. Under Area in the Color section, click on the color yellow for your column fill.

   Notice in the Sample area of the Patterns tab that Excel lets you preview how your data series column will look.

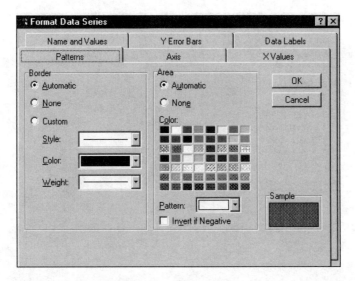

FIGURE 9.15 THE PATTERN TAB OF THE FORMAT DATA SERIES DIALOG BOX.

6. Click **OK** to accept the edits.

Notice that not only did the columns for the Total Income change, but the legend has also changed correspondingly. If you used a yellow field area with a red border your chart should be looking pretty good.

DISPLAYING DATA LABELS

We use the numbers along the value (y) axis to identify certain values on the charts. Sometimes, however, it is unclear exactly what amount our data series represents. Excel allows you to place data labels within your chart to make the chart more descriptive. Let's go back to the Format Data Series dialog box to display data labels.

1. Double-click inside the chart area to elect it with a thick border if it isn't already selected.
2. Double-click on one of the income columns in the chart. The Format Data Series dialog box appears.
3. Select the **Data Labels** tab as illustrated in Figure 9.16.

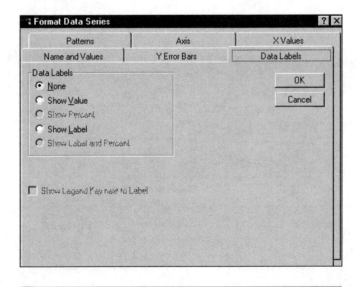

FIGURE 9.16 THE DATA LABELS TAB OF THE FORMAT DATA SERIES DIALOG BOX.

4. We want to show the value of our Total Income columns. Therefore, select **Show Value** then select **OK**.

You can further format the data label numbers by double-clicking on them to change their appearance. Experiment with this to get more familiar.

Now your chart is really looking pretty fancy. With the data labels added you know exactly what the columns represent. This feature can be useful for various applications.

BASIC DRAWING TECHNIQUES

Excel provides an amazing array of drawing tools (see Figure 9.17) for adding lines, arrows, circles and even additional text that isn't one of the normal chart title elements. These drawing tools can be used in your worksheets as well as on your charts.

All of the tools basically work in the same manner: you select the tool you want to use and then click at a location on the chart or worksheet where you want the object drawn, then drag the tool. You can use this technique with several of the drawing tools on the Drawing Toolbar, namely, rectangles, ellipses, text boxes, buttons, arcs, lines and arrows. Figure 9.18 shows the Drawing Toolbar.

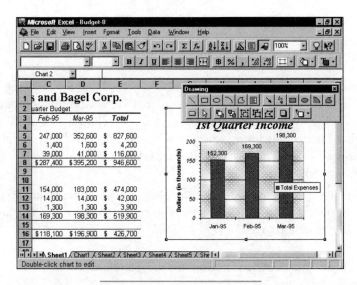

FIGURE 9.17 THE DRAWING TOOLBAR.

If you want to use a drawing tool several times in succession, just double-click on it and you won't have to reselect it the next time. When you are through using that tool, just click on it again.

SHORTCUT

You can also draw lines freehand, that is, every movement of the mouse creates a line. You can use the Freehand tool to write your name if you have a steady hand.

Creating polygons uses a slightly different technique from the click-and-drag technique used for circles and squares. For polygons, you would first select the **Freeform** tool. Find a location on the worksheet where you want the polygon to be and click once. That action marks the location at which the polygon anchor is placed. Then you move your mouse pointer to a different location and click once again. That click will cause a line to be drawn from the anchored position to the second location you selected. From this point, you can continue selecting locations to click on which will allow Excel to continue drawing straight lines from one location to the next.

You can turn the Freeform tool into a Freehand tool by pressing and holding the left mouse button while dragging.

N O T E

DRAWING, MOVING AND SIZING OBJECTS (ELLIPSE)

Let's spruce up our chart with drawings and objects using the Drawing Toolbar. You can draw circles and squares freehand, that is click on the appropriate tool and then click and drag the circle or square. Sometimes, however, you may want to draw perfect circles and perfect squares. This can be accomplished by holding down the **Shift** key as you click and drag the circle or square tool onto your chart or worksheet.

Let's place a freehand circle (ellipse) around March's Total Expanse of 169,300, because it represents the largest expense. You'll circle the amount in order to bring attention to it.

1. Click on the **Drawing** button on the Standard Toolbar to display the Drawing Toolbar.
2. Click on the **Ellipse** tool in the Drawing Toolbar to select it.

3. Place the mouse pointer above and to the left of March's Expense data label and drag the mouse pointer over the data label and release, as shown in Figure 9.18.

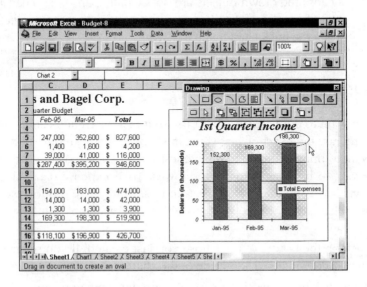

FIGURE 9.18 PLACING CURSOR TO DRAW A CIRCLE.

Don't worry if your data label isn't centered in the ellipse or if your ellipse is too small or large. We'll move and alter it in the next steps.

Notice that the circle contains small black size boxes. Circles, as with any object, can be moved to various locations on the worksheet. If the data label is not completely centered in your circle, perform the following steps.

4. Click and hold the border of the ellipse with your mouse.

5. As you move the mouse, an ellipse dotted outline will be displayed. Release the mouse button when the ellipse outline is positioned properly.

6. If your circle is too small or too large, you can resize it by dragging one of the size boxes to a different position.

7. Click once outside of the chart area to see your new ellipse.

NOTE When you double-click your chart to select different chart elements, all objects on the chart drawn from the Drawing Toolbar will disappear. When the chart is deselected, the objects will reappear. This is because the drawn objects are not actually part of the chart itself. To make them part of the chart, you can draw them onto a selected chart (when the thick chart frame is active).

COPYING OBJECTS (ELLIPSE)

When you want to duplicate an object to use it in a different location, instead of trying to redraw the exact object, you can simply copy it. In our chart, not only do we want to bring attention to the highest Total Expense data point value, but we also want to bring attention to the lowest Total Expense data value. To do this we want to copy the circle object and use it to circle the lowest expense data label in January. The following procedures will accomplish this.

1.   Click on the border of the ellipse you just created. If you select the chart by mistake, single-click outside of the chart area and try again.
2.   Right-click the mouse button to bring up the shortcut menu.
3.   Select **Copy.**
4.   Right-click the mouse to bring up the short-cut menu and select **Paste**.
     The new ellipse should be somewhere on your screen already selected.
5.   Point to the border of the ellipse then click and drag to January's Total Expense data label. Your chart should now look like Figue 9.19.

NOTE There is actually an easier way to copy objects. By holding the **CTRL** key down before selecting the object, a copy is made. Simply drag the copy to the new location after selecting it.

Now you have two identical ellipses on your chart.

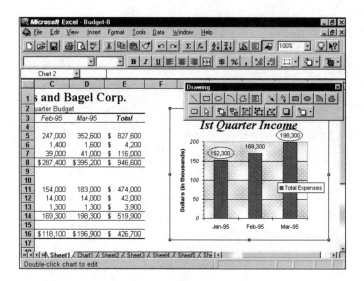

FIGURE 9.19 CHART WITH TWO ELLIPSES.

DRAWING ARROWS

We need to bring even more attention to the highest Expense data series. Let's draw an arrow that will overlap our circle slightly and really bring attention to this area. In order to draw an arrow, simply follow these procedures.

1. Click on the **Arrow** button on the Drawing Toolbar then position the mouse pointer, which is now a crosshair, up and to the right of the ellipse that circles the highest expense in the February column.

2. Click and drag the crosshair toward the circle until it is slightly inside the circle and release the mouse button to create the arrow, as seen in Figure 9.20.

   The handles on the end of the arrow indicate that it is selected and can be moved or sized. You can also format the arrow. Let's take a look at how you can format your arrow.

3. Double-click on the arrow to display the Format Object dialog box, as displayed in Figure 9.21. Click on the **Patterns** tab if it isn't already selected.

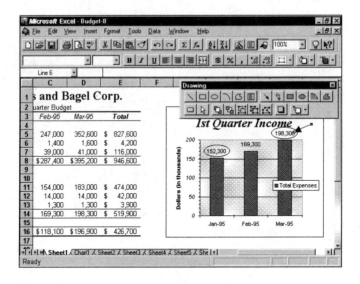

FIGURE 9.20 COMPLETED ARROW.

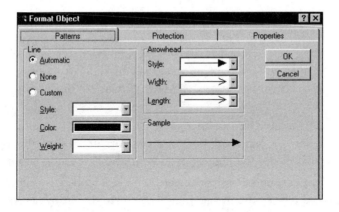

FIGURE 9.21 THE PATTERNS PORTION OF THE FORMAT OBJECT DIALOG BOX.

The dialog box is specific to the type of object you are formatting. In this case, we can change the type of arrowhead or its line. Make the line thicker by changing its weight.

4. Click on the arrow next to the Weight drop-down list to display the available options, as pictured in Figure 9.22.

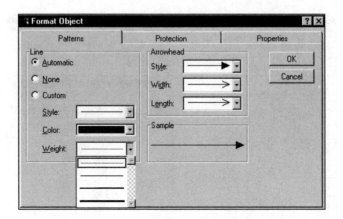

FIGURE 9.22 AVAILABLE LINE WEIGHT CHOICES.

5. Click on the thickest line at the bottom of the list.

6. Now click on the arrow next to the Color drop-down list to display the available colors and select your favorite color (I'm selecting purple).

    The Sample area of the dialog box displays a sample arrow with the selected line weight and color.

7. Click **OK** button to accept the changes, and click outside of the chart area.

CREATING TEXT BOXES

When you create a chart you have learned that Excel helps create and place certain text on the chart for you. For example, in creating your chart, you were able to have a chart title, legend and other pertinent text. Suppose you wanted to add additional text that is not part of the ChartWizard's procedures. Let's add a statement at the bottom of your chart to indicate it was prepared by you.

1. Select the **Text Box** button on the Drawing Toolbar.

2. Create a rectangular text object by clicking and dragging near the lower right-hand corner of your chart, as illustrated in Figure 9.23.

3. Type **Prepared by {enter your name here}**. Enter your name as the preparer of this chart.

4. If all the text does not fit in your text box, click and drag the middle size box (by the letter "P" in Prepared) to the left. Readjust it to the right if necessary.

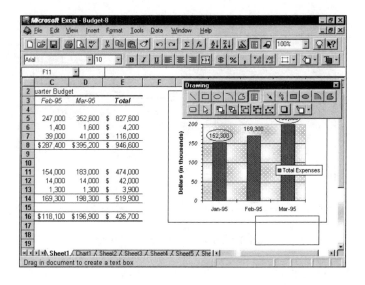

FIGURE 9.23 DRAWING A TEXT BOX.

Your chart should be similar to the one shown in Figure 9.24.

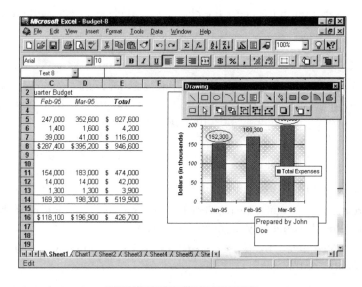

FIGURE 9.24 CHART WITH TEXT BOX.

5. If the text box is not placed properly in the lower right-hand corner, simply click and drag the entire text box.

   You may find that the text in your text box is too large and you may want to reduce it to a smaller size. The following steps will reduce the font in your text box.

6. Double-click directly on the border of the text box to bring up the Format Object dialog box.

7. Click on the **Font** tab if it is not already selected.

8. In the Size list, select **8** and click **OK**.

   While your text box is still selected, let's add a drop shadow to it.

9. From the Drawing Toolbar select the **Drop Shadow** button.

10. Click once outside of the chart area so that you can view the entire chart. Your final chart should look like Figure 9.25.

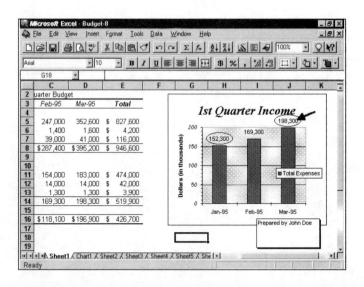

FIGURE 9.25 THE CHART WITH TEXT BOX AND DROP SHADOW.

When text is placed inside of text boxes, it can be edited directly in the text box itself. We will not edit our text box but the following steps are use to perform this function.

1. Click once on the text box.

2. Click once more to place the cursor inside of the text box.

3. Perform any edits necessary and then click outside of the text box area to accept the changes.

A Final Thought

You have learned to turn numbers into dazzling charts that are sure to add punch to your presentations and help you persuade the most skeptical. In the next chapter you'll learn to enhance and customize your charts using Excel's powerful chart formatting features.

CHAPTER 10

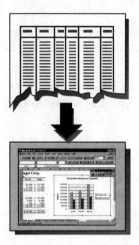

MANAGING DATA

- ◆ Database basics
- ◆ Setting up a database
- ◆ Entering data
- ◆ Searching the database
- ◆ Deleting and editing records
- ◆ Sorting the database
- ◆ Filtering the database

DATA BASICS

In addition to the worksheet and charting capabilities, we've worked with in the beginning chapters of this book, Excel provides a powerful facility for creating and manipulating databases.

So what is a database? A *database* is a collection of information (data) orga-nized to make it easy to find and use the data you are looking for. An example of a database you use every day is the phone book. The white pages of the phone book contain several categories of data: Last Name, First Name, Address, and Phone Number.

In database terms, each of these categories is called a *field*. All the field entries for one person make up a *record*. On one page of the phone book, there are four fields and perhaps several hundred records. The phone book makes it easy for you to find the data you want by sorting the records into alphabetical order. With Excel databases, you can sort and search the data in a wide variety of ways. You can even perform calculations on the data in an Excel database, just as you can with any worksheet data.

WHEN TO USE EXCEL AS A DATABASE

How can you determine when or if you need to use Excel as a database? As we discussed in the previous section, if you maintain data with many records and fields, like a phone book does, then you would benefit greatly using Excel's database management tools. Of course, your data doesn't have to be as massive as a phone book to use Excel as a database.

Let's look at some benefits of using Excel as a database and see if some of these benefits appear to fit your needs.

One benefit is that you'll be able to easily add and remove records or data from a data range. With the phone book example, new names and addresses are added and some are deleted. If you find yourself doing a similar tasks with your data (adding and deleting records), then you should seriously consider using Excel's database management tools.

Another benefit is the ease with which data can be changed. Again, using our phone book example, sometimes phone numbers change and have to be updated. If you find yourself having to update your data and records, an Excel database management tools will provide you with easy procedures to accom-plish the task.

A third benefit in using Excel as a database management tool is if you find the need to look at subsets of your data. Using our phone book again, we could print out the entire book, or if we wanted to look at only a subset. For instance, we could find just those people who live on a certain street. If you need to see different subsets of your data and records, then Excel database would work great for you.

One other benefit is that you will have the ability to do statistical analysis on a subset or on all of your database. You'll be able to create charts and pies and other visual presentation of your data. You know the saying, a picture is worth a thousand words. Well, using excel as a database management tool can create your data in picture form.

If any of these benefits apply to your tasks, then you should seriously consider using Excel as a database. Excel uses a neat dialog box called the *data form* that makes adding, removing, changing, sorting, subsetting, and searching your database range very easy and user-friendly. We'll talk more about the data form later in this chapter.

SETTING UP A DATABASE

To create a database, you first enter field names in the first row you want to use for your list. Each row below the field name or header row is a *record*. There can't be any blank rows between records, and all the cells in a field should be formatted the same way to facilitate sorting and database manipulation.

There are a few rules to follow when choosing a field name. Every field name must be unique. For example, if you were creating a name and address list in which you needed two fields for the address to accommodate suite and apartment numbers, they couldn't both be called ADDRESS. You could solve this situation by calling the first field ADDRESS1 and the second field ADDRESS2.

N O T E   It's best to keep field names as short as possible, yet descriptive enough that you know what should be entered in the field. If you need to use a field name that is longer than the column width, consider formatting the text to wrap so it occupies multiple lines instead of requiring an inordinately wide column. To wrap text, choose **Format Cell** from the cell's shortcut menu and click in the **Wrap Text** check box.

In setting up your database, you should follow certain guidelines to assure yourself that your database will maintain integrity:

♦ Make absolutely sure that each field name, sometimes called *column headings*, are unique. You'll run into trouble manipulating your data if you use the same name more than once for a field or column heading.

♦ Remember that your field name has a limited number of characters. No field name can be longer than 255 characters. A good rule of thumb is to try to keep your field names as short as possible, but at the same time descriptive enough so that you know what the name refers to.

♦ Each row should contain a new record. Records are delineated by rows. Also, you should never have a blank row in your database range. Moreover, each row/record should be unique from other rows and records. You should always have at least one field in your record that is unique from any other record.

♦ Format your header row or field names differently from your rows that contain data. You may want to change the justification, font type, and font style of your field names to distinguish them from your records. This way, Excel knows automatically where the first row of your data begins.

♦ Give your database plenty of breathing room. Since databases tend to grow, make sure that your database is located on the worksheet where records can be easily added and not run into limitation problems. If possible, use one entire sheet for your entire database.

CREATING A DATABASE

Now that you know the basics of a database, how about some hands-on experience in actually creating a database. Once you create your own database and try out some of the neat database management tools, it'll be much easier for you to determine if and when you should use Excel as a database. Let's start creating a partial inventory list database for the Spokane Locks and Bagel Corp.

1. Start Excel and open the BUDGET workbook if it isn't already on your screen.

2. Click on **Sheet2** at the bottom of the worksheet to move to a clean worksheet in the same workbook.

Keeping related worksheets in the same workbook is one of the reasons Excel uses workbooks in the first place. We could put the inventory list in a new workbook, but then when we want to work with our various data from Spokane Locks and Bagel, we'd have to open two workbooks instead of one.

N O T E

3. Enter the field names and data for the first record in the appropriate cells, as displayed in Table 10.1.

TABLE 10.1 THE FIELD NAMES AND THE DATA FOR THE FIRST RECORD OF OUR INVENTORY DATABASE

	A	B	C	D	E
1	ITEM	TYPE	COST	QTY	TOTAL
2	Small Paddock	Hardware	4.33	42	=C2*D2

The formula in E2 multiplies the item's cost by the quantity.

The fastest way to enter the data in this range is to select the entire range first (A1 through E2) and press **Enter** after each cell entry to move to the next cell in the selection.

N O T E

Next we'll format the cells containing the field names as center-aligned and first record cells to display the numbers properly.

4. Select the range A1 through E1 and format the cells as center-aligned. You can right-click on the selection to display the shortcut menu, then choose **Format Cells**, click on the **Alignment** tab, and select the **Center** option button in the Horizontal portion of the dialog box.

5. Format cell C2 with the comma format by clicking on the **comma** format button in the toolbar.

6. Format cell E2 with the currency format using the **currency** format button.

7. Double-click on the right border of each of the column headings to adjust the column widths to accommodate the cell entries.

You'll need to do this again after entering data that is wider than the current column widths. Your screen should now look like Figure 10.1.

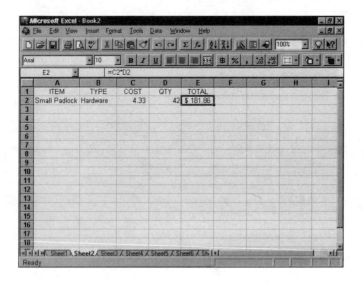

FIGURE 10.1 THE FIELD NAMES AND FIRST RECORD OF THE DATABASE.

Entering Database Records

You already entered data in a database when you entered the first record. You can enter data directly into the database in the same way to add as many records as needed. However, the following steps show a useful trick for entering database records, saving you time and effort.

1. Approximate the number of records you plan to enter and then highlight the range to accommodate that number of records under the last record in your database.

2. Enter your data into the first cell of your range and press the **Tab** key when you finish entering the first cell.

3. Excel will move you to the next cell, horizontally, while keeping the range highlighted. Continue to enter your data in the specified field and

pressing **Tab.** Excel will automatically move to a new line when you are finished entering a record.

Using the Data Form

Excel provides an even slicker method for entering data in a database—the data form.

Once you've started the database, you can use the data form, which includes text boxes for the fields requiring data entry and also displays the results of calculated fields.

N O T E There's no right or wrong way to enter data in an Excel database. You may decide that entering data directly into the database and bypassing the data form is the easiest method for you. One advantage of using the data form to enter data is that the cell formatting for the previous record automatically applies to the next record, thus eliminating the need to format more than one record.

Let's enter the next record using the data form.

1. Be sure one of the cells in the database is active and choose Data, Form to display the data form dialog box, as displayed in Figure 10.2.

    The title bar in the dialog box displays the name of the sheet where the database is, in this case Sheet2. If the sheet were renamed something more relevant to the database, such as INVENTORY, that name would be displayed in the title bar.

    The data for the first record is displayed in the text boxes for each field. Notice that the data for the TOTAL field isn't in a text box since, being a calculated field, it can't be edited. The scroll bar to the right of the text boxes is used if you have more fields than can be displayed in the dialog box at one time. The dialog box also displays the number of the record you are currently viewing and the total number of records in the database in the upper-right corner of the dialog box.

    Let's add the next record in the data form now.

2. Click the **New** button to clear the text boxes for the new record entry.

    As you enter new records, the dialog box displays the text New Record in the upper-right corner.

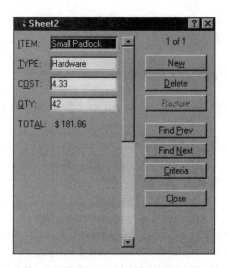

FIGURE 10.2 THE SHEET 2 DATA FORM DIALOG BOX.

3. Type **Bagel Dogs, Food, 1.27, 375** in the ITEM, TYPE, COST, and QTY text boxes. You can press the **Tab** key to move the insertion point from one text box to the next.

If you need to correct a typo in a text box you've already done, you can click in the text box you need to edit, or press **Shift-Tab** until the field you need to edit is highlighted and type the correct data.

N O T E

4. Click on the **New** button to add this record to the bottom of the database and clear the text boxes for the next record.

    The new record is added and you'll notice that the cell formatting was copied from the first record. If the dialog box is obscuring too much of the database, you can drag it out of the way by its title bar.

    Next, we'll enter the remaining records for the inventory database.

5. Enter the data for the records, displayed in Table 10.2.

When you finish entering the data for the last field in a record, the fastest way to confirm the entry and clear the text boxes for the next record is to press the **Enter** key. This way you don't need to move your hands from the keyboard as you enter a series of records.

SHORTCUT

TABLE 10.2 THE DATA FOR THE RECORDS

Item	Type	Cost	Qty
Plain bagels	Food	.22	456
8 oz. Cream cheese	Food	1.33	78
BMW keys	Hardware	.87	26
Mercedes keys	Hardware	.47	73
Ferrari keys	Hardware	.56	37
Garlic bagels	Food	.25	133
Jalapeño bagels	Food	.27	277
Chocolate bagels	Food	.32	76
Large padlock	Hardware	3.42	44

6. Click on the **Close** button to clear the dialog box from the screen and readjust the column width of column A to accommodate the new entries.

Your screen displays all the records, as shown in Figure 10.3.

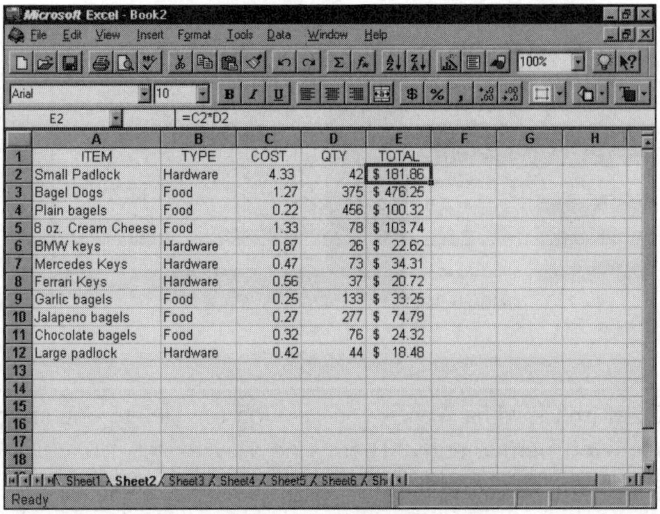

FIGURE 10.3 ALL THE RECORDS IN THE DATABASE.

DELETING AND EDITING RECORDS

As with any other data on a worksheet, you can delete and edit records directly. If you wanted to delete a record directly, you could select a cell in its row and choose **Edit, Delete, Entire Row**. Editing a record's data directly is simply a matter of moving to the cell you want to edit and making the change, just as you would in any cell.

Another way to edit and delete records is with the data form dialog box. An advantage of using the dialog box is that you can combine editing and deleting with the search capabilities which we'll cover later in the chapter. For example, if you wanted to edit all the records that matched certain comparison criteria: you could specify the criteria, click the **Find Next** button, perform the edits in the text boxes, and click on **Find Next** to display the next record you want to edit.

Let's delete one of the records using the data form dialog box now.

1. Click on **Find Next** or **Find Prev** until the Small Padlock record is displayed in the data form dialog box.

2. Click the **Delete** button.

   The message box, as shown in Figure 10.4, is displayed to let you know that what you are about to do can't be undone.

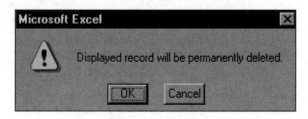

FIGURE 10.4 THE WARNING MESSAGE BOX.

WARNING Excel isn't kidding. When you click on the **Delete** button, the record is removed permanently. There's no way to get it back. Don't let the grayed-out **Restore** button in the data form dialog box fool you either. That only works for restoring an *edited* record to its original state prior to confirming the edit. So be careful before deleting a record in this way.

There is one safety measure you can take before doing something dangerous like deleting a record—save your work. If you save your work just before deleting the record, you can always close the workbook without saving changes and then open the saved version to get back to where you were before the deletion.

3. Click **Cancel** to close the dialog box without deleting.

4. Click the **Close** button to clear the data form dialog box.

SORTING THE DATABASE

At the beginning of the chapter, you saw how the phone book makes it easy to find a particular entry. The records are sorted in alphabetical order. When you add records to the database list, you don't need to worry about entering them in the correct order. Excel makes it easy to sort the list in a variety of ways.

NOTE

Your list doesn't even have to be a database for Excel to sort it. Any rectangular area consisting of rows and columns of related data can be sorted in the same manner as database data.

One sorting concept that is important to understand is the *sort key.* The key is the basis for the sort, and you can sort by up to three keys. In the phone book example, the first sort key is the last name. A second sort key (the first name) is used as a tie breaker. If there is more than one entry of a particular last name, those last names are sorted by first names.

Let's perform a simple sort on the inventory database. First we sort the list in alphabetical order by the ITEM field. This is so easy you won't believe it.

1. Make any cell in the database in column A (the ITEM field) the active cell.

2. Click on the **Sort Ascending** toolbar button.

Voila! The list is instantly sorted, as displayed in Figure 10.5.

The *Ascending* in Sort Ascending means from lower to higher. For an alphabetical sort such as this, it means A through Z. For a numerical sort, ascending would be 1 through 100. The toolbar button to the right of the

Sort Ascending button is the **Sort Descending** button which performs a sort from higher to lower.

	A	B	C	D	E	F	G	H
1	ITEM	TYPE	COST	QTY	TOTAL			
2	8 oz. Cream Cheese	Food	1.33	78	$ 103.74			
3	Bagel Dogs	Food	1.27	375	$ 476.25			
4	BMW keys	Hardware	0.87	26	$ 22.62			
5	Chocolate bagels	Food	0.32	76	$ 24.32			
6	Ferrari Keys	Hardware	0.56	37	$ 20.72			
7	Garlic bagels	Food	0.25	133	$ 33.25			
8	Jalapeno bagels	Food	0.27	277	$ 74.79			
9	Large padlock	Hardware	0.42	44	$ 18.48			
10	Mercedes Keys	Hardware	0.47	73	$ 34.31			
11	Plain bagels	Food	0.22	456	$ 100.32			
12	Small Padlock	Hardware	4.33	42	$ 181.86			

FIGURE 10.5 THE SORTED DATABASE.

It's a good idea to save your work before performing a sort so you can get back to the original sort order later if you need to.

WARNING

If you perform a sort and want to return the list to its original order, you can choose **Edit, Undo Sort** before taking any other actions in Excel.

A trick you can use if you think you will need to return to the original sort order more than once is to add a field for record numbers. In one column in the database, type **1**, and then use the fill handle with the **Ctrl** key to increase the numbers in ascending order down the column. With the records numbered, you can get back to the original order any time you want by performing a sort by the column containing the record numbers.

Let's sort the list in descending order by the COST field.

3. Move to any cell in the database range in column C and click on the **Sort Descending** toolbar button.

Sorting with Multiple Keys

Finally, we sort the database by two sort keys. Sorting by two fields isn't quite as easy as clicking on a toolbar button. But it is still pretty easy.

We use the TYPE field as the first sort key, which groups the food and hardware items separately. Because there are several records for each of the two types of items, we have Excel use the ITEM field as the second sort key.

1. Be sure that any cell in the database is the active cell and then choose **Data, Sort** to display the Sort dialog box, as shown in Figure 10.6.

    Notice that the entire list is selected, excluding the column headings and the field name in the Sort By list box is ITEM, which is the first column in the database. This isn't what we want to use for the first Sort By, so we change it now.

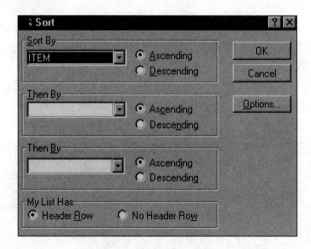

FIGURE 10.6 THE SORT DIALOG BOX.

2. Click on the **Arrow** next to the Sort By drop-down list to display all the field names in the database, as shown in Figure 10.7.

3. Click on **TYPE** in the drop-down list to select it as the first field to sort by.

    Each field we choose to sort by can be sorted in ascending (the default) or descending order. We accept ascending for both of our sort keys.

4. Click on the **Arrow** next to the Then By drop-down list and click on **ITEM**.

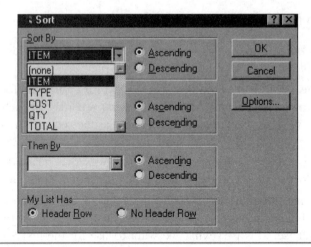

FIGURE 10.7 THE SORT DIALOG BOX DISPLAYING THE DROP-DOWN LIST OF FIELD NAMES.

Since there are no duplicate item names, there is no need for a third sort key, so we leave the bottom Then By list blank.

5. Click **OK** to perform the sort.

The list is sorted with all the food items at the top and the item names alphabetized within the food group. Next, the hardware item names are alphabetized within the hardware group, as shown in Figure 10.8.

FIGURE 10.8 THE LIST SORTED BY TWO SORT KEYS.

NOTE Excel can only use three sort keys, which could be a serious limitation for some complex lists. However, as with most limitations in Excel, there is a way around it. If your sort requires more than three sort keys, simply sort multiple times. Specify the first three keys for the first sort, and then choose up to three more and perform a second sort.

SEARCHING THE DATABASE

In the database, we have created, there is no need to use any fancy searching techniques because there are so few entries and all of them are visible at the same time. However, as the number of records increases to hundreds or thousands, it can be difficult, if not impossible, to find the records you want by visually scanning the list.

Excel provides a couple of ways to find records that meet certain criteria. Later in the chapter, you'll learn to use Excel's filtering system to display the records that meet your specifications. But the most straightforward way to find records you are looking for is to use the data form dialog box.

Using the data form dialog box does not change the database in any way. As you perform the search, the dialog box displays the records in the database that meet the search criteria, one at a time. Let's use the data form dialog box to search for some records.

1. Be sure one of the cells in the database is still active, and choose **Data, Form**.

   The data form dialog box displays 1 of 11 in the upper-right corner, indicating that the data for the first of eleven records is presented.

   The three dialog box buttons used for searching the database are: **Find Prev**, **Find Next**, and **Criteria**. If you don't specify any criteria, the Find Prev and Find Next buttons display the data for the previous or next record in the list. Using the Criteria button, you can tell Excel which records to search for, and then the Find Prev and Find Next buttons display the previous or next records that meet your criteria.

   Let's use the Criteria button to provide Excel with search specifications.

2. Click the **Criteria** button.

   The upper-right corner of the dialog box now displays Criteria indicating that you can enter search conditions called comparison criteria in the text boxes. When you perform the search, Excel compares the comparison criteria with the records in the list and displays the first one that matches.

The other difference between this and the normal data form dialog box is that even the calculated TOTAL field has a text box. This is because you can specify search criteria on any field, including calculated fields.

Let's enter criteria to search for the BMW keys.

3. In the ITEM text box, type **bmw** and then click the **Find Next** button.

N O T E The comparison criteria are not case sensitive, which means that you can type your conditions in uppercase or lowercase and it won't affect the outcome of the search.

The data form now displays the data for the BMW keys record and, in the upper-right corner, displays 7 of 10 indicating that this is the seventh record in the hardware category. If you click the **Find Next** button, your computer is likely to beep at you and won't display any other records.

Now, let's try finding records that match the multiple criteria.

4. Click the **Criteria** button again so you can enter new criteria.

The ITEM text box is highlighted so you can start typing to enter new criteria for the ITEM field, or delete what's there. We delete it since we won't be using the ITEM field as part of our next search.

The first comparison criterion we use is HARDWARE to locate only records that have HARDWARE entered in the TYPE field.

5. Press the **Delete** key to delete the highlighted text, then press the **Tab** key to move the insertion point into the TYPE text box and type **HARD-WARE**.

If you enter comparison criteria in more than one text box, the record must meet both conditions. We search for records that fall into the Hardware category and also have a total value more than $100.00.

6. Click in the **TOTAL** text box and type **>100**

The > (greater than) symbol is one of Excel's comparison operators that can be used to compare values. The other comparison operators are:

♦   = (equal to)

♦   < (less than)

♦   >= (greater than or equal to)

♦   <= (less than or equal to)

♦   <> (not equal to)

These operators can only be used with numeric values, not text data.

7. Click the **Find Next** button to display the first record that meets both of the comparison criteria.

    Only two records match both criteria. You can click on **Find Prev** to display the other match.

Filtering the Database

The major limitation to using the data form to find records that meet certain criteria is that you can only display one record at a time. There may be times when you want to be able to view and manipulate a subset of the list. Excel's filter capability permits you to do just that.

By filtering the database, Excel automatically hides all records that do not meet your specifications, leaving only the records you want to see displayed on your screen. Just as in sorting, you can have multiple criteria for filtering the database.

Let's use Excel's AutoFilter feature to display only the food records.

1. With one of the cells in the database as the active cell, choose **Data, Filter, AutoFilter**.

    Drop-down arrows appear next to each field name at the top of each column, as shown in Figure 10.9.

2. Click on the drop-down **Arrow** next to the TYPE field name.

    The drop-down list provided by the AutoFilter Arrows display all the unique entries for that field, as shown in Figure 10.10.

    You would select **All** in the drop-down list to cancel a filter selection for that field. Selecting **custom** lets you specify more complex filter specifications, including the use of the comparison operators we use in the data form dialog box. The Blanks choice tells Excel you want to display all records that have no entry in that field. NonBlanks excludes records with no entry in that field.

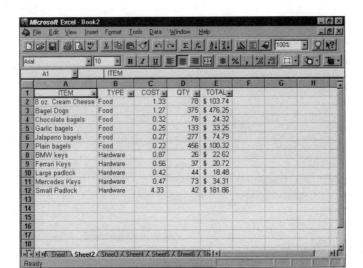

FIGURE 10.9 THE LIST WITH THE AUTOFILTER DROP-DOWN ARROWS DISPLAYED.

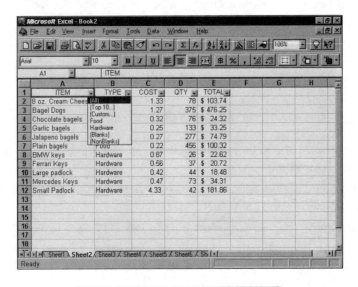

FIGURE 10.10 AN AUTOFILTER DROP-DOWN LIST.

3. Click on **Food** in the drop-down list.

    Instantly, all the records that don't meet the food criterion are hidden, as shown in Figure 10.11.

You cannot tell from the figure, but if you look at your screen, you'll notice that the arrow next to the TYPE heading is blue. This indicates that a filter criterion has been specified for this field. If you display the list again and choose **All**, the hidden records reappear and the arrow loses the blues.

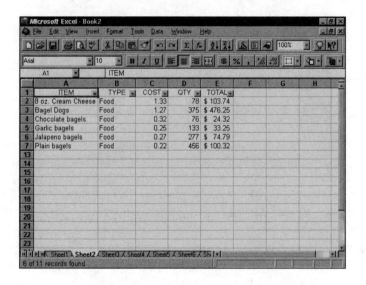

FIGURE 10.11 THE LIST WITH JUST THE FOOD ITEMS.

If you have a very long list of field entries from which to choose, you can move to the desired field quickly by typing the first few letters of its name.

SHORTCUT

Using Custom Filters

Let's specify a filter criterion for another field. This time we only allow Excel to display records from the filtered list that have quantities of greater than 100 and less than 400.

1. Click on the drop-down **Arrow** next to the QTY column heading.

   We need to create a custom filter for this field to specify the range of acceptable values.

2. Click on **Custom** to display the Custom AutoFilter dialog box, as shown in Figure 10.12.

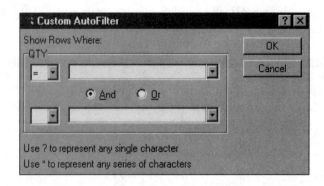

FIGURE 10.12 THE CUSTOM AUTOFILTER DIALOG BOX.

The comparison operators must be chosen from their own drop-down list in the dialog box, instead of being typed in the text box as we did in the data form dialog box.

3. Click on the drop-down **Arrow** next to the box with = in it (just below QTY) in the dialog box to display the list of comparison operators, as shown in Figure 10.13.

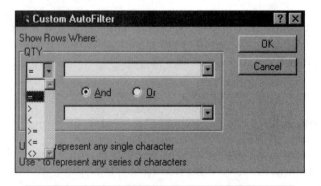

FIGURE 10.13 THE DROP-DOWN LIST OF COMPARISON OPERATORS.

4. Click on > (greater than symbol) in the drop down list, then click in the text box to the right of the comparison operator list and type **100**.

5. Leave the And option button selected, then choose < (less than symbol) from the bottom drop-down list of comparison operators and type **400** in the bottom text box.

6. When the Custom AutoFilter dialog box is displayed as in Figure 10.14, click **OK**.

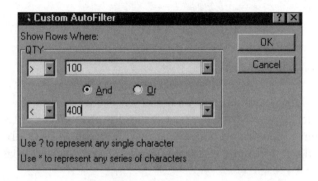

FIGURE **10.14** THE CUSTOM AUTOFILTER WITH THE FILTER SPECIFICATIONS ENTERED.

Your screen, as displayed in Figure 10.15, should now have three records matching the two filter criteria.

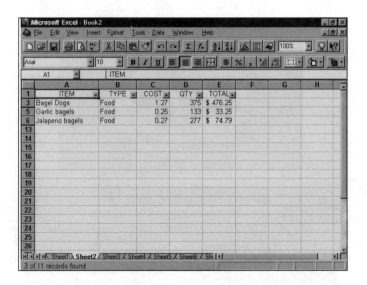

FIGURE **10.15** THE LIST AFTER ENTERING THE TWO FILTER CRITERIA.

We are finished with the filtered list, so let's turn off AutoFilter and redisplay all the records.

7. Choose **Data, Filter, AutoFilter** to remove the check mark in front of the AutoFilter and reveal the hidden records.

8. Save your work and exit Excel if you aren't moving on to the next chapter now.

A FINAL THOUGHT

As you work with Excel, you will find yourself using the database creation and manipulation techniques you have learned in this chapter more frequently than you can imagine. You will also discover that many of these database concepts also apply to the full-featured database programs used for larger database applications.

In the next chapter, you learn to use some of Excel's worksheet, data proofing and analysis tools.

CHAPTER 11

PROOFING AND ANALYZING WORKSHEET DATA

♦ Using the Spell Checker
♦ Working with PivotTable Wizard
♦ Using "What If"
♦ Using Scenario Manager
♦ Outlining worksheets

You should be sure that the final version of any document is as error-free as possible and presents the data you want to present, whether from a spreadsheet program, a word processor or a database. Excel provides several tools for making sure your worksheet is accurate and for looking at the data in various ways.

247

USING THE SPELL CHECKER

The most obvious place to start ensuring accuracy is with Excel's spell checker. Spelling errors can contribute to a perception that your entire worksheet and even the logic you used to prepare it is sloppy. If you want to convince your readers that the data in your worksheet is accurate and your conclusions are correct, you want to be absolutely sure any spelling errors (and typos) are corrected.

Many cells in a worksheet contain only values or formulas. You may be wondering how the spell checker deals with these cells. That's easy. Excel ignores the contents of these cells.

So far, we've been entering only correctly spelled data into our worksheets, so we should not have to worry about checking the spelling. Of course, it is still a good idea to check the spelling in case there are some typos. Just to be sure we have something to correct, let's edit one of the cell entries to that it is intentionally misspelled.

1. Start Excel and open the BUDGET workbook if it is not already on your screen. Make sure Sheet2 (the database sheet) is active. If it isn't, click on the **Sheet2** tab.

2. Edit the contents of cell B2 from Food to **Foood**.

3. Click on **Spelling** in the toolbar to start the spell check process.

    The Spelling dialog box appears, as shown in Figure 11.1, with the cell value of the first misspelled word displayed in the lower-left portion of the dialog box above the two check boxes.

    Because the **Always Suggest** check box is checked, the dialog box offers suggestions for correcting the misspelled word. The word in the Change To box is the suggestion Excel thinks is most likely the correct spelling of the word you had in mind. In this case, the Change To box does, in fact, contain the correct spelling. If the spelling of the misspelled word had been too badly mangled, Excel might not have been able to make a correct guess. In such a case you could click on one of the other suggestions in the Suggestion list, or edit the word in the Change To box.

N O T E   Having Excel make suggestions every time it stops at a misspelled word can slow down the process, so you might consider clicking in the **Always Suggest** check box to remove the check mark. If Excel stops on a particular word and you want suggestions, you can click on the **Suggest** button.

If you find that eliminating suggestions does not improve the speed noticeably, it might be more convenient to have Excel always provide you with suggestions.

You may also want to use the **Ignore UPPERCASE** check box to have the spell checker ignore any work that is in all uppercase letters. This option might be useful if, for example, you had a list of names or other words that would not be in the dictionary, in all uppercase.

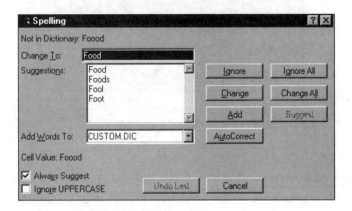

FIGURE 11.1 THE SPELLING DIALOG BOX.

The Add Words To box displays the name of the custom dictionary where you can add the word if it is correctly spelled, but isn't a word in the normal dictionary. The default dictionary for adding words is CUS-TOM.DIC, but you can create other dictionaries for use with various types of documents. If you add a word to the dictionary, the spell checker won't stop on that word as a misspelled word in other documents. Examples of the kinds of names you might want to add to the dictionary are your name, your company's name, or other special names or terms you use in your business.

4. Click the **Change** button to replace the cell contents with the word in the Change To box.

Excel stops next on Jalapeno, which is spelled correctly but is not in the regular dictionary. We have several appropriate choices. The **Add** button would add the word to the custom dictionary. If you are sure the word is correctly spelled, this might be the best choice. The **Ignore** button would leave the word as is. **Ignore All** would leave the word as it is and ignore any other occurrences of the word in this document.

5. Click on the **Ignore** button.

Excel continues checking the spelling until it reaches the bottom of the worksheet and then displays the message dialog box, shown in Figure 11.2, asking if you want to continue checking from the beginning of the sheet.

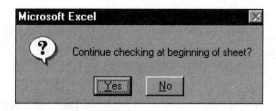

FIGURE 11.2 A SPELLING MESSAGE DIALOG BOX.

6. Click **Yes**.

If there are no typos in your document, Excel displays the message dialog box shown in Figure 11.3.

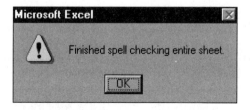

FIGURE 11.3 THE END OF SPELL CHECK MESSAGE.

7. Correct any other spelling errors Excel finds and then click **OK** in the message box to end the spell check session.

WARNING A common error some people make is to assume that if the spell checker doesn't find any errors, everything is spelled correctly. Wrong! What the spell checker does is to make sure each word in your worksheet matches a word in it regular or custom dictionary.

If there is a word in your document that is a correctly spelled word, but just not the word you mean, the spell checker won't catch it as a misspelled word. For example, if you type the word *pane* but you meant *pain*, the spell checker won't catch your error.

The moral of this warning is that, even when you use the spell checker, you still need to proofread your document. Better yet, have someone else do it. It's hard to spot your own errors.

WORKING WITH PIVOTTABLE WIZARD

The PivotTable command lets you analyze and view data in a list or database by producing tables that are easy to understand. Your database may contain hundreds of pieces of raw data in the form of records and fields. One way to analyze your database is by viewing one record at a time (or even one field at a time). But this could take days, if not years, depending on the size of your database. Furthermore, you can never gain an *overall* summary of your data in this manner.

The PivotTable command allows you to summarize your database results in a nice presentation that will be useful to you. A company, for example, may use a database for keeping various data relating to their sales, products, salespersons, buyers, etc. However, the marketing, sales, and warehouse departments all must have reports and tables tailored from this one database that will suit their particular needs. A useful summary table for the marketing department, for example, may not be useful for the warehouse department.

This is why the PivotTable command is such a powerful database tool. It allows you to easily manipulate and create tables that are relevant for different needs. It doesn't matter that the raw data is the same for various departments. The PivotTable concerns itself with how you want your data summarized and presented to provide meaningful and useful tables.

Now that you understand the concept behind PivotTables, let's get to work creating the data for our PivotTable. Let's start fresh with a new sheet.

1. Click on a new sheet tab.
2. Type the information in Table 11.1 so that your new worksheet looks like Figure 11.4. Center your column headings (field names) within the cell. If needed, expand the column width so you can see all your data.

TABLE 11.1 THE FIELD NAMES AND DATA FOR CURRENT AND PAST YEAR INVENTORIES

A ITEM	B TYPE	C COST	D QTY	E YEAR
Small Padlock	Hardware	4.33	42	1995
Bagel Dogs	Food	1.27	375	1995
Plain bagels	Food	0.22	456	1995
8 oz. Cream Cheese	Food	1.33	78	1995
BMW keys	Hardware	.87	26	1995
Mercedes Keys	Hardware	.47	73	1995
Ferrari Keys	Hardware	.56	37	1995
Garlic bagels	Food	.25	133	1995
Large padlock	Hardware	3.42	44	1995
Small Padlock	Hardware	4.01	34	1994
Bagel Dogs	Food	1.31	55	1994
Plain bagels	Food	0.44	834	1994
8 oz. Cream Cheese	Food	.99	75	1994
BMW keys	Hardware	.87	22	1994
Mercedes Keys	Hardware	.40	80	1994
Ferrari Keys	Hardware	.51	5	1994

3. With one of the cells in the list as the active cell, choose **PivotTable** from the Data menu to display the first of four PivotTable Wizard dialog boxes, as shown in Figure 11.5.

4. Because the data source we're using is from an Excel worksheet, "Microsoft Excel List or Database" is the correct and default option. Otherwise you would select a different option depending on your data source. Click **Next** to move to Step 2 the PivotTable Wizard.

5. The PivotTable Wizard places a dashed line around the data it thinks you want to use for the PivotTable and asks you to confirm (or modify) the range (see Figure 11.6). One way to modify the range is to type the range

in the range box. Or you can click on the worksheet and highlight a new range which places the range automatically into the range box. Accept the range PivotWizard selected by clicking **Next** to move to Step 3.

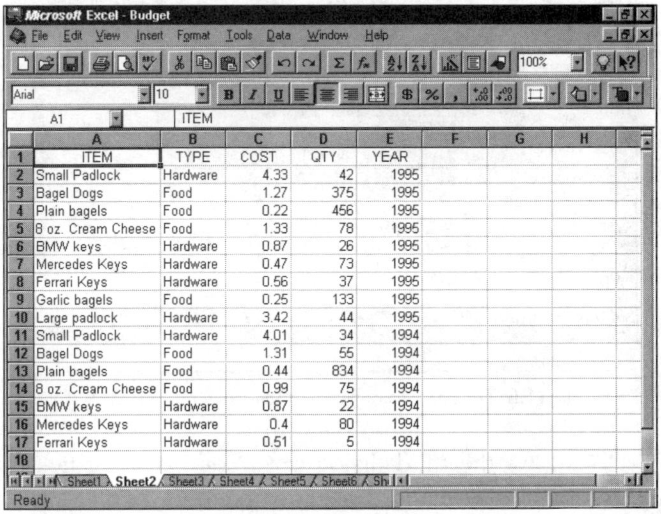

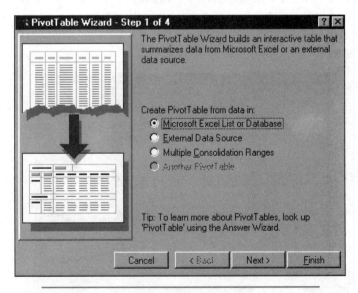

FIGURE 11.4 THE FIELD NAMES AND RECORDS OF THE INVENTORY DATABASE.

FIGURE 11.5 THE PIVOTTABLE WIZARD DIALOG BOX—STEP 1 OF 4.

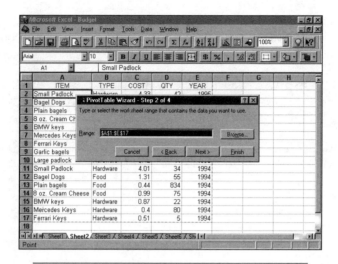

FIGURE 11.6 THE PIVOTTABLE WIZARD DIALOG BOX—STEP 2 OF 4.

6. Figure 11.7 shows the third dialog box. You can drag field names from the right edge of the dialog box into the ROW, COLUMN, DATA, and PAGE portions of the dialog box to determine which data is summarized. This will produce the layout of the PivotTable. We want to summarize the data by TYPE. Therefore, drag the **TYPE** field name button into the ROW portion of the dialog box and then drag the **YEAR** field name button into the COLUMN portion of the dialog box. Finally drag the **COST** field name button into the DATA box.

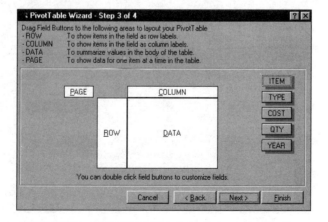

FIGURE 11.7 THE PIVOTTABLE WIZARD DIALOG BOX—STEP 3 OF 4.

7. When your dialog box is displayed, as shown in Figure 11.8, click on the **Next** button.

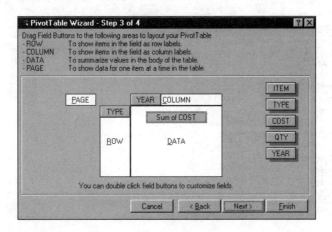

FIGURE 11.8 THE FIELD BUTTONS IN PLACE FOR THE PIVOTTABLE WIZARD.

8. Figure 11.9 displays the final PivotTable Wizard dialog box. In the PivotTable Starting Cell box, type **A19** to have the PivotTable placed a couple of rows below your list. Note that you can also click a worksheet tab to have your table housed in its own sheet. Click the **Finish** button when you are done. The table is placed in your worksheet, as shown in Figure 11.10.

FIGURE 11.9 THE PIVOTTABLE WIZARD DIALOG BOX—STEP 4 OF 4.

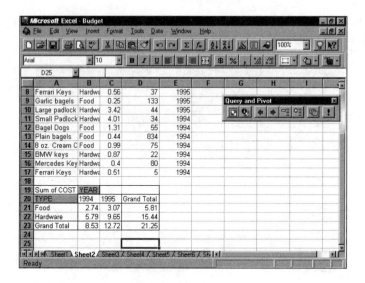

FIGURE 11.10 THE PIVOTTABLE DISPLAYED BELOW THE LIST.

WARNING

If you do not specify a starting cell in this dialog box, the PivotTable replaces the database, which may not be what you have in mind.

The Query and Pivot toolbar also appears with the PivotTable so you can work with the PivotTable more conveniently. You may want to drag the Query and Pivot toolbar to a new location if it obscures part of the PivotTable or is too far away from the PivotTable.

You have just created a simple table from your database which summarizes and compares the cost of the items in your inventory from the current year to the previous year. Let's add another piece to the puzzle. Suppose the hardware department wants to see a summary cost of the hardware items over the past two years, and the food department wants to see a summary cost of the food items over the past two years. Let's create one table that will work for both departments.

1. First, let's copy your data into a new worksheet. Highlight your database (cells A1 through E17). Press the right mouse bottom to bring up the short-cut menu and then press **Copy**. Click on a new sheet in the work-

book. Place the mouse pointer in cell A1, click the right mouse button to display the short-cut menu again, and press **Paste**. While the database is still highlighted, double-click between the column header labels to adjust the width of the columns. You've just copied your database into a new sheet.

2. With one of the cells in the list as the active cell, choose **PivotTable** from the Data menu to display the first of the PivotTable Wizard dialog boxes.

3. Because the data source we're using is from an Excel worksheet, "Microsoft Excel List or Database" is the correct option. Click **Next**.

4. The PivotTable Wizard has correctly placed a dashed line around the data we are going to use for the PivotTable. Click **Next**.

5. Drag **TYPE** and then **ITEM** into the ROW portion of the dialog box. Then drag **YEAR** into the COLUMN portion of the dialog box. Finally drag **COST** into the DATA portion of the dialog box. When the dialog box is displayed, as shown in Figure 11.11, click the **Next** button.

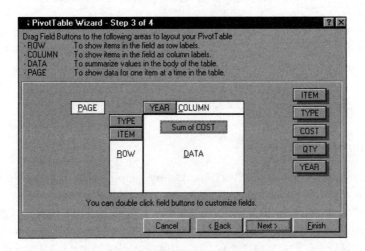

FIGURE 11.11 ANOTHER PIVOTTABLE SETUP.

6. In the PivotTable Starting Cell text box, type **A19** to have the PivotTable placed a couple of rows below your data. Click the **Finish** button when you are done. Use the scroll bar to see your new table. It should look like the table in Figure 11.12. (Note that the worksheet gridlines have been removed so we can see the table more clearly.)

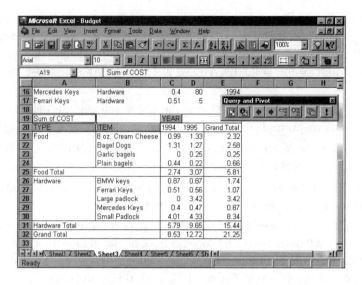

FIGURE 11.12 THE COMPLETED PIVOTTABLE—READY FOR REARRANGING.

You have just created a table that summarizes and categorize both the food items and the hardware items. The table can now be given to both the hardware and food departments, because the data is arranged to be meaningful for each department.

Save your work before proceeding with the next section.

Rearranging the Table

Rearranging and altering the PivotTable is very simple. You may decide that you want your table to have a slightly different look. All that is needed to alter an existing PivotTable is to drag the field heading markers in the existing PivotTable to different locations. Excel automatically updates the changes and produces the new table. Let's try a very simple rearrangement so that you'll get a feel for it.

1. Using the table you just created, click on the **YEAR** file heading button and drag it until it is on top of the TYPE file heading button. Notice that the rectangular shape changes from a horizontal shape, representing column headings, to a vertical shape, representing row headings.

2. Release the mouse button; Excel automatically rearranges the table. You may have to select **Zoom** from the View menu, select **75%** magnification

in the custom window, and then press **OK** to see the whole table. Your table should look like Figure 11.13.

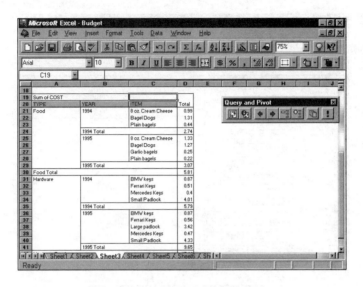

FIGURE 11.13 REARRANGING THE PIVOTTABLE.

Try creating other PivotTables and rearranging them from the sample database you've created. For example, try rearranging the order of the three PivotTable buttons as shown in Figure 11.14. This is done by dragging the buttons into the desired arrangement. The concepts of the PivotTable become clearer the more you practice it.

USING "WHAT IF"

One of the main reasons people enjoy using Excel worksheets is that it allows you to analyze your data by doing *what if* tests on variable data. For example, you may have a savings account and want to know the future value of the account in 5 years if you systematically deposited a certain amount. But suppose you want to play *what if* with the amounts you deposit. Suppose you want to test depositing $100 a month, or $125 a month or $75 a month. What would the future value in five years be for each amount?

There are a number of powerful tools in Excel that you can use to play *what if* to determine the results of different scenarios. You will have to determine the *what if* tool that is right for your analysis. Following is a brief outline and description of these tools.

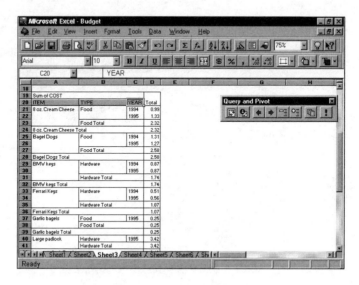

FIGURE 11.14 REARRANGING THE PIVOTTABLE AGAIN.

Single-Variable Data Tables

The single-variable data tables will help you analyze how a variable will change the result of a formula. For instance, suppose you knew the bank was paying .75% interest. You also knew that you wanted to make an equal deposit each month for the next 3 years. This would equal 36 deposits. How much would you earn if you deposited $100 a month, or $125, or $150, or $175? Let's create a single-variable table using the Future Value function (FV) to find out. The following steps create the single-variable table using the Function Wizard.

1. Click on a new sheet and enter the data shown in Figure 11.15.
2. In cell B4 do the following procedures:
   ♦ Click in cell **B4**.
   ♦ Click the **Function Wizard**.
   ♦ Click **Financial**.
   ♦ Click **FV**.

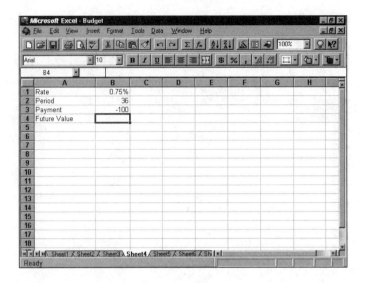

FIGURE 11.15 SETTING UP THE DATA TABLE WORKSHEET.

◆ Click **Next**.

◆ Click cell **B1** for rate and press **Tab**.

◆ Click **B2** for number of periods and press **Tab**.

◆ Click **B3** for amount and press **Finish**. (You may have to widen your columns as needed.)

Basically, you've just used the Function Wizard to create the FV formula in cell B4. The complete details of using the Function Wizard are provided in Chapter 5.

3. Click in cell D2 and type **=B4**.

This is the first cell of the table we are going to create. The starting cell will be the same as the result of the FV function.

4. Starting in cell C3, let's list the *what if* variables. In cell C1 type **Test Values**. Then enter the values shown in Figure 11.16. Adjust column widths as necessary.

5. Highlight C2 through D6, which will make up our table.

6. Select the **Table** command from the Data menu.

7. Since we want data to appear in column format, Tab to Column Input Cell. Although we're setting up this input table in rows, you can set tables up in columns also.

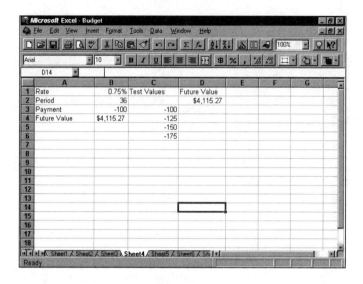

FIGURE 11.16 ENTERING TEST VALUES FOR THE TABLE.

8. Click in cell **B3** because this is the variable data we're using. (An absolute reference to the cell will be displayed in the Column Input Cell window.)

9. Press **OK** and the table with the variable deposits are created showing how much you would earn depending on your monthly payment. Your table should look like Figure 11.17. You should format the cells using the currency format.

Double-Variable Data Tables

Sometimes you may want to use the *what if* in more complex instances where you have two variables instead of just one. Excel can produce data tables using double variables. In order to create a double-variable table, you must enter variable amounts in both rows and columns. Suppose we wanted to analyze different number of payments AND different payment amounts. Let's use our previous example to demonstrate double-variable tables.

1. Select cells A1 through C6. Choose the **Copy** command from the Edit menu, then move to cell A10 and select the **Paste** command from the Edit menu.

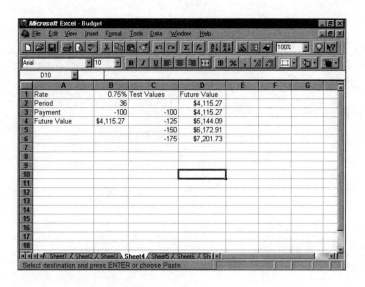

FIGURE 11.17 THE COMPLETED SINGLE-VARIABLE DATA TABLE.

2. Enter the following:

◆ Cell D11 enter **36**

◆ Cell E11 enter **42**

◆ Cell F11 enter **54**

    (36 represents 36 months, 42 represents 42 months, and 54 represents 54 months.)

3. In cell C11 we want to duplicate the Future Value Function in cell B13. Simply type **=B13**. Your screen should now look like Figure 11.18.

5. Highlight the entire table (cells C11 through F15).

6. Select **Table** from the Data menu. Click on cell **B11** (number of periods) for the Row Input Cell. This indicates that the number of periods are listed across the top row of the table. Click on cell **B12** (payment amount) for the Column Input Cell. This indicates that the payment amounts are listed down the column of the table. Figure 11.19 shows the dialog box filled in. When finished, click **OK**.

7. To format your data to currency format, highlight cells **D12–F15**, then click on the **Currency Format** button in the toolbar.

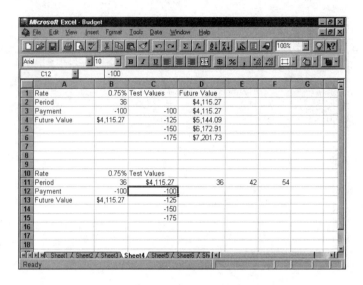

FIGURE 11.18 THE DOUBLE-VARIABLE TABLE BEING SET UP.

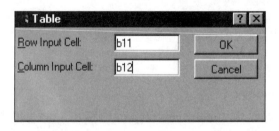

FIGURE 11.19 THE DOUBLE-VARIABLE DIALOG SETUP.

8. Expand the width of your columns to see your data. Your table should look like Figure 11.20.

You have just created a double-variable table for finding the future value using the number of payments as one variable and the amount of payments as another variable.

USING SCENARIO MANAGER

Playing *what if* is one of the spreadsheet's most useful facilities. You can change values in various cells of the worksheet to see the effect the changes will have.

For example, what would happen if January sales increased by $100,000? You could just enter the new value in the January sales cell. But you'd have to re-enter the original value, then the new value to switch between the scenarios.

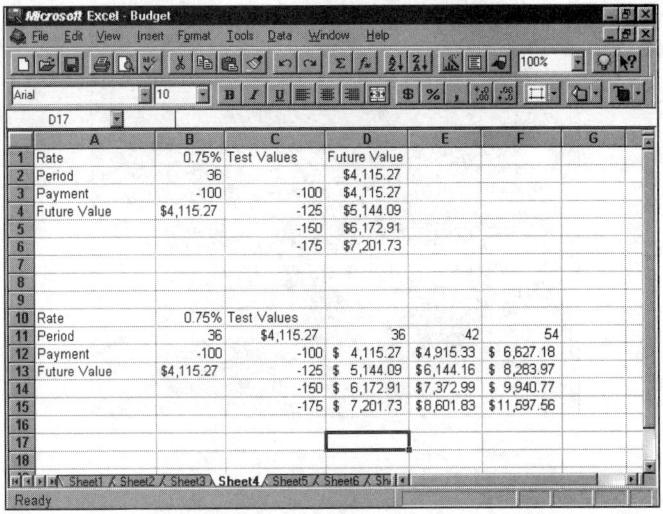

	A	B	C	D	E	F	G
1	Rate	0.75%	Test Values	Future Value			
2	Period	36		$4,115.27			
3	Payment	-100	-100	$4,115.27			
4	Future Value	$4,115.27	-125	$5,144.09			
5			-150	$6,172.91			
6			-175	$7,201.73			
7							
8							
9							
10	Rate	0.75%	Test Values				
11	Period	36	$4,115.27	36	42	54	
12	Payment	-100	-100	$ 4,115.27	$4,915.33	$ 6,627.18	
13	Future Value	$4,115.27	-125	$ 5,144.09	$6,144.16	$ 8,283.97	
14			-150	$ 6,172.91	$7,372.99	$ 9,940.77	
15			-175	$ 7,201.73	$8,601.83	$11,597.56	

FIGURE 11.20 THE FINISHED DOUBLE-VARIABLE TABLE.

Or you could use a data table as described earlier in this chapter. But data tables are useful only when you are inserting different variables into a formula to change the result of a single formula. There may be times when you want to experiment with many values on your worksheet—setting up scenarios for best-case budgets, or worst-case projections.

Excel's Scenario Manager makes switching between various what-if scenarios a breeze by letting you name the scenarios and then choosing the one you want to see from a list in the dialog box. Let's create scenarios for our budget worksheet to allow us to switch among a couple of sales possibilities.

1. Click on the **Sheet1** tab to make the budget worksheet data visible and then choose **Tools**, **Scenarios** to display the Scenario Manager dialog box, as shown in Figure 11.21.
2. We do not have any scenarios defined yet, so click the **Add** button to add a scenario. The Add Scenario dialog box appears, as shown in Figure 11.22.

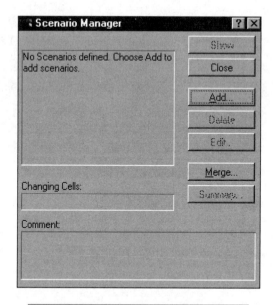

FIGURE 11.21 THE SCENARIO MANAGER DIALOG BOX.

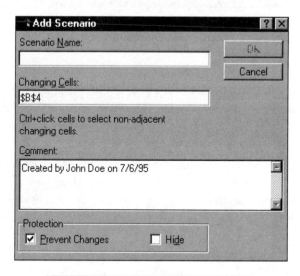

FIGURE 11.22 THE ADD SCENARIO DIALOG BOX.

3. In the Scenario Name text box, type **Best Guess**.

4. Press **Tab** twice to highlight the entire comment that says "Created by Your Name on MM/DD/YY" and type **This is what I expect sales to be.**

5. Drag the dialog box by its title bar down far enough so cells B5, C5 and D5 are visible, then double-click in the **Changing Cells** text box.

    This is where we define which cells will have different values for the scenario.

N O T E   The cells you specify as the Changing Cells should not contain formulas, but rather be cells containing values that formulas depend on. For example, B5 is the cell containing the January sales value, but several formulas in the worksheet depend on this value for their results. Therefore, B5 is a good choice for a Changing Cell.

6. Click on cell **B5**, then hold down the **Ctrl** key while you click on **C5** and then **D5**.

7. When the dialog box is displayed, as shown in Figure 11.23, click **OK**. The Scenario Values dialog box appears, as shown in Figure 11.24, where you can enter the values for this scenario. For our Best Guess scenario, we leave the values as they are.

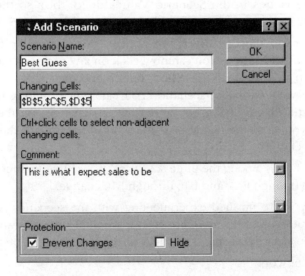

FIGURE **11.23** THE COMPLETED ADD SCENARIO DIALOG BOX.

8. Click the **Add** button to display the Add Scenario dialog box and try another scenario.

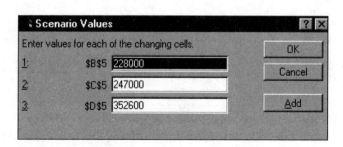

FIGURE 11.24 THE SCENARIO VALUES DIALOG BOX.

9. In the Scenario Name text box, type **Wishful Thinking**, and edit the Comment box so the comment is **Not a chance**, then click **OK**.

10. Edit the values in the Scenario Values dialog box so the values are **328,000** for B5, **347,000** for C5, and **410,000** for D5, then click **Add** again so we can add one more scenario.

11. In the Scenario Name text box, type **The Sky is Falling!** and edit the Comment box so the comment is **We're in big trouble**. Then click **OK**.

12. Edit the values in the Scenario Values dialog box so the values are **128,000** for B5, **147,000** for C5 and **210,000** for D5.

The Scenario Manager dialog box appears once again, this time with the three scenarios listed. You can now click on any of the scenario names in the Scenarios list. Click the **Show** button and the worksheet changes to see the values for that scenario. You can switch among the scenarios while still in the dialog box and view the changes on the worksheet. When you close the dialog box, the worksheet displays the values from the last chosen scenario.

As you switch among the three scenarios, notice that the numbers in cells E5, B13 through E13, and B16 through E16 change.

13. When you are finished experimenting with the scenarios, switch to the Best Guess scenario to return to our original numbers and then click **Close** to clear the Scenario Manager dialog box.

14. Save your work.

Your scenarios are saved with the workbook so they are available whenever you are working with this worksheet in the workbook.

N O T E

OUTLINING WORKSHEETS

As your skills improve and your applications for Excel expand, there will be times when you'll need to manage worksheets, and probably workbooks, containing massive data. Managing and tracking large worksheets can be very difficult and confusing. Excel has a feature called outlining that consolidates portions of your worksheet's data, and thereby makes large worksheets more manageable. Let's explain what outlining is and then give you some hands-on steps in creating outlines.

Excel 95 is designed on the premise that most people use their worksheets to calculate totals. After all, that's a worksheet's chief application. We calculate totals in columns and in rows to come up with subtotals. Then we calculate our subtotals to come up with grand totals. We then calculate these grand totals to come up with grand-grand totals. Before long, our worksheet contains a massive grand total in cell A16384, (the last row of an Excel worksheet), while the data for this grand total starts in cell A1. Managing such a worksheet, or a similar scenario, can be a nightmare.

Outlining is a feature in Excel that allows you to consolidates all your subtotals, totals, grand totals, grand-grand totals, and so on. Outlining will display only the totals you choose, without displaying the accompanying data used to make up these totals. Having the ability to display only totals and not the data that makes up the totals is why this feature is called outlining.

Before you try your hands at outlining, lets talk a little about levels of data. Most worksheets employ a natural hierarchy as it relates to levels of data. The lowest level of data is a simple value in a cell. These value are not formulas—they're simply values. The next level of data are formulas that calculate these lowest level of data. Then we move to the next level of data which are more formulas that calculate the previous formulas, and so on.

The outlining feature main task is to view selected levels of data without having to view all the data. Let's do an illustration to help you better understand outlining.

1. In Figure 11.25 you'll see a worksheet with several levels of data. Re-create this worksheet by entering the data into your worksheet as shown. You may want to click on a fresh worksheet tab.

2. Using your **AutoSum** button, let Excel calculate the sums of the Level Two Totals for Jan, Feb, and Mar. Highlight cells **B5**, **C5**, and **D5**, then double-click the **AutoSum** button. Repeat this for the totals in rows 9, 13, and 14.

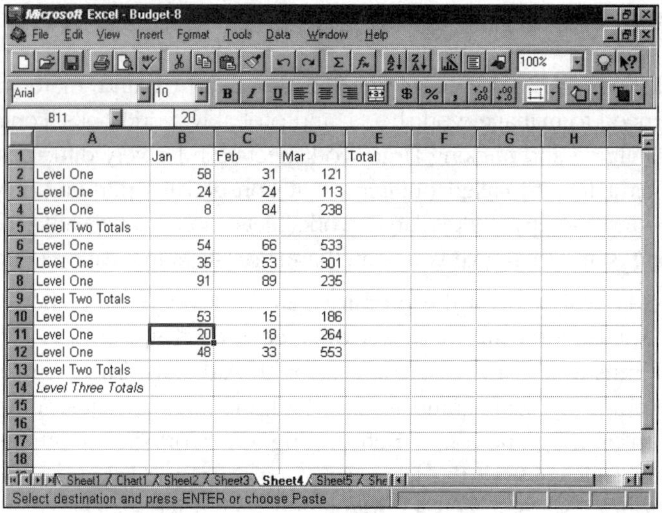

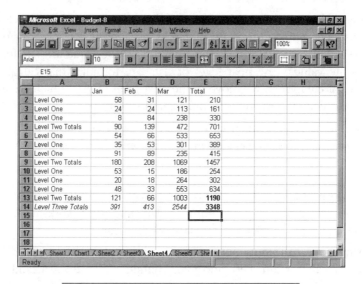

FIGURE 11.25 DATA FOR WORKSHEET WITH LEVELS OF DATA.

3. Highlight the cells under Total (E2:E14) and double-click the **AutoSum** button to calculate the row totals. Your worksheet should look like Figure 11.26.

FIGURE 11.26 A WORKSHEET WITH MANY LEVELS OF DATA.

4. Highlight cells A2 through E14. This is the data and formulas we want to outline.

5. From the Data menu, choose **Group** and **Outline**. Then select **AutoOutline**. Your screen should look like Figure 11.27.

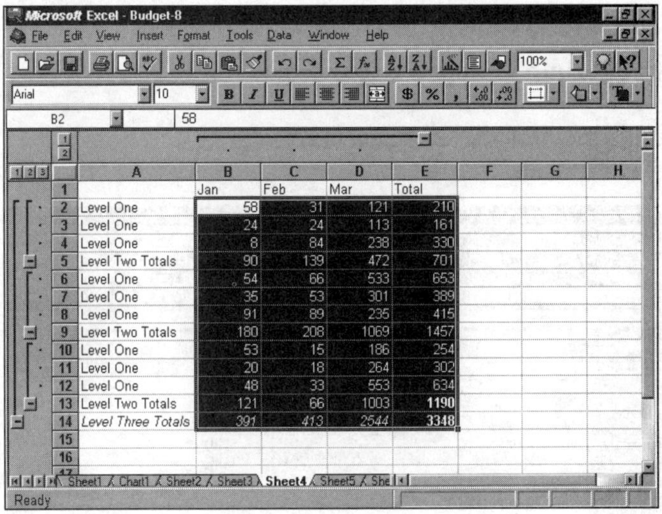

FIGURE 11.27 OUTLINED DATA.

You have just had Excel automatically outline your worksheet. You'll notice it has placed outlining symbols on the top and right side of the worksheet. The symbols allows you to determine what level of data you want to see and what level of data you don't want to see.

Let's look a little closer at the outlining symbols and tools. You can see that the basic outlining symbol is a line with a bracket on one end and a box attached to the other end with a minus sign in the middle of it. Each cell that contains a formula (total) has an outlining symbol indicating which cells contain the data that makes up the total. For example, if you look at Level Two Totals in cell B5, and then look over to the left to the outlining symbol, you'll notice that rows 2 through 5 are bracketed. This is because the total of rows 2 through 4 are contained in row 5—B5 to be exact. Notice that rows 6 through 9 and rows 10 through 13 are also bracketed. The totals are in row 9 and in row 13 respectively.

The box, with the minus sign inside of it, is the outlining tool called the Group Collapse/Expand button. The minus sign indicates that the group is fully expanded. To collapse a group and hide the data in the group, simply click on the **Group Collapse/Expand** button.

Follow these steps to collapse your worksheet.

1. Click the **Group Collapse/Expand** button for row 5.
2. Click the **Group Collapse/Expand** button for row 9.
3. Click the **Group Collapse/Expand** button for row 13.

Your worksheet should look like Figure 11.28.

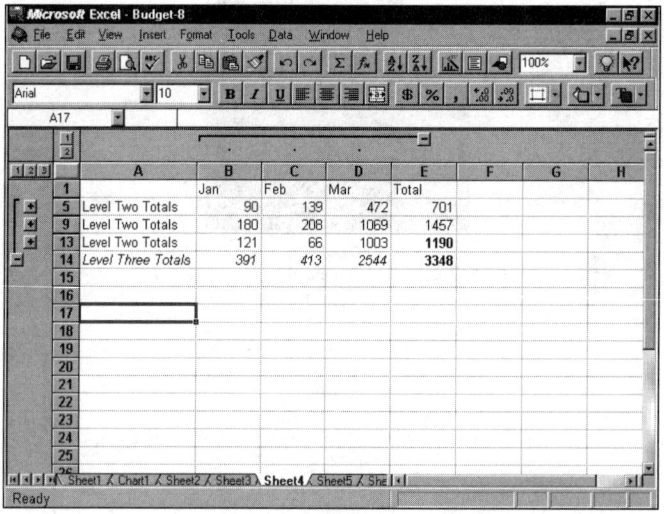

FIGURE 11.28 COLLAPSED WORKSHEET.

Excel has hidden all the data in each group and displays only the group totals. The minus sign inside the box has been replaced with a plus sign to indicate that the group can be expanded to display more data.

We only had one Level Three Total. Notice it brackets the entire worksheet. Larger worksheets of course would contain more Level Three Totals as well as Level Four Totals, etc.

You can gain a sense of how useful consolidation can be with a large worksheet. It simplifies your data and lets you see only what you want to see. It allows you to choose the level of data that's important to you.

Another benefit in outlining is that sometimes you only want to print totals, without having to print the entire worksheet (which could expand several pages of data). Moreover, you'll want those totals on only one page. Outlining allows you to suppress the data you don't need and print only the totals that are relevant for you.

Now, note the outlining symbol above the worksheet. Since our example used only one column total there's only one outlining tool. If we had used more column totals, then we would have had more outlining symbols for the columns.

◆ Click the **Group Collapse/Expand** button on the top of the worksheet. Your worksheet should look like Figure 11.29.

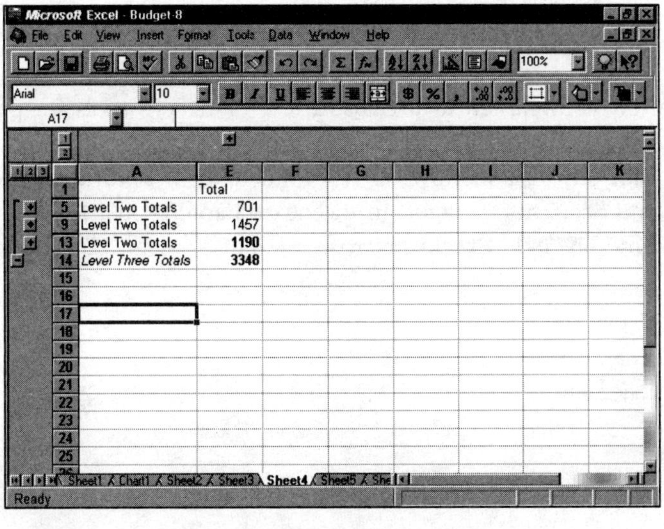

FIGURE 11.29 COLLAPSED COLUMNS.

Notice that all the data columns for the group were collapsed (Jan, Feb, March) and only the total column remained.

One final explanation before we leave this topic. Have you wondered what the two vertical buttons numbered one and two are for? Or the three horizontal buttons numbered one, two, and three are for? These buttons are called the Row Level button and the Column Level button. You can click the **Row Level** button to display the highest level of data you want to see. You may also click the **Column Level** button to display the level of data you want to see in your columns.

Suppose we want to see all level of data in our sample worksheet. Do the following:

1. Click box **2** on the Column (vertical) Level button.
2. Click box **3** on the Row (horizontal) Level button.

These steps told Excel to display the columns by 2 data levels, which is the maximum in our example, and display the rows by 3 data levels, which is again the maximum in our example.

Add more data to your worksheet, especially column totals, and practice using the outlining feature of Excel.

A FINAL THOUGHT

In this chapter, you learned to use just a few of Excel's tools for proofing and analyzing your worksheet data. You now know how to ensure that your data is free of spelling errors and how to view the data in a variety of ways using PivotTable and Scenario Manager. In the next chapter you'll learn about one of the biggest time savers in Excel—Macros.

CHAPTER 12

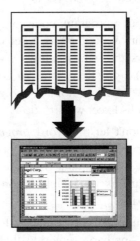

AUTOMATING YOUR WORK WITH MACROS

- ♦ Understanding macros
- ♦ Planning a macro
- ♦ Storing macros
- ♦ Recording a macro
- ♦ Running a macro
- ♦ Unhiding the personal macro workbook
- ♦ Assigning macros to menus, shortcut keys, buttons, and objects

Understanding Macros

Without a program, your computer is nothing more than a big, expensive paper-weight. A program is a set of instructions, in a language your computer can understand, which allows your computer to perform useful (or so one would hope) tasks. Excel is a big computer program that tells your computer what to do. A *macro* is nothing more than a little program (in this case, inside Excel) that tells Excel what to do.

Don't let the word *program* scare you. You can use Excel macros to cut time-consuming, repetitive tasks down to size without knowing the first thing about programming. Excel lets you record any series of Excel actions for later use, just as you would record a series of sounds on a tape recorder for future playback.

Suppose you routinely format groups of selected cells in some particular ways—perhaps centering their contents, surrounding them with a border, and adjusting the column width to accommodate the longest entry. To do this manu-ally, you have to perform three separate tasks requiring many mouse actions or keystrokes. However, if you record these tasks as a macro, you can perform all these tasks at once with a couple of mouse clicks or keystrokes to run (play) the macro. You even learn a few tricks for assigning macros to menus, buttons, and shortcut keys so they are even easier to use.

Another common use for a macro is to automate the typing of frequently entered text, such as your name, address, or company name. Recording fre-quently entered text as macros saves time and eliminates typos—assuming you typed it correctly while recording the macro.

This cell formatting example is a very simple example of what you can do with macros. Literally any series of tasks can be consolidated into a single macro. No series of tasks is too simple or too complex to be turned into a macro. Consider the toolbar buttons. You have likely noticed that they are short-cuts for performing tasks with just the click of a mouse.

Some buttons, such as the Open button, do not save you much time. Instead of clicking on the **Open** button, you could simply choose **File**, **Open**. It may hardly seem worth the effort to use a button to save one keystroke or mouse click. However, because opening files is something that is repeated many times during a typical Excel session, the button can accumulate a savings in time that is worthwhile.

Let's discuss the issue of programming. You don't need to know anything about programming to make good use of macros. However, if you take the time to learn a little about Excel's programming language, you can extend your macros' potential flexibility and complexity enormously.

Even if you don't do any programming and just use Excel's macro recorder, you are actually programming. Huh? Let me explain. When you turn on the macro recorder and perform the tasks you want included in the macro, Excel creates a computer program for you and runs the program when you run the macro.

N O T E The programming language Excel uses to create your macro is called *VBA* (Visual Basic for Applications). This language is an extension of the ubiquitous BASIC programming language that comes with many computers. In fact, you may already have some familiarity with BASIC. If you already know a little about any version of BASIC, you won't have any trouble adapting to VBA. If you have no clue about the ins and outs of programming, but have some healthy curiosity, you can quickly learn some simple VBA programming from the documentation included with Excel.

PLANNING A MACRO

To start recording, simply choose **Tools**, **Record Macro**, **Record New Macro** and then enter a macro name, description, and perform the tasks you want included. There are a couple of things to take into account before you start recording. The first is planning.

When you record a macro, everything you do (including mistakes) is recorded in the macro and turned into program code. If you start recording a macro while in one worksheet and then realize that you want to use the macro on another worksheet, you switch to the other worksheet and start performing the tasks you want to be part of the macro. The problem is, whenever you run the macro, the first thing it does is switch to a different worksheet, which probably isn't what you want to do at that point. Recording a macro with a lot of mistakes can also slow down the execution of the macro.

If you want the macro to manipulate some selected cells, you want to perform the macro recording tasks on a single active cell in the worksheet. Select that cell before starting the recording process. This way, when you run the macro, it performs on the current selection.

You want to consider whether the macro uses relative or absolute referencing. The concept is the same as the absolute versus relative referencing discussed in copying formulas. If your active cell is A1 when you start recording the macro using absolute referencing and you click on cell D6, the first thing the macro does when played is move to cell D6. If you were using relative referencing—which is the default—the macro would move three columns to the right and five rows down, which is D6's relative position from A1. As a general rule, relative referencing allows your macros to operate correctly in a variety of situations.

STORING MACROS

Macros are stored on what are called *module sheets*. Module sheets are very much like worksheets but their only purpose is to maintain macros and their instructions. Module sheets can be stored as one of the sheets of the workbook you're working in or can be stored in the Personal Macro Workbook. You instruct Excel where to store your macros.

When macros are stored in the workbook you are working with, they are called *local macros*. When you select the **Store in This Workbook** option, Excel creates a module page as the last page of the workbook and the macros are stored there. They are called local macros because they can only be executed in the workbook they are stored in.

On the other hand, when macros are stored in the Personal Macro Workbook, they are called *global macros*. When you select the **Store in Personal Macro Workbook** option (we'll show you where you would select this option later), Excel stores your macro in this hidden workbook. When you open any workbook, the Personal Macro Workbook also opens, albeit as a hidden file. The macros are called global or Personal macros because the macros can be executed from any workbook.

If you needed to actually see the Personal Macro Workbook, possibly for editing macros in it, you can unhide the file by using the **Unhide** command in the Window menu. Don't forget to hide the Personal Macro Workbook when you finish with any edits. The Personal Macro Workbook is created by Excel when you store your first global macro. If, when you go to unhide the Personal Macro Workbook, and the Unhide command does not appear, it simply means that no macros have been created and stored there yet. Create a simple one, and then you'll be able to unhide it. This will become clear as you progress through this chapter.

In planning your macros, you should decide if the macro will only be used for one workbook or if it's a macro that will be used for various workbooks. For example, if you planned a macro that creates PivotTables exclusively from the data in your **SALES.XLS** file, then you should store your macro as a local macro in the **SALES.XLS** file by choosing the **Store in This Workbook** option. However, if you planned a macro that generates your company name, centers it, bolds it, and italicizes it, this macro can be used in more than one workbook, and you should store this macro as a global macro by choosing the **Store in Personal Macro Workbook** option. You'll see where this option appears as you work through the example in this chapter.

NOTE You can also store macros in a New Workbook, but in order to use the macros, you would always have to open the New Workbook where the macros are stored. It's better to store them locally in the workbook you will use them in, or globally.

RECORDING A MACRO

Let's start recording the cell formatting macro now.

1. Start Excel and open the **BUDGET** workbook if it isn't already on your screen. Click on a clean sheet so we can record this macro on a fresh worksheet.

    It isn't necessary to record the macro on an unused sheet, but doing so ensures that you won't mess up any existing worksheet data while recording your macro.

2. Click on cell **B2** to make it the active cell and then choose **Tools**, **Record Macro**, **Record New Macro** to display the Record New Macro dialog box, as shown in Figure 12.1.

    For this macro, any active cell works. Using a cell that is at least one row down and one column over allows us to see all sides of the border the macro adds.

    You could allow Excel to name the macro for you (in this case Macro1) but that's not very descriptive, so we give it a new name.

3. With the Macro Name text box highlighted, type **CellFmt** and press the **Tab** key to highlight the contents of the Description box.

4. In the Description box, type **Formats selection center aligned, places border and AutoFits column width**.

FIGURE 12.1 THE RECORD NEW MACRO DIALOG BOX.

This macro works on any group of selected cells, so we want to make sure it's available whenever we need it.

5. Click the **Options** button to expand the dialog box so the Record New Macro options are visible, as shown in Figure 12.2.

FIGURE 12.2 THE EXPANDED RECORD NEW MACRO DIALOG BOX.

We'll cover the Assign To portion of the dialog box later in the chapter. For now, let's make sure we are storing the macro in the Personal Macro Workbook. This ensures that the macro is available on any worksheet we may open now or in the future.

N O T E

The Language section of the dialog box lets you choose whether you want to record the macro in Visual Basic or the MS Excel 4.0 Macro language. Unless you are sharing macros with users who haven't upgraded to version 5 yet, you should always use Visual Basic. Not only is Visual Basic a more powerful language, but it is also the language that will become the standard for all future Microsoft applications. You might as well get used to it.

6. Click on the **Personal Macro Workbook** option button and then click **OK** to begin the macro recording session.

   You can tell you are recording a macro because the status bar displays the message <u>Recording</u>. There is also a little toolbar floating on the screen with a Stop Recording Macro button, as displayed in Figure 12.3.

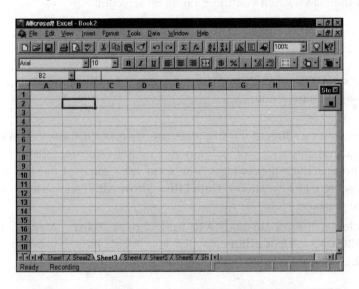

FIGURE 12.3 THE STOP TOOLBAR AND THE STATUS BAR DISPLAYING RECORDING.

Before performing the macro tasks, we need to make sure we are using Relative References so the macro works on any group of selected cells and not just B2.

7. Choose **Tools**, **Record Macro**, **Use Relative References**, unless there is already a check mark in front of Use Relative References. If there is already a check mark, press **Esc** three times to back out of the menu.

Now, we proceed to format the active cell for center alignment, place a single-line border around it, and AutoFit the selection.

8. Display the shortcut menu for the active cell by right-clicking on it. Choose **Format Cells**, click on the **Alignment** tab, and choose **Center** in the Horizontal area of the dialog box. Don't click OK yet.

9. Click on the **Border** tab, then click **Outline** in the Border section of the dialog box, and click **OK**.

10. Choose **Format, Column, AutoFit Selection**.

11. Click on the **Stop Recording Macro** button in the floating Stop toolbar, and then click on another cell so you can see the border around the cell.

    You cannot tell if the type in the cell is centered or the width is adjusted to accommodate it, since the cell is empty. You see the complete results of the macro when you run it on a real selection.

RUNNING A MACRO

Now that we've recorded a macro, let's select some cells in the sheet containing our database and try it out.

1. Click on the **Sheet2** tab (the database sheet) to display it. If you already adjusted the width of column A and B to accommodate the largest entries, reduce their widths now so at least some of the text in each is obscured. Finally, choose **Data Filter Show All** to show all the records in the database.

2. Select cells A2 through A12 and choose **Tools, Macro**. Click on **PERSONAL.XLS!CellFmt** so that it is highlighted, as shown in Figure 12.4.

NOTE Your Macro dialog box may contain the names of other macros if there are any others stored in the PERSONAL.XLS dialog box or on any other open workbook.

3. Click the **Run** button to execute the macro.

    The list of items in column A is now center-aligned, with a border around it and with the column width adjusted to fit the largest entry.

That's all there is to running a macro from the Macro dialog box. Next let's take a look at ways to make it even easier to run a macro.

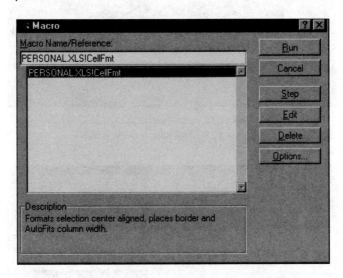

FIGURE 12.4 THE MACRO DIALOG BOX.

UNHIDING THE PERSONAL MACRO WORKBOOK

Let's change the options for the CellFmt macro in the PERSONAL.XLS workbook. The PERSONAL.XLS workbook is hidden, so before we can make any changes to the CellFmt macro, we have to unhide the PERSONAL.XLS workbook.

1. Choose **Window**, **Unhide** to display the Unhide dialog box, as displayed in Figure 12.5.

   If there are any other open but hidden workbooks, these are listed along with PERSONAL.XLS.

2. Click on **PERSONAL.XLS** if it isn't already highlighted, and then click the **OK** button.

   The PERSONAL.XLS workbook with one tab, Module1, is displayed, as shown in Figure 12.6.

   If other macros have been recorded and stored on the PERSONAL.XLS workbook, they may be displayed on your screen and you may need to scroll down to view the CellFmt macro.

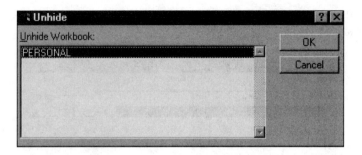

FIGURE 12.5 THE UNHIDE DIALOG BOX.

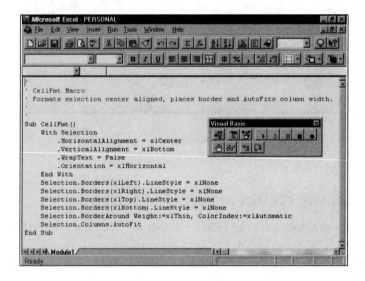

FIGURE 12.6 THE PERSONAL.XLS WORKBOOK.

With the macro displayed, you could edit it to correct mistakes or add functionality. Even if you do not know the first thing about programming, you may find it interesting to look over the macro. You'll be surprised at how easily you'll understand what's going on.

WARNING

Unless you know what you are doing and have a reasonable understanding of Visual Basic, you should not edit the macro in any way. Even making some seemingly innocuous changes could leave the macro completely useless.

ASSIGNING MACROS TO MENUS AND SHORTCUT KEYS

Now that the workbook containing our macro is unhidden, we can switch back to the Budget workbook and change the macro's options. In the expanded Record New Macro dialog box, there is an Assign To area. This area lets you assign the macro to a menu option, a shortcut key, or both.

1. Choose **Window**, and then click on **BUDGET.XLS** in the bottom portion of the menu.

2. Choose **Tools**, **Macro** and click on **PERSONAL.XLS!CellFmt**, then click the **Options** button to display the Macro Option dialog box, as shown in Figure 12.7.

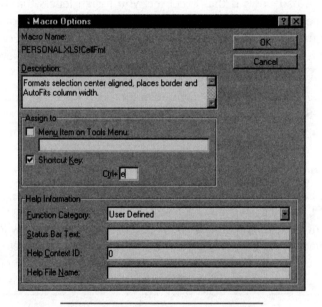

FIGURE 12.7 THE MACRO OPTIONS DIALOG BOX.

The Assign To portion of the Macro Options dialog box is the same as in the expanded Record New Macro dialog box. You can do everything before you start the recording process in exactly the same manner as you do after the macro is recorded.

By default, the Shortcut Key check box is unchecked, but Excel assigns **Ctrl** plus the next available letter for the shortcut key combination. You can use any of the 26 alphabet letters in either uppercase or lowercase, giving you 52 possible shortcut key combinations. To change the shortcut key, you highlight or delete the letter in the box and type the letter you want. If you want to use the letter in uppercase, press **Shift** plus the letter. We accept the shortcut key Excel suggests, which is probably **Ctrl-e**. If "e" does not appear in your box, simply type it in.

WARNING

When Excel chooses the shortcut key, it's looking for the next *available* letter. Available does not necessarily mean the next consecutive letter. After Ctrl-e is used, Excel skips to Ctrl-g because Ctrl-f is already assigned as the keyboard shortcut for Find. Press **Ctrl-f** and the Find dialog box is displayed.

The bad news is that Excel lets you assign letters that have already been assigned. If you choose Ctrl-f as the shortcut key combination for a macro, then **Ctrl-f** is no longer the shortcut for Find. For this reason, it is usually best to accept Excel's choice for a shortcut key.

We assign this macro to a menu item on the Tools menu and put a check in the **Shortcut Key** check box. In real life, you probably would not use both a shortcut key and assign the macro to a menu item. You'd most likely choose one or the other.

3. Click on the **Shortcut Key** check box if it is not already checked.

NOTE

If Excel has assigned a different shortcut key to this macro, that's OK, but make a note of it so you'll be able to remember how to invoke the macro later. In fact, it's not a bad idea to keep a complete listing of all your macros and their shortcut keys handy. You could create the list in an Excel database or in your word processing program.

4. Click on the check box in front of **Menu Item** on the Tools menu and then click in the text box below and type **Center/Border/AutoFit**. Click **OK** and then the **Close** button of the Macro dialog box.

The text you typed—Center/Border/AutoFit—is the text that appears in the Tools menu. The menu width will adjusts to accommodate as much text as fits on one line across the screen. However, it's best to keep the menu text reasonably short so the menu does not obscure too much of the screen.

The whole point of using macros is to save time. That being the case, choosing **Tools**, **Macro**, clicking on the macro name, and then the **Run** button is a far too tedious process for executing a simple macro. We now have two new ways to run the macro, from the Tools menu and the shortcut key. Let's use them both.

1. Select cells B2 through B11 (the category column) and choose **Tools** to display the Tools menu, as shown in Figure 12.8.

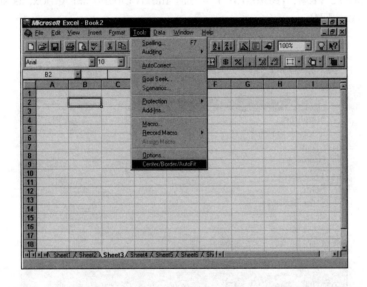

FIGURE 12.8 THE TOOLS MENU WITH THE NEW CHOICE AT THE BOTTOM OF THE MENU.

2. Click on **Center/Border/AutoFit** in the bottom portion of the menu.

   There now, wasn't that easier? To use the shortcut key on a column that needs reformatting, we close the Budget workbook without saving it, and then open it again.

3. Close the Budget workbook by choosing **File**, **Close** and click on **NO** when asked if you want to save BUDGET.XLS. Then reopen the Budget workbook.

4. Once again, select cells B2 through B11 and press the shortcut key combination, **Ctrl-e** (or whatever your shortcut key is).

ASSIGNING MACROS TO TOOLBAR BUTTONS

This is getting just a bit too easy, don't you think? Well, we're still not finished making life easier with macros. Next, assign the macro to a button, which we will then add to the Formatting toolbar.

1. Close the Budget workbook again without saving and reopen it, as before.

2. Choose **View**, **Toolbars** to display the Toolbars dialog box, as shown in Figure 12.9.

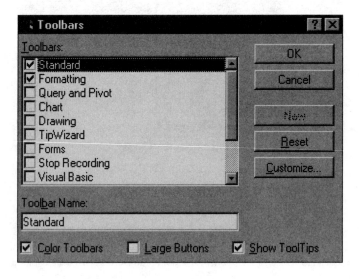

FIGURE 12.9 THE TOOLBARS DIALOG BOX.

N O T E From this dialog box, you can add or remove any toolbars you want displayed on the screen by clicking in the check box next to the toolbar name. Remember, the more toolbars you display, the less screen real estate you are able to see.

3. Click the **Customize** button to display the Customize dialog box, as shown in Figure 12.10.

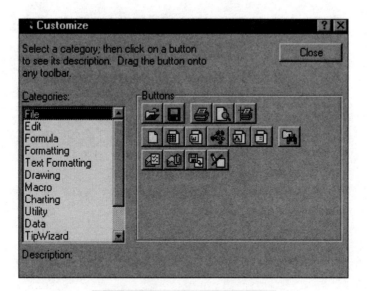

FIGURE 12.10 THE CUSTOMIZE DIALOG BOX.

You can use the Customize dialog box to assign macros to any of the button icons used in any of the toolbars. Instead of using a button that is already used in another toolbar, it makes more sense to choose a button from the group of custom buttons that Excel supplies.

4. Scroll down to the bottom of the Categories list and click **Custom** to display the group of buttons, as shown in Figure 12.11.

    You can add any button to any visible toolbar by dragging it to the position you want on the toolbar. We will drag a button onto the Formatting toolbar.

N O T E

You can create some space on a toolbar for your new macro buttons, (or just remove some clutter) by simply dragging the button you want to remove down onto the worksheet and releasing the mouse button. We have enough room to add another button to the Formatting toolbar, so we won't remove any buttons from it.

---

5. Drag the button you want to add—let's use the smiley face that's on the right side of the third row of buttons—to the Formatting toolbar, between the Underline and the Align Left buttons. Release the mouse button to accept the new button position and display the Assign Macro dialog box, as shown in Figure 12.12.

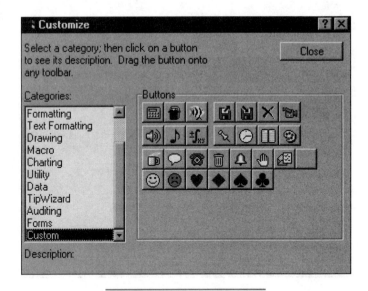

FIGURE 12.11 THE CUSTOM BUTTONS.

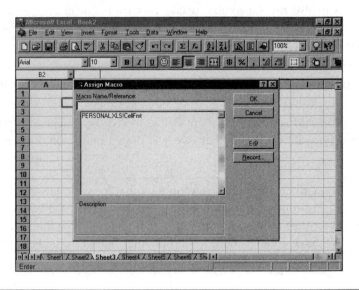

FIGURE 12.12 THE NEW BUTTON ON THE FORMATTING TOOLBAR AND THE ASSIGN MACRO DIALOG BOX.

You can assign any available macro in the Macro Name/Reference list to the button.

6. Click on **PERSONAL.XLS!CellFmt** and then click **OK**.

7. Click the **Close** button of the Customize dialog box to complete the toolbar button assignment.

8. Select B2 through B11 again and then click on your new smiley-face macro button.

ASSIGNING MACROS TO BUTTONS ON THE WORKSHEET

If you thought assigning macros to a toolbar was neat, wait until you assign a macro to a button on the worksheet. You may have occasion where you'd like a *floating* button. Floating macro buttons are good when you want the button to stay in a particular area of the worksheet, namely close to the chart or data that the macro is designed to manipulate. Try the following exercise and see what you think.

1. Close the Budget workbook again without saving and reopen it, as before.

2. Place the mouse pointer over any button on the toolbar that is displayed, right-click the mouse button to display the shortcut menu, and choose **Forms** to display the Forms toolbar, as shown in Figure 12.13.

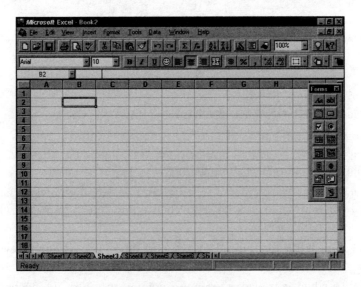

FIGURE 12.13 FORMS TOOLBAR.

3. Click on the **Create Button** button by clicking it and then releasing it. Create Button is the button with the empty square in the middle of it.

4. Place the mouse pointer near B2 through B11. Click and drag the mouse to the approximate size you want the button, but don't obscure cells B2 through B11. (Don't make your button too small or you will not be able to read the temporary name that Excel gives it.)

5. The Assign Macro dialog box will appear, as shown in Figure 12.14. Again, you can assign any available macro in the Assign Macro dialog box.

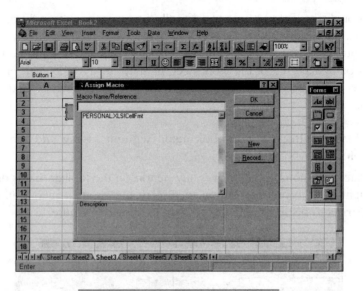

FIGURE 12.14 THE ASSIGN MACRO DIALOG BOX.

6. Click on **PERSONAL.XLS!CellFmt** and then click **OK**.

   Your floating button is probably named Button 1 and is currently selected. When the button is selected you can change the size, name, or font of the button. Let's change the name before we execute it.

7. Click inside the button and type **CellFmt**. Delete the previous name from the button. When you have finished typing the new name, click anywhere on the worksheet.

8. Select cells B2 through B11 again and then click on your new floating Worksheet Button to execute the macro.

   Notice when you place the mouse pointer on top of the floating button, the thick cross pointer changes to a pointing finger pointer. When the mouse pointer is a pointing finger, you can click on the floating button to activate the macro.

9. Scroll down the worksheet and watch your floating macro button scroll with the worksheet. Scroll back up to have it reappear on the screen.

N O T E To select a floating button that's attached to a worksheet in order to cut, copy, paste, clear, format, change the name, move to back, or bring to front, you must first right-click the button with your mouse, which will bring up the shortcut menu. An easier way, however, is to hold the **Ctrl** key before clicking on the floating button.

ASSIGNING MACROS TO DRAWING OBJECTS

Now the fun really begins. You can assign macros to any worksheet object or drawing object. You can even import graphical objects from other programs into Excel and turn them into macro buttons. Using objects as macro buttons, your designs and choices are virtually limitless. We'll use a simple oval shape object in our demonstration, but you can use your creativity in the future.

1. Close the Budget workbook again without saving and reopen it, as before.

2. Place the mouse pointer over any button on the toolbar that is displayed, right-click the mouse button to display the shortcut menu, and choose **Drawing** to display the Drawing toolbar, as shown in Figure 12.15.

3. Click on the **Oval** button by clicking it and then releasing it. The Oval button is the third button on the Drawing toolbar.

4. Place the mouse pointer near B2 through B11. Click and drag the mouse to the approximate size you want the button but don't obscure cells B2 through B11.

5. Click on **Tools**, **Assign Macro** to display the Assign Macro dialog box as shown in Figure 12.14. Again, you can assign any available macro in the Assign Macro dialog box.

6. Click on **PERSONAL.XLS!CellFmt** and then click **OK**.

7. Select cells B2 through B11 again and then click on your new floating oval object to execute the macro.

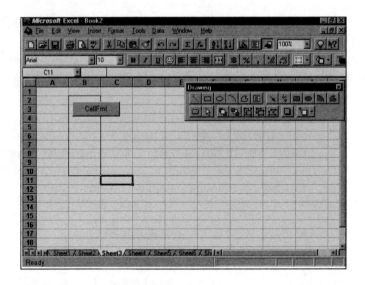

FIGURE 12.15 DRAWING TOOLBAR.

That's all there is to making macros easier to execute. You should have no excuses for avoiding them anymore, even though they involve that nasty programming stuff.

1. Choose **Window**, click on **PERSONAL.XLS**, and then choose **Window**, **Hide**.

2. **Save** your work and exit Excel if you are not proceeding to the next chapter now. If exiting, click on the **Yes** button to save the changes to the Personal Macro Workbook.

A FINAL THOUGHT

This chapter covered the basics of planning, recording and executing macros. We strongly encourage you to invest more time and energy exploring the vast power of macros and macro programming. It is time well spent.

The next chapter looks at the process of linking worksheets.

CHAPTER 13

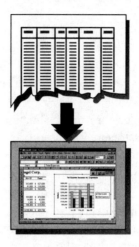

LINKING WORKSHEETS

- ♦ Understanding linking concepts
- ♦ Creating links
- ♦ Updating links
- ♦ Linking with pictures
- ♦ Consolidating worksheets

UNDERSTANDING LINKING CONCEPTS

You may or may not have been working in only one workbook throughout the exercises we've covered so far. You have probably, however, been working in more than one worksheet throughout these exercises. The worksheets we've been creating have no special relationship to each other, except that some contain information about a single company.

There are many situations that call for tying data from two or more workbooks together. This process of tying data together is called *linking*. You can also link data between worksheets in the same workbook.

There is nothing magical or mysterious about linking. When you link data from one worksheet to another, you are simply using the referencing concepts that have been discussed since we started creating formulas. However, when you create links to other worksheets—whether they are in the same or a different workbook—the reference includes the workbook name (if it's a different workbook), the sheet name, and then the cell address or range.

Linking is commonly used for a couple of different purposes. You can use linking to break a large, complex worksheet into smaller, more manageable chunks. You might want to keep some confidential data in a separate worksheet to keep prying eyes away, or you may want to segregate your worksheet by company, department, or activity.

A very good reason for linking to worksheets in different workbooks is to summarize data from several company divisions. Suppose your company has offices in three cities and each creates a worksheet detailing weekly sales activity. By linking, the manager at each location could send a disk containing the workbook to company headquarters, where the new numbers could be brought into the summary, or master worksheet.

N O T E

Of course, you don't have to place confidential information in a separate sheet. You can hide any portion of a worksheet that you do not want in plain sight. However, it can be less cumbersome to place the data in another worksheet so that it is available to you by switching to that sheet, rather than having to unhide and rehide it every time you want to see it.

When you create links, you are dealing with at least two worksheets: a source worksheet and a dependent worksheet. The *source worksheet* contains the data that you want to bring into the dependent worksheet. After a link is created, the linked data in the *dependent worksheet* is automatically updated when the linked data in the source worksheet is updated.

Linking worksheets is different from a simple copy-and-paste operation. If you copy a value from one worksheet and then paste it into another, you are simply copying the value and not establishing a link. If the value in the source worksheet (the one you copied from) changes, the value in the dependent worksheet does not change.

If you try to use copy and paste to copy a formula from one worksheet to another, it does not work at all. The requisite workbook and worksheet portions of the reference are not copied; you end up with an invalid formula.

CREATING LINKS

If the worksheets you want to link are already created, you can simply open them and create the link references from the source worksheets to the dependent worksheet. In our case, the worksheets and workbooks we want to link are not created. So we need to create them before we can discuss linking them. The following section will guide you through creating multiple workbooks.

Creating Multiple Workbooks

Before we can demonstrate how to link workbooks and worksheets, we must first create multiple workbooks to use in our linking examples. We'll create three simple worksheets in separate workbooks to track sales data for Spokane Locks and Bagels' three locations. These are the source worksheets. We'll then create a dependent worksheet to let us summarize the data from the source worksheet.

1. Start Excel. If the BUDGET workbook or any other workbooks containing data are on your screen, close them and then click on the **New Workbook** toolbar button to open a fresh workbook. Double-click on the **Workbook** icon to open a new workbook.

2. In cell A1, type **SALES**.

3. In cell A3, type **Total Sales**, press **Enter** to confirm the entry, and then double-click on the column heading border of column A to adjust the width to accommodate the entries.

Let's copy the worksheet to two other sheets in two new workbooks. This worksheet is simple enough that we can enter the data manually into the other worksheets. But copying the worksheet can be a real time saver when you want to create multiple worksheets with an identical structure.

4. Choose **Edit, Move or Copy Sheet** to display the Move or Copy dialog box, as shown in Figure 13.1.

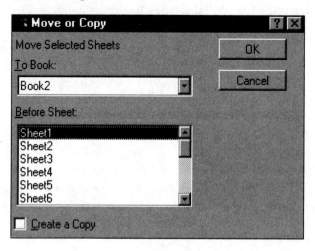

FIGURE 13.1 THE MOVE OR COPY DIALOG BOX.

5. Click on the **Arrow** next to the text box under To Book to display the list of books to which you can move or copy the worksheet, as shown in Figure 13.2.

6. Click on **(new book)**. Then click the **Create a Copy** check box and click **OK** to make the copy.

    Let's create our third source workbook by copying our current worksheet, but this time we'll use the shortcut menu to perform the copy.

7. Place the mouse pointer on the active sheet tab at the bottom of the worksheet and press the right mouse button to bring up the shortcut menu.

8. Select **Move or Copy** to display the Move or Copy dialog box, as shown in Figure 13.1.

9. Click on the **Arrow** next to the text box under To Book to display the list of books to which you can move or copy the worksheet, as shown in Figure 13.2.

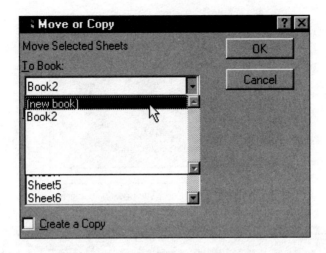

FIGURE 13.2 THE MOVE OR COPY DROP-DOWN LIST OF AVAILABLE WORKBOOKS.

10. Click on **(new book)**. Then click the **Create a Copy** check box and click **OK** to make the copy.

11. Click on the **New Workbook** toolbar button to display a new empty workbook so we can enter the structure for our summary sheet.

12. In cell A1, type **MASTER SALES SHEET**.

13. In cell A3, type **Downtown**; in A4, type **Valley**; and in A5, type **Northside**. Press **Enter** to confirm the entry.

Adding Data to the Workbooks

Now that we have created multiple workbooks, let's create the data for each worksheet. Once we have entered our data, we can begin linking our source worksheet to our dependent worksheet. We could switch to each of them one at a time, but it's often easier to be able to see a portion of all of the worksheets at once. To do this we use Windows' ability to organize the four workbook windows into four equal-sized tiles on the screen.

1. Choose **Window**, **Arrange** to display the Arrange Windows dialog box, as shown in Figure 13.3.

2. The Tiled option is the default, so just click the **OK** button to tile the four windows, as shown in Figure 13.4.

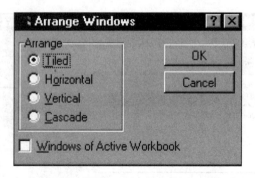

FIGURE 13.3 THE ARRANGE WINDOWS DIALOG BOX.

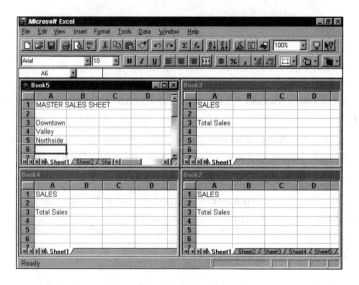

FIGURE 13.4 THE TILED WINDOWS.

You can easily tell which window is active. It is the one with the high-lighted title bar and the scroll bars. You can change active windows by choosing **Window** and then the name of the window you want. The easiest way to change active windows is to simply click on it.

Let's add location and sales information in cells B1 and B3 of each of the source windows.

3. Click anywhere in the window in the upper-right portion of the screen. In Figure 13.4 it is Book3.

4. In cell B1, type **DOWNTOWN**. In B3, type **$31,000** and then click anywhere in the window below (Book2) to make it the active window.

5. In cell B1, type **VALLEY**. In B3, type **$27,500** and then click in the window on the lower left (Book4) to make it the active window.

6. In cell B1, type **NORTHSIDE**. In B3, type **$58,000** and then click in the Master Sales window in the upper-left.

Creating Linking Formulas

In order to link workbooks together, we must create linking formulas. As with any other Excel formula, the linking formula starts with an equal sign. Also, as with any other Excel formula, once the equal sign is entered, Excel allows you to click into cells and cell ranges to have their address included in the formula. In creating linking formulas you can also click into cells from a different workbook and have their address entered into your formula. We have tiled the three source workbooks and the one dependent or Master Sales workbook to illustrate this.

1. Click on the **MASTER SALES SHEET** to activate it. Then click in cell B3, where the Downtown sales figure will be. Type **=**.

2. Make the Downtown sheet (Book3 in the figure) active by clicking in it, then click in cell B3 and click in the confirm box on the formula bar to accept the entry.

N O T E When creating a link reference, clicking on another worksheet does not *really* make it the active window. It just allows you to include references from the window and use scroll bars to find the portion of the sheet you want.

The formula in the formula bar is =[Book2]Sheet1!B3. Next we add the other links.

3. Press the **Down Arrow** key to make B4 (the Valley sales cell) active and type **=**. Click in the Valley window and then on cell B3 of the Valley window, and press **Enter**.

4. With cell B5 in the Master Sales sheet selected, type **=**. Click in the Northside window, then click on cell B3, and click on the confirm box to accept the entry.

The sales numbers for each location are now linked to the master sheet, as shown in Figure 13.5.

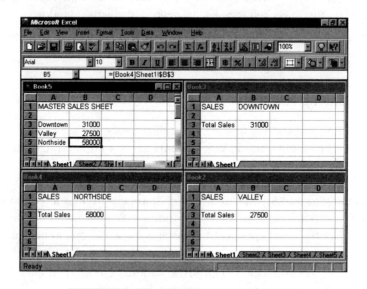

FIGURE 13.5 THE TILED WINDOWS WITH SALES NUMBERS.

If any of the sales numbers in the source sheets change, the numbers in the dependent Master Sales sheet also change. Let's try changing one of the numbers to see if it works.

5. Change the sales number in the Downtown sheet to **$41,000** and notice the number in the Master Sales window change.

Not only can you create links between different workbooks, but you can also create links within the same workbook between separate worksheets or pages. To link within a workbook you would start with the equal sign as in the above example of linking between separate workbooks. Then click on the desired page tab within the workbook to activate the page. Finally, click on the desired cell to create a link between the sheets. The actual linking formula references the worksheet name and the cell address as shown in Table 13.1. Table 13.1 also gives you examples of how referencing formulas look in different examples within Excel.

TABLE 13.1 LINKING USING CORRECT REFERENCING

Type of Reference	Example of How Referencing Should Appear
Normal reference	=C6
Worksheet reference in same workbook	=Sheet1!C6
Workbook reference	=[Workbook1]Sheet1!C6

In the above illustration of linking, we arranged four separate workbooks so that each was visible at the same time by tiling them. This made creating the linking formula easier because we simply had to click on the appropriate workbook and cell address.

If you want to create a link within the same worksheet, you should use Excel's Split command to view your active worksheet in two or four panes. Once the worksheet is split, say in half, you can use one half to select the cell where the linking formula will be housed and type the equal sign. Then you could use the other half to select the cell that is being linked and click on it to have it entered into your linking formula. To activate the split command, select **Split** from the Window menu. Placing the mouse pointer in the first row cells or the first column cells or in a cell totally surrounded by other cells will determine if the window will split into two or four panes, and will split vertically or horizontally. You can play with the splitting command to get a sense of it.

If you want to create a link within a workbook, you should use Excel's New Window command to view multiple pages of the same workbook. When you have two or more copies of your workbook, then you can view different pages simultaneously. To create a new window of your current workbook, simply select **New Window** from the Window menu. The title bar will show the original workbook name followed by a colon and the number of the new window. For example, the second window of your SALES.XLS workbook would be named SALES.XLS:2. The original workbook will be temporarily renamed SALES.XLS:1. Then use the **Arrange** command from the Window menu to view both SALES.XLS:1 and SALES.XLS:2.

Maintaining Links

You'll often make changes in your linked worksheets that require them to be updated. If you save these workbooks and name them something other than Book1 through Book4, the link references are no longer correct. However, when you open the dependent document later, you are given an opportunity to have Excel automatically update the links.

Let's save and close the workbooks now.

1. Close the Downtown workbook, saving it with the name **Downtown**. Close the Northside workbook and save it with the name **Northside**. Use the name **Valley** to save the Valley workbook and, finally, save the Master Sales workbook with the name **Master**.

   Open the Master and Valley workbooks to see how Excel updates the links.

2. Open the MASTER.XLS workbook.

   Excel prompts you with a message dialog box asking if you want to update the automatic links, as shown in Figure 13.6.

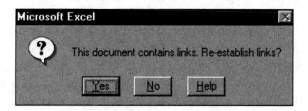

FIGURE 13.6 THE EXCEL MESSAGE DIALOG BOX TO UPDATE LINKS.

3. Click the **Yes** button to update the links and open the workbook.

4. Click on cell B4 and notice that the reference in the formula bar now indicates the VALLEY.XLS workbook.

5. Open the VALLEY.XLS workbook and try changing the sales number to assure yourself that the link has been maintained.

6. Close all open workbooks.

So why wouldn't Excel just assume that you want all links maintained at all times and stop asking you that annoying question when you open a worksheet that contains links? Well, you might want to make changes to one of the individual worksheets without affecting the Master worksheet yet. You can make these changes without having the Master worksheet open. The Master worksheet will not automatically show the updated figures until you give Excel permission to update the links. This could come in handy.

Converting Formulas to Values

You may have occasion where you want linking to be discontinued—or you might want to turn a formula into its value and remove the underlying references. With Excel you can convert and replace any formulas to their values, including linking formulas. Once converted, the formulas remain regular values. Let's do an exercise in turning off linking.

To turn off linking by converting linking formulas to their values, follow these steps.

1. Open up MASTER.XLS and DOWNTOWN.XLS.
2. Make cell B3 of the MASTER.XLS workbook the active cell. Notice the linking formula displayed in the formula bar.
3. Click into the formula bar and select the entire formula by highlighting it.
4. Press **Ctrl-=**. Then press **Return**.

The highlighted formula is calculated and converted into a value. Make cell B3 the active cell. Notice the value has replaced the linking formula in the formula bar.

Just to make sure that linking has been deactivated, make DOWNTOWN.XLS the active workbook and click into cell B3. Type **$85,000**. Notice the MASTER.XLS workbook Downtown value did not change, but remained $41,000.

LINKING BY PICTURES

Sometimes linking via a linking formula may not be the best approach to join data together. Excel provides an exciting additional method for linking data from one worksheet to another, or from one application to another. We'll call this method linking by pictures.

Linking by pictures involves highlighting a range of data you want to take a picture of. Once the picture is taken from the source worksheet, it can be placed in the dependent worksheet. Any changes done to the data from the supporting worksheet will automatically changed in the dependent worksheet.

Linking by pictures has two major differences from linking through normal external reference. The first difference is that the picture is an object, similar to a graphical object. As such, objects can be resized, moved, copied and over-lapped. The second difference is that the picture does not reference any particular cell(s), but refers to an *area* of the source or supporting worksheet. Therefore, any object that appears in the specified area becomes part of the picture, including all formatting.

You may be wondering what's the advantage linking by pictures as oppose to using linking formulas. One advantage has already been alluded to. With picture linking, you can include the formatting as well as the data. When the format changes in the source worksheet, then the picture automatically changes. This is not possible using linking formulas.

A second advantage has also been alluded to. That is, any object that resides in the "area" of the original or source worksheet will be pictured in the dependent worksheet. Remember, linking by pictures is not concerned with particular cell addresses, but with a particular area you designate. All objects in this area appear in the dependent worksheet. This feature is helpful in creating forms.

Another advantage is that since pictures are objects, you can manipulate them in various ways. You can resize them, move them, group them, etc. You'll be surprise at some of the looks you can achieve by reshaping objects.

Finally, a tremendous advantage of linking via pictures is that once the data is linked into the dependent worksheet, you cannot alter the data from the dependent worksheet. The data can be altered from the source worksheet, of course, but the resulting copy is not changeable. The advantage is that you can create documents (like forms) where in certain areas you do not want the data altered. Using pictures will achieve this whereas normal linking does not.

Let's try a very simple illustration to demonstrate linking data by pictures. You should start fresh by closing any workbooks you currently have open. We're going to create new workbooks. Follow the steps as we demonstrate various features of linking data by pictures.

1. Close any existing workbooks that are open and create two new work-books. Let them be the only two workbooks open for this illustration.

2. Tile the workbooks by selecting **Range** from the Window menu and then selecting **OK** for Tiled.

3. Using the **Save As** command from the Edit menu, save but do not close the workbook on the left as **PICTURE1.XLS** and the workbook on the right as **PICTURE2.XLS**.

4. In the PICTURE1.XLS workbook, cell A1 type **Product**; cell B1 type **Cost**; cell C1 type **Sale**; and cell D1 type **Profit**.

5. In the PICTURE2.XLS workbook, type the following data: cell A3 type **Paper**; cell A4 type **Pen**; cell A5 type **Stapler**; cell B3 type **$2.00**; cell B4 type **$0.25**; cell B5 type **$3.05**; cell C3 type **$2.50**; cell C4 type **$1.25**; cell C5 type **$5.25**; cell D3 type **$.0.50**; cell D4 type **$1.00**; and cell D5 type **$2.20**.

   Your screen should look like Figure 13.7.

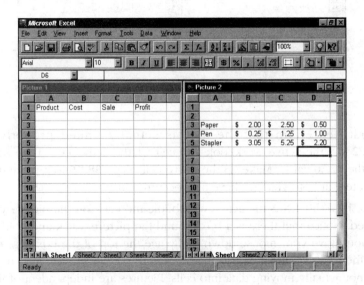

FIGURE 13.7 TILED WORKBOOKS WITH DATA.

6. Highlight and copy the data in PICTURE2.XLS (A3 through D5) using the **Edit**, **Copy** command.

7. Make PICTURE1.XLS the active workbook and cell A3 the active cell.

8. Click the **Edit** menu while holding down the **Shift** key, then select **Paste Picture Link** (don't confuse the Paste Picture command with Paste Picture Link).

   You have just successfully linked data using pictures. Your screen should now look like Figure 13.8.

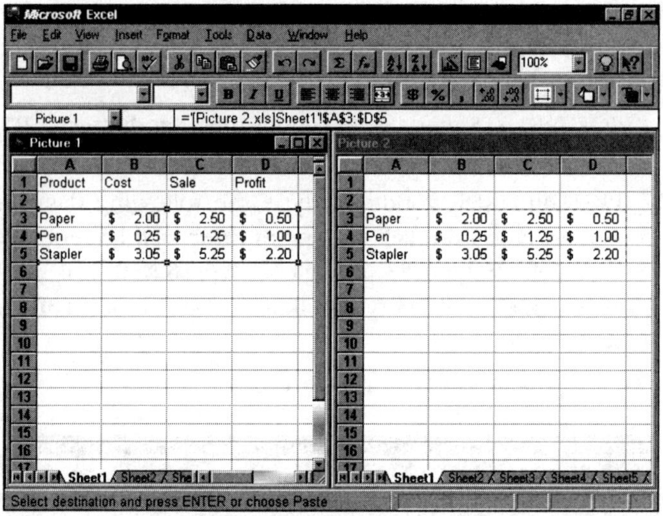

FIGURE 13.8 TWO WORKBOOKS LINKED VIA PICTURES.

Let's first be certain that the data is actually linked properly. Make PICTURE2.XLS the active workbook and cell C1 the active cell. Type **$10.75** to replace the $2.50 value. Make C3 the active cell. Type **$8.75** to replace the $0.50 value. Note that both changes have also occurred in PICTURE1.XLS.

Make PICTURE1.XLS the active workbook and click on the picture you have just pasted. Notice that there is a box around the picture. Click and hold the picture as you move your mouse down and place the top of the box near cell A12. Release the mouse button. Notice that the entire picture moves. Also notice that you are not actually moving data into cells. Pictures are independent of the cells.

Since your picture is really an object like any other graphical object, you can use the drawing tool bar to alter its look. Click on the tool bar button. While your picture is selected, click on the **Drop Shadow** button on the drawing tool bar. Click away from the picture, anywhere in the workbook, so you can see the effects of the drop shadow on the picture.

You have probably noticed the handles on the box surrounding the picture. Although we will not use them in this illustration, they are used to reshape your picture. You can click and hold any handle and move it in the direction you desire. It alters the shape of your picture which can be useful with certain applications, but not too useful with this particular one.

For more information on how to link between Excel and other applications, please see Chapter 17. For more information on manipulating objects and pictures in Excel, refer to Chapter 9.

N O T E

CONSOLIDATING WORKSHEETS

We have discussed consolidating data by creating links and through external referencing of several workbooks and worksheets. *Consolidation* is simply the process of combining data from several sources into a summarized form. Let's look at some other ways in which Excel consolidates data from many worksheets into a summary worksheet.

Consolidating Manually

One of the simplest ways of consolidating data from several worksheets is to create a summary sheet where you paste the data from the individual worksheets onto the summary sheet. This is a fairly straightforward method, as long as you don't have too many individual worksheets to copy from. When pasting, however, you must remember to use the **Paste Special** command.

The following are steps used to consolidate worksheets using the **Copy** and **Paste Special** commands.

1. Activate one of the worksheets that contains the data you want included in the consolidated or summary sheet. Highlight the range of cells to be copied.

2. Select **Copy** from the Edit menu.

3. Activate the summary worksheet as well as the cell in the upper-left range where the data is to be copied to.

4. Choose **Paste Special** from the Edit menu and then select **Add** from the Paste Special dialog box.

5. Continue to activate, one by one, each worksheet you want to copy data from and consolidate on the summary sheet. Paste and add the copied data directly on top of the existing data in the summary sheet.

As you continue copying your data on top of the existing data in the summary sheet, Excel continues to add the new data with the existing summary sheet data. Again, this is one of the simplest ways of consolidating data. The only main drawback to this method is that the summary sheet you create is not linked to the original individual sheets. Consequently, if the data in the original sheets change, then the summary sheet is outdated. The only way of updating your summary sheet is to repeat the consolidation process.

Automatic Consolidation

Excel has a built-in consolidation feature which is also fairly simple in consolidating several worksheets into one summary worksheet. With the consolidation feature, you can even have Excel automatically create links to the summary worksheet. You instruct Excel which worksheets and ranges to consolidate by clicking on them or typing their names in the Consolidate dialog box.

Let's try some hands-on with this particular method of consolidating. The following are the steps used to consolidate worksheets using the Consolidate dialog box.

1. Make sure no previous workbooks are open. Create two new workbooks by clicking the **New** button on the standard tool bar. Tile the two workbooks horizontally by selecting **Arrange** from the Window menu and then selecting **Horizontal** from the Arrange Window dialog box. Click **OK**.

2. Use the top workbook, Sheet1, for the Summary worksheet you're creating. Activate the Summary worksheet and activate cell A1 as the starting position of the consolidated data.

3. Click on the bottom workbook. Let's enter data into three of the worksheets. In Sheet1, cell A1 type **111**; cell B1 type **111**, cell C1 type **111**; and cell D1 type **111**. Type the same data across cells A2 through D2; A3 through D3; and A4 through D4. Figure 13.9 shows how your worksheet should look at this point.

4. Click on Sheet2 in the bottom workbook and follow the same procedures as step 3 above, but this time use the number **222** throughout.

5. Click on Sheet3 of the bottom workbook and follow the same procedures as step 3 above, but this time use the number **333** throughout.

6. Activate Sheet1. Select **Consolidate** from the Data menu. Figure 13.10 shows a Consolidate dialog box.

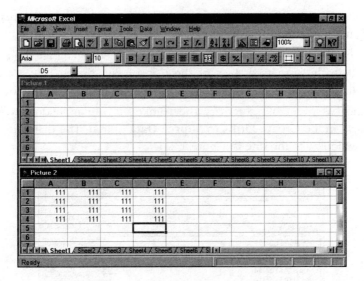

FIGURE 13.9 WORKSHEET WITH PARTIAL DATA.

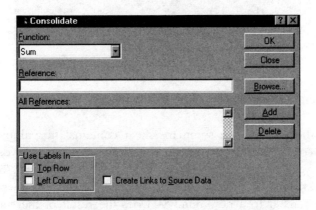

FIGURE 13.10 CONSOLIDATE DIALOG BOX.

7. Highlight the range A1 through D4. This is the data we want to consolidate. (The Consolidate dialog box may be in your way. Simply drag it to another position.) As you highlight the range, the range reference is entered in the Reference box of the Consolidate dialog box.

8. Click the **Add** button. The selected range is added into the All References box of the Consolidate dialog box.

9. Click on Sheet2 and Sheet3 separately and repeat the procedures in steps 7 and 8, clicking the **Add** button between each one.

10. Since we want to sum our data, we do not need to change the Sum function in the upper-left box of the Consolidate dialog box. You should note, however, that you can select a different function if desired.

11. Since we want our summary sheet linked to our individual worksheets, click on the **Create Links to Source Data** option. The dialog box should now look like the one in Figure 13.11.

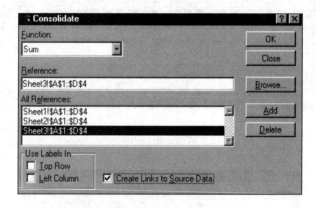

FIGURE 13.11 THE FILLED-OUT CONSOLIDATE DIALOG BOX.

12. Click **OK** to consolidate the data you selected.

Notice that the cells of the summary sheet contains the value 666. This is because we consolidated Sheet1, Sheet2, and Sheet3. In other words, for each cell in the range of A1 through D4, we added 111+222+333=666. To make sure that the worksheets are linked, click on any number on the lower worksheet. Change that number to a new number. Does the result of the summary sheet change? Yes it does. This indicates that the worksheets are linked.

A FINAL THOUGHT

In this chapter, you learned to take advantage of some of Excel's powerful features for working with multiple workbooks. In the next chapter, you learn about some of the ways you can customize Excel to make your working environment suit your requirements.

CHAPTER 14

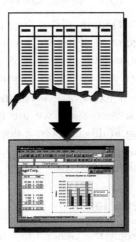

CUSTOMIZING EXCEL

♦ Setting Excel's options

♦ Using AutoSave

♦ Changing views

This chapter covers various ways of customizing your Excel environment. It is also something of a potpourri of Excel information that did not have a clearly logical location in any of the other chapters.

Some of the sections of this chapter, such as using AutoSave, can allow you to work in Excel with greater confidence knowing your data is automatically protected, even if you forget to save. Other sections show you how to specify such options as how Excel calculates formulas, whether you are prompted for summary information when saving workbooks and how many sheets there are in a workbook by default.

You also learn to alter your perspective of the worksheet by changing view options.

313

SETTING EXCEL'S OPTIONS

Excel's Options dialog box provides tremendous flexibility and allows you to change most of the ways you interact with the program. We'll examine some of the more interesting options in the dialog box without changing them. However, I will offer some of my recommendations for these options.

Start Excel, if it isn't already running. Make sure there is a worksheet on your screen. Since we are not stepping through the procedures we are discussing in this chapter, it doesn't matter which worksheet is on the screen. Let's take a look at some of Excel's flexible options by starting with the General worksheet tab.

General Tab

To display the General tab of the Options dialog box, choose **Tools**, **Options**, and then click on the **General** tab, as shown in Figure 14.1.

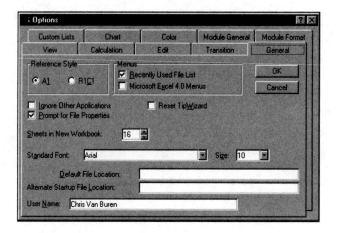

FIGURE 14.1 THE GENERAL TAB OF THE OPTIONS DIALOG BOX.

♦ **A1 or R1C1 Reference Style**. You have a choices of selecting either A1 or R1C1 Reference Style on the General tab. The reference style determines how you refer to cells in the worksheet. You want to leave this as the default, A1, unless you are more comfortable with a fairly old spreadsheet program from Microsoft called Multiplan. Even if you are more familiar with Multiplan, you are still better off sticking with the default since that is the way all modern spreadsheet programs refer to cells.

◆ **Recently Used File List**. The Recently Used File List in the Menu area of the General tab allows you to turn off the display of the last four recently used files at the bottom of the File menu. I cannot think of any reason to turn this option off.

◆ **Microsoft Excel 4.0 Menus**. The Microsoft Excel 4.0 Menus option in the Menu area of the General tab lets you use the menus from the previous version of Excel, version 4.0. Again, I cannot think of a good reason to use this option. You may as well get used to the 5.0 menus since this book and all the documentation that comes with Excel 95 refers to them.

◆ **Prompt for Summary Info**. The Prompt for Summary Info option on the General tab may be turned off if you are not entering any information into the Summary dialog box and are not having trouble locating your files from their file names.

◆ **Sheets in New Workbook**. The Sheets in New Workbook option on the General tab defaults to 16 sheets. You can always add or delete worksheets from a workbook, so the value in this option does not matter too much. However, if you consistently use more or fewer worksheets in a workbook, you may want to increase or decrease the value to save you the trouble of doing it later.

◆ **Standard Font** and **Size**. The Standard Font and Size options on the General tab allows you to specify which of your available fonts and sizes you want to use for future worksheets. Changing the defaults does not change the fonts or sizes on existing worksheets. You might consider changing the font or size if you find the default difficult to read on your screen. Keep in mind that, if you change to a larger size, you are not able to see as much data on your worksheet at one time.

◆ **Default File Location**. The Default File Location option on the General tab allows you to specify which directory you want to use for your Excel files. The directory appears when you choose **File, Open**. I recommend specifying a directory for Default File Location so your files are always where you expect them to be. To enter a Default File Location, click in the text box and type the complete path where your files are stored. For example, if your files are stored on drive C in a directory called MYFILES, which is one level below the Excel directory, you would enter **C:\EXCEL\MYFILES** in the text box.

◆ **Alternate Startup File Location**. Did you know that any Excel file placed in the XLSTART directory will automatically open when you startup Excel? This shortcut feature is very useful if you find yourself working on the same documents often. If, however, you want to open files from a directory other than XLSTART when you startup Excel, you should type the full pathname of the directory location in the Alternate Startup File Location box.

You do not have to manually close a workbook that automatically opens up at the start of Excel. Opening another workbook at the start of Excel will cause the default workbook to automatically close.

T I P

♦ **User Name**. The User Name option on the General tab displays the name that was entered when Excel was first installed on the computer. If you are not the person who installed the software, you can simply delete the name in the text box and enter yours. They can always change it back when they return from vacation.

♦ **Reset Tip Wizard**. The Reset Tip Wizard option on the General tab allows you to reset tips you may have already seen in the current session (a session begins when you start Excel and ends when you exit Excel). The Tip Wizard remembers which tips it has offered during each session of Excel. After a tip is displayed, it will not be displayed again in that particular session. By clicking an **X** in the Reset Tip Wizard box, you reset the Tip Wizard so that all tips can be redisplayed.

Edit Tab

To display the Edit tab on the Options dialog box, choose **Tools**, **Options**, and then click on the **Edit** tab, as shown in Figure 14.2.

♦ **Edit Directly In Cell**. The Edit Directly In Cell option on the Edit tab allows you to edit your data directly in the cell, as opposed to having to click on the formula bar and editing your data there. Editing your data directly in the cell is usually the fastest way to make changes to your worksheet. I can't see why anyone would not want this feature active.

♦ **Allow Cell Drag And Drop**. The Allow Cell Drag And Drop option on the Edit tab really makes using your mouse with Excel in windows worthwhile. When the Allow Cell Drag And Drop option is selected, the mouse pointer changes from a plus sign to an arrow when it is placed near the border of cells. This allows you to use your mouse for tasks like copying, pasting, moving, and selecting cells. Otherwise these tasks would have to be done from the keyboard.

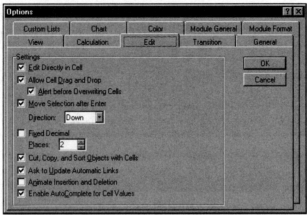

FIGURE 14.2 THE EDIT TAB OF THE OPTIONS DIALOG BOX.

♦ **Alert Before Overwriting Cells**. The Alert Before Overwriting Cells option on the Edit tab is probably a good option to keep selected. When selected, Excel will inform you if you are copying or moving data to an area that already contains data. This option prevents data from being accidentally overwritten.

♦ **Move Selection After Enter**. The Move Selection After Enter (the default) option on the Edit tab causes the active cell to move one row down after you accept an entry by pressing **Enter**. If you want to be able to press **Enter** without changing the selected cell, click in the check box to remove the check.

♦ **Fixed Decimal**. The Fixed Decimal option on the Edit tab is useful if you almost always enter numbers with a certain number of decimal places. It can save you time if you do not have to enter the decimal point. If you specify a certain number of decimal places (2 is the default) and click in the **Fixed Decimal** check box, Excel enters your decimal point for you. You can always override this option by manually entering a decimal point.

♦ **Cut, Copy, and Sort Objects with Cells**. The Cut, Copy, and Sort Objects with Cells option on the Edit tab is for advanced users. Basically, Excel allows objects (usually graphics like circles, squares, triangles, etc.)

and text to be "attached" to one particular cell. You may have a column of objects attached to separate adjacent cells. The Cut, Copy and Sort Objects with Cells allows for deleting, copying, and sorting to be performed on cells that have objects and text attached to them.

◆ **Ask to Update Automatic Link**. The Ask to Update Automatic Link option on the Edit tab activates a dialog box when you open a document that is linked with other documents. Sometimes the linked documents are saved under a different name than the name they were originally saved and linked with. With the Ask to Update Automatic Link activated, documents can be relinked. (See Chapter 13 for more information on linking.)

Calculation Tab

To display the Calculation tab on the Options dialog box, choose **Tools**, **Options**, and then click on the **Calculation** tab, as shown in Figure 14.3.

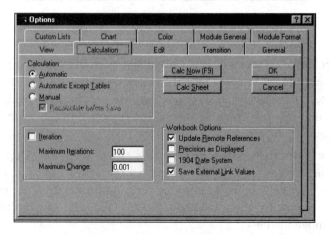

FIGURE 14.3 THE CALCULATION TAB OF THE OPTIONS DIALOG BOX.

◆ **Calculation**. The options in the Calculation area on the Calculation tab lets you choose whether Excel calculates automatically (the default) or manually. You can also choose to have Excel calculate automatically except for tables (such as PivotTables).

As you have worked through the steps in this book, you probably noticed that when you changed numbers that formulas referred to, the recalculations occurred almost instantly. This is because the examples in the book are very simple and very small. However, if you are working with larger, more complex worksheets containing many formulas and functions requiring recalculation when numbers are changed, there can be quite a long delay while Excel performs the calculations.

The actual length of time required for calculations depends on the size and complexity of the worksheet, as well as the speed of your computer. If your computer is fast enough, even very large worksheets may recalculate fast enough to satisfy you. However, when you find that the delays become burdensome as you are entering or editing worksheet data, consider switching to manual recalculation by clicking in the **Manual** option button.

Be sure to keep the **Recalculate Before Save** check box checked so the numbers are brought up-to-date when you save the workbook. However, even if you've selected **Manual** calculation, Excel normally recalculates when you're saving anyway. Deselecting the Recalculate Before Save option will prevent Excel from updating or recalculating the worksheet.

♦ **Iteration**. The Iteration option on the Calculation tab deals with circular references of the type where a formula in the first cell references a formula in a second cell, and the formula in the second cell references the formula in the first cell. This causes a circular reference error message. However, selecting the Iteration option, Excel will calculate the formulas based on 100 iterations (you can increase or decrease this number) or until the values change to be less than 0.001 (the default which can also be changed), whichever comes first.

♦ **Calc Now (F9)**. The Calc Now (F9) option on the Calculation tab is used to calculate all open workbooks. You can also calculate all open workbooks by pressing **F9** on your keyboard.

♦ **Calc Sheet**. The Calc Sheet option on the Calculation tab is used to calculate the active worksheet only. The shortcut key is **Shift-F9**.

♦ **Updating Remote References**. The Updating Remote References option of the Calculation tab refers to linking workbooks with other applications. When you open a workbook that is linked by remote reference to a document or application other than Excel, you have the option to relink and update the references (calculate the formulas) to the documents that are no longer linked. (See Chapter 13 for more on linking.)

♦ **Precision as Displayed**. The Precision as Displayed option on the Calculation tab is used to determine how certain rounded values are displayed. For example, look what rounding does if you were to add

5.006+5.006=10.012. When formatted as currency (rounded) you would get $5.01+$5.01=$10.01. Although the rounded result is correct, it may not be acceptable for presentation purposes. By selecting the Precision as Displayed option, the values are converted to $5.01+$5.01=$10.02.

WARNING When using the Precision as Displayed option, be very careful because the underlying values are permanently changed to the displayed values. You will not be able to changed them back to their original values. For example, 5.006 would permanently changed to 5.01.

◆ **1904 Date System**. The 1904 Date System option on the Calculation tab allows you to change the base date of January 1, 1990 (the first date that coincides with the serial value of 1), which is used by Microsoft Excel for Windows, to the base date of January 2, 1904, which is used by Microsoft Excel for Macintosh. (See Chapter 3 on Entering Dates & Times for more on dates and serial values.)

◆ **Save External Link Values**. The Save External Link Values option of the Calculation tab saves copies of values contained on an external document linked to your worksheet. A worksheet that has massive links to external documents can take a long time to open and take up a lot of disk space. By selecting **Save External Link Values**, you can reduce the space needed for your worksheet and cause the worksheet to open faster.

View Tab

To display the View tab on the Options dialog box, choose **Tools**, **Options**, and then click on the **View** tab, as shown in Figure 14.4.

The View tab of the dialog box is a bit different than the other tabs of the Options dialog box we have looked at so far. Any changes to the settings in the other tabs of the dialog box become the new default settings for new workbooks. This is also true of the changes made in the Show area of the View tab in the Options dialog box. However, changes made in areas outside of the Show area of the View tab only affect the current worksheet.

This dialog box lets you turn on or off various screen elements that can make it easier to navigate in Excel, but can also add clutter to your screen. A good rule of thumb is to remove any elements that you don't use. Let's explain each of the options on the View tab.

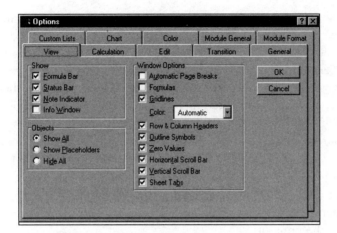

FIGURE 14.4 THE VIEW TAB OF THE OPTIONS DIALOG BOX.

♦ **Formula Bar** and **Status Bar**. The Formula Bar and Status Bar options in the Show area on the View tab is to suppress the Formula Bar and Status Bar from displaying. Although you have the option to remove these tools, it becomes very difficult and awkward to navigate in your worksheet without them.

♦ **Note Indicator**. The Note Indicator option in the Show area on the View tab, when activated, informs you of the location of any notes you may have attached to your worksheet. The indicator, which is actually a red dot in the upper-right-hand corner of the cell where the note is attached, can be viewed by selecting this option. (See Chapter 3 for more about how to add, delete and enter notes.)

♦ **Info Window**. The Info Window option in the Show area on the View tab, which is not checked by default, can be activated and viewed by selecting this option. The Info Window is an actual window that displays the current active cell reference, any formula it contains, and any attached note. The Info Window does not take up any screen real estate since you have to switch to it to see it, which you can do from the Window menu.

SHORTCUT

All the options in the Show area of the View tab of the dialog box, except the Info Window option, can be turned on and off from the View menu. Since you may want to turn these elements off and on while working in a particular worksheet, the View menu is the fastest way to make these changes.

♦ **Show All**. The Show All option in the Objects area on the View tab allows you to see all the objects in your worksheet. The objects in question here are graphic elements, such as charts and pictures. Showing all of them (the default) presents you with the most accurate representation of what your printed page will look like. Not surprisingly, though, it can slow down your navigation through the worksheet, especially on a slower computer.

♦ **Show Placeholders**. The Show Placeholders option in the Objects area on the View tab is used when you do not necessarily need to see your objects on the screen but need to know where they are on your worksheet. This option replaces your objects with gray rectangles as a placeholder. Showing only the placeholder can speed things up and does not affect the printout.

♦ **Hiding All**. The Hiding All option in the Objects area on the View tab allows for when you do not want to see your objects and do not want a placeholder for the objects. You can make them completely disappear by using the Hiding All option. The Hiding All option also prevents the objects from printing. Don't worry, you can have your objects back by selecting either **Show All** or **Show Placeholders**.

You can toggle between displaying objects, displaying placeholder, and hiding objects by using the shortcut key, **Ctrl-6**.

SHORTCUT

♦ **Automatic Page Breaks**. The Automatic Page Breaks option in the Windows Options on the View tab allows you to choose whether Excel displays horizontal and vertical lines where your printed pages end. This can be a very useful option for determining where portions of your worksheets fall on the printed pages as you enter and edit data, without having to use Print Preview.

♦ **Formulas**. The Formulas option in the Windows Options on the View tab can be especially useful for finding and displaying all the formulas on a worksheet without selecting one cell at a time. It is easy to forget where you placed your formulas, particularly in larger worksheets, and this can shed some light on the situation. Figure 14.5 shows a portion of the budget worksheet with the formulas displayed.

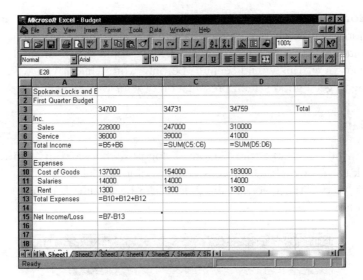

FIGURE **14.5** PART OF THE BUDGET WORKSHEET WITH FORMULAS DISPLAYED.

- ◆ **Gridlines**. The Gridlines option in the Windows Options on the View tab allows you to remove all gridlines in the selected worksheet and view the worksheet on a clean white screen. This can be useful when you do not want the individual cells to clutter your view.

- ◆ **Color**. With the Color (Gridlines) option in the Windows Option on the View tab you can change the color of your gridlines in your workbook by selecting a color from the Color drop-down list box and selecting **OK**.

- ◆ **Row and Column Headers**. The Row and Column Headers in the Window Options on the View tab will suppress the letter headings across the columns and the number headings down the rows.

- ◆ **Outline Symbols**. The Outline Symbols option in the Window Options on the View tab allows for selection and deselection of Outlining Symbols. (A discussion on outlining and outlining symbols can be found in Chapter 10.)

- ◆ **Zero Value**. The Zero Value option in the Window Options on the View tab suppresses (does not display) any cell that has a zero value in it. If a formula returns a zero value to a cell, the zero in that cell is also suppressed.

♦ **Horizontal Scroll Bar**, **Vertical Scroll Bar**, and **Sheet Tabs**. The Horizontal Scroll Bar, Vertical Scroll Bar, and Sheet Tabs options in the Window Options on the View tab removes both scroll bars and sheet tabs from view. This would seem to be only worthwhile if you were attempting to get a good screen presentation of your worksheets.

Color Tab

To display the Color tab of the Options dialog box, choose **Tools**, **Options**, and then click the **Color** tab. On Excel's default Color tab palette you'll find a selection of 56 colors. The colors in the palette can be modified. Figure 14.6 shows the Color tab.

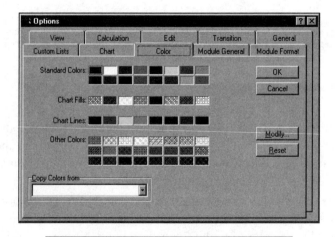

FIGURE 14.6 THE COLOR TAB OF THE OPTIONS DIALOG BOX.

♦ **Standard Colors**. The Standard Colors on the Color tab consist of every solid color that makes up a palette.

♦ **Chart Fills**. The Chart Fills colors on the Color tab depict the default colors used for the filling sections on charts. It also depicts the default order in which the colors are used.

♦ **Chart Lines**. The Chart Lines colors on the Color tab represent the default colors used for chart lines. It also depicts the default order in which the colors are used.

♦ **Other Colors**. The Other Colors on the Color tab are blended colors that are available on a particular palette.

♦ **Modify**. The Modify button on the Color tab allows you to change the colors on your existing palette. Once the Modify button is clicked, a Color Picker dialog box appears with two pointers. Moving the two pointers with the mouse will determine how the color will be modified.

♦ **Reset**. The Reset button on the Color tab will return the Color tab to its default status.

♦ **Copy Colors From**. The Copy Colors From dialog box on the Color tab allows you to copy a custom palette from one workbook to another in order to achieve a consistent look. Once both workbooks are open and the destination workbook is active, clicking on **Copy Colors From** and selecting the source workbook will copy the custom palette to the source workbook.

Transition Tab

To display the Transition tab of the Options dialog box, choose **Tools**, **Options**, and then click the **Transition** tab, as shown in Figure 14.7. The Transition tab was developed to help Lotus 1-2-3 users make an easier transition to Excel.

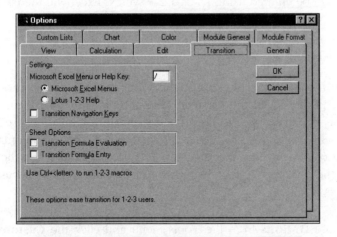

FIGURE 14.7 THE TRANSITION TAB OF THE OPTIONS DIALOG BOX.

♦ **Microsoft Excel Menu** or **Help Key**. The Microsoft Excel Menu or Help Key options in the Settings area on the Transition tab allows you to change the keyboard character that activates the menu bar. The default character is the slash key. If you want the key to activate the Help For

Lotus 1-2-3 Users dialog box instead of Microsoft Excel Menus, select **Lotus 1-2-3 Help** in the Settings section of the Transition tab.

SHORTCUT A shortcut for accessing the menu bar is to press the **Alt** key along with the letter on the menu bar that is underlined. This will activate the menu and display the commands. You can then simply type the underlined letter of the command to activate the command.

♦ **Transition Navigation Keys**. Selecting the Transition Navigation Keys option in the Settings section on the Transition tab alters how the keyboard shortcuts and function keys will perform.

♦ **Transition Formula Evaluation**. The Transition Formula Evaluation option in the Sheet Options section on the Transition tab manages the way calculations are done in a Lotus 1-2-3 worksheet that is opened in Excel.

♦ **Transition Formula Entry**. The Transition Formula Entry option in the Sheet Options section on the Transition tab allows for Lotus 1-2-3 functions to be entered using Lotus 1-2-3 syntax. Excel will then automatically convert the Lotus 1-2-3 function to an Excel function.

Custom Lists Tab

To display the Custom Lists tab of the Options dialog box, choose **Tools**, **Options**, and then click the **Custom Lists** tab, as shown in Figure 14.8. The Custom Lists tab allows you to create and maintain lists that are used in Excel's automatic series feature. As discussed in Chapter 3, Excel will automatically create a series of values when you enter the first value and then use the fill handle to extend the first entry into other cells. Let's create and use a custom list to illustrate this feature.

1. Choose **Options** from the Tools menu and click the **Custom Lists** tab. The **NEW LIST** option should be highlighted; if not, click once on it to highlight it.

2. Type **Ten, Jack, Queen, King, Ace** into the space marked List Entries.

3. Click the **Add** button, then click **OK**.

4. Move to cell G3 and type **Ten**.

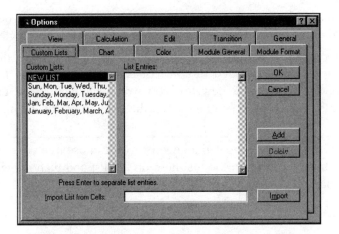

FIGURE 14.8 THE CUSTOM LISTS TAB OF THE OPTIONS DIALOG BOX.

5. Click on the lower-right edge of cell (the pointer should change to an arrow shape), then drag to highlight through cell K3. Release the mouse when finished. Your custom list will appear as shown in Figure 14.9.

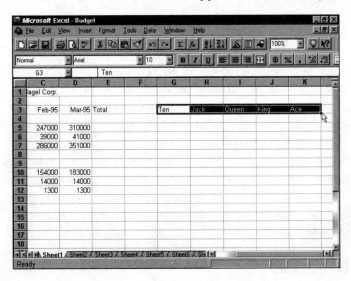

FIGURE 14.9 ADDING A CUSTOM LIST.

♦ **Custom Lists**. The Custom Lists box on the Custom Lists tab stores the names of custom lists that are created. The names of the lists are actually the first few names on the list. Excel has created four lists by default (they are day and month lists) and you can create more by choosing **NEW LIST**.

◆ **List Entries**. The List Entries box on the Custom List tab displays the actual list of the selected Custom List names in the Custom Lists box. If you were to create a new list, you would highlight **NEW LIST** in the Custom Lists box and enter the list in the List Entries box, then press **Add**.

Once you have created a new list, you can use it in your Excel worksheet by typing in the first item on the list and then dragging the fill handle of the cell to display the remaining list entries.

SHORTCUT

◆ **Import List from Cells**. The Import List from Cells option on the Custom List tab allows for lists developed in worksheets to be imported as a custom list that can be automatically reproduced for future use. Highlighting a list in your worksheet that you want to import and opening the Custom List tab, then selecting the **Import** button will produce your new custom list.

Module General Tab

To display the Module General tab of the Options dialog box, choose **Tools**, **Options**, and then click the **Module General** tab, as shown in Figure 14.10. We will not go through the features of this tab. However, for an overview, the Module General tab gives options for use with macros and Visual Basic, the programming language used with Excel.

The Module General tab basically provides options for how modules will both perform and be displayed. For instance, you can have and set automatic indents as you create the modules, Excel can inform you when syntax errors exits, the program can pause at each error it encounters, and Excel can notify you when variables are required.

Module Format Tab

To display the Module Format tab of the Options dialog box, choose **Tools**, **Options**, and then click the **Module Format** tab, as shown in Figure 14.11. This tab, as with the Module General tab, contains options used with macros and Visual Basic, the programming language used with Excel.

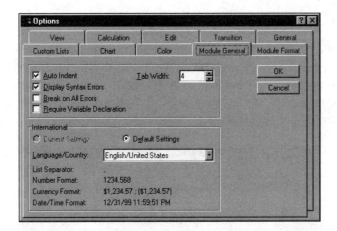

FIGURE 14.10 THE MODULE GENERAL TAB OF THE OPTIONS DIALOG BOX.

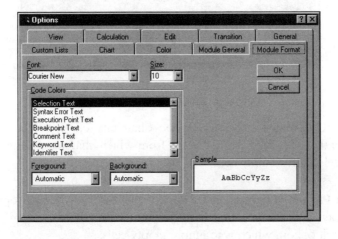

FIGURE 14.11 THE MODULE FORMAT TAB OF THE OPTIONS DIALOG BOX.

The Module Format tab allows you to change the color of the foreground and background of all text in a module as the text is displayed on your monitor. Excel has set many Code Colors as automatic and others with specific colors. The colors can be changed by using the pull-down menus.

You can also set the default of the font and font size to be used when you create new modules.

Chart Tab

To display the Chart tab of the Options dialog box, choose **Tools**, **Options**, and then click on the **Chart** tab, as shown in Figure 14.12. The Chart tab allows you to control how worksheets are plotted and charted. To see these options, you must have a chart selected prior to choosing the **Options** command from the Tools menu. For more information about creating and selecting charts, see Chapter 8.

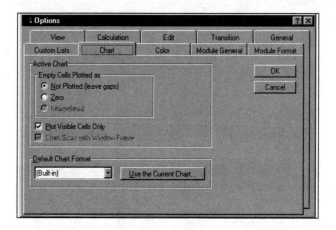

FIGURE 14.12 THE CHART TAB OF THE OPTIONS DIALOG BOX.

The Empty Cells Plotted As area on the Chart tab tells Excel how to handle empty cells that are included in a range from which charts are created from. By default Excel ignores empty cells.

- ♦ **Not Plotted (Leave Gaps)**. The Not Plotted (Leave Gaps) option of the Empty Cells Plotted As section on the Chart tab is the same as Excel's default option, which is to ignore empty cells.

- ♦ **Zero**. The Zero option of the Empty Cells Plotted As section on the Chart tab treats empty cells as if they contained a value of zero.

- ♦ **Interpolated**. The Interpolated option of the Empty Cells Plotted As section on the Chart tab instructs Excel to interpolate values for the cells and then plot them.

- ♦ **Plot Visible Cells Only**. The Plot Visible Cells Only option of the Active Chart area on the Chart tab instructs Excel to include cells in hidden rows and columns as part of the data series, or not to include them.

♦ **Chart Size With Window Frame**. The Chart Size With Window Frame option of the Active Chart section on the Chart tab instructs Excel if the chart size should be adjusted when the document window size is adjusted.

USING AUTOSAVE

A host of extra little programs are included, designed to enhance Excel. We have already used one of these, the Scenario Manager, earlier in the book. Other add-ins include a program for creating slide shows from Excel screens, which you can use for presentations. There is a program for querying external databases that can be quite useful when data is kept in files created by other programs, such as dBase or Access.

The add-in we are going to discuss here is AutoSave. There is no more important procedure in Excel, or any other computer program for that matter, than saving your work. It does not matter which other skills you master or what sort of elaborate worksheets you create if you lose them to a power failure or some other computer mishap.

Of course you can save your work manually, but anything that can be done to automate the process and relieve you of that burden is welcome. AutoSave does just that. With AutoSave you can instruct Excel to save your work automatically at specified intervals.

Let's take a look at AutoSave now. You can skip the first two steps if AutoSave is already one of the choices on your Tools menu.

1. Choose **Tools**, **Add-Ins** to display the Add-Ins dialog box, as shown in Figure 14.13. Note that this command was added to the Tools menu because you activated the AutoSave add-in.

   This dialog box displays the add-in programs on your computer's hard disk. The ones with checks in their check boxes are currently available to Excel.

2. Click the **AutoSave** check box (if it is unchecked) and then click **OK** to make AutoSave available.

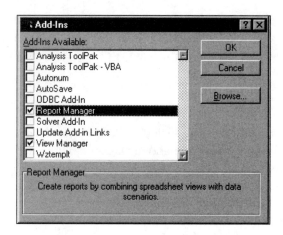

FIGURE 14.13 THE ADD-INS DIALOG BOX.

N O T E

Browse through the other add-ins to familiarize yourself with their functions. You can also use the **Help** button to learn more about each of them.

In addition to the add-ins included with Excel, several companies offer other add-in programs for performing many specialized tasks. You'll see ads for and reviews of these in some of the popular computer magazines. You may also receive offers for some of these through the mail after you send in your registration form.

3. Choose **Tools**, **AutoSave** to display the AutoSave dialog box, as shown in Figure 14.14.

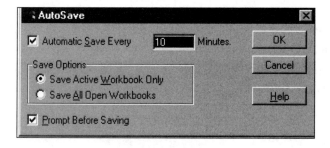

FIGURE 14.14 THE AUTOSAVE DIALOG BOX.

By default, the check box in the upper-left portion of the AutoSave dialog box is checked and the default save interval is ten minutes. The rule of thumb for how often you should AutoSave is the same as for how often you should save manually. Save often enough that if you lose your work just before the next save, you won't be too upset. For most folks, that is between 10 and 20 minutes.

The Save Options area of the dialog box lets you choose whether AutoSave saves only your active workbook (the default), or all open workbooks. Since saving all open workbooks could cause each save to take a few extra precious seconds, it is usually best to have AutoSave just save the active workbook.

The final check box lets Excel prompt you before proceeding with a save. I strongly recommend that you use this option. In this way, if you have made some changes to the worksheet that you do *not* want saved, you can cancel the save.

If you choose to be prompted before the save, Excel displays the AutoSave confirmation dialog box, as shown in Figure 14.15, after the specified number of minutes.

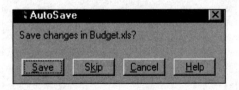

FIGURE 14.15 THE AUTOSAVE CONFIRMATION DIALOG BOX.

If you want to proceed with the save, click on the **Save** button. If you do not want to save, click on **Cancel**. The **Skip** button also works, but its primary purpose is to allow you to skip saving certain workbooks and save others when you've chosen to have AutoSave save all open workbooks.

WARNING

Just because your work is saved to your computer's hard disk often, do not feel too secure about the safety of your data. If you have important data stored on your computer, you must also back it up to floppy disks or tape (if you have a tape back-up system). This is critical, because things can go wrong that are more serious than a power failure.

If your computer breaks altogether, is stolen, or burned in a fire, you can at least restore your important data to another computer from your backups.

CHANGING VIEWS

There are a couple of options for changing the view of your worksheet that are not part of the Options dialog box. The first of these we discuss is another add-in called View Manager.

As you work with larger worksheets, you may find yourself jumping back and forth between the far reaches of the worksheet to view and edit different portions. You can use the Go To method we discussed earlier, but even that method can become confusing. An easier way to move around the worksheet is to assign names to the various views you want to move to in the View Manager.

To add a named view, move to the portion of the worksheet you want to be able to return to and then use View Manager to assign it a name. Let's take a look at View Manager.

1. Choose **View**, **View Manager** to display the View Manager dialog box, as shown in Figure 14.16.

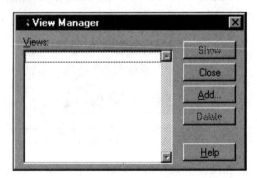

FIGURE 14.16 THE VIEW MANAGER DIALOG BOX.

2. Click on the **Add** button to display the Add View dialog box, as shown in Figure 14.17.

3. Enter a name for the view and click on **OK**.

   You usually want to keep the print settings and hidden rows and columns with your views, so keep these check boxes checked.

Figure 14.18 displays an example of the View Manager dialog box with several views from which to choose.

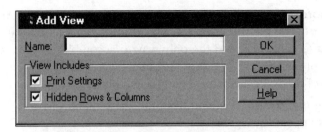

FIGURE 14.17 THE ADD VIEW DIALOG BOX.

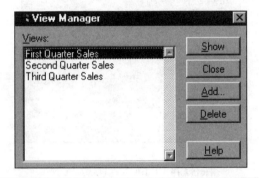

FIGURE 14.18 THE VIEW MANAGER DIALOG BOX WITH SEVERAL NAMED VIEWS.

N O T E

The views you name in the View Manager only relate to the active worksheet. You can use View Manager to switch among workbooks, or even among worksheets in the active workbook.

After you have added views, you can move to them by choosing **View**, **View Manager**, highlighting the desired view, and clicking on the **Show** button.

Zooming the Workbook

Let's take a look at one other useful feature for changing the view of your work-sheet. Until now, we have been looking at our worksheets at the default (100%) zoom. If you want to step back from your worksheet to get a bigger picture, you can zoom out to a smaller percentage. You can also zoom in to see more detail in a smaller portion of the worksheet.

The **Zoom** command on the View menu is used to either magnify your worksheet or demagnify it, whichever you choose. Sometimes you may want to see your entire worksheet and the only way to accomplish that task is to shrink it so that it all fits into the window. At other times you may want to magnify a certain area of the worksheet, maybe to have a better view of that section.

Selecting the **Zoom** command from the View menu displays the Zoom dialog box as it appears in Figure 14.19.

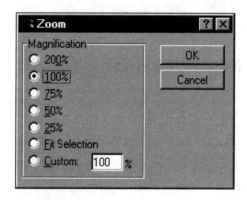

FIGURE 14.19 THE ZOOM DIALOG BOX.

The Zoom dialog box consists of one enlargement feature (200%), three reduction features (75%, 50%, and 25%), a Fit Selection feature (this option will determine the best fit to view the highlighted portion of your worksheet so that it fills the window), and Custom feature (which allows you to choose a percentage between 10% and 400% for enlargement or reduction).

The following steps will guide you through magnifying or demagnifying your worksheets.

1. Choose the **Zoom** command from the View menu. The Zoom dialog box appears.

2. Choose the **200%** enlargement option, one of the three reduction sizes (**75%**, **50%**, or **25%**), the **Fit Selection** option, or enter a custom size into the custom window.

3. Select **OK**.

   The larger the number, the less worksheet area you are able to see. Figure 14.20 displays a portion of the budget worksheet zoomed to 200%.

N O T E

You can also use the Zoom Control box on the Standard toolbar to quickly select your desired magnification. By selecting the pull-down menu you can select one enlargement option, three reduction options, or one Selection option which will fill the screen by given you the best fit for any selected cell(s).

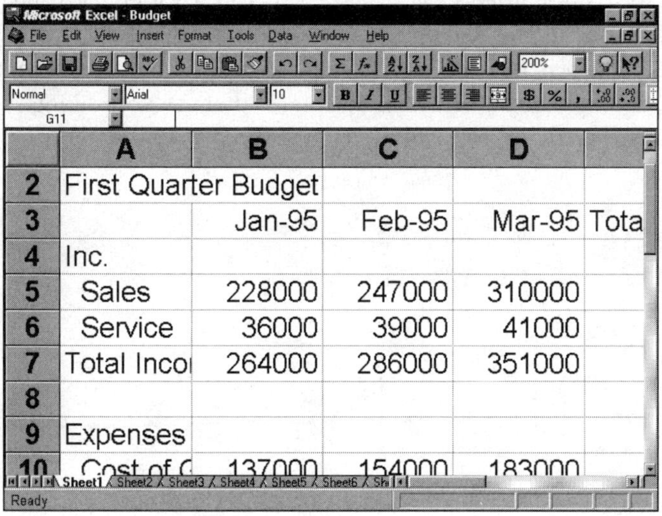

FIGURE 14.20 AN EXAMPLE OF A 200% ZOOM.

The zoom percentage you choose only affects the appearance of your screen. It has no effect on what is printed.

Also, zoom percentages are saved as a part of your named views in View Manager.

N O T E

If you find yourself zooming in and zooming out often, you should probably place the Zoom In and Zoom Out buttons on your toolbar to quickly change the display of your worksheet. The Zoom In and Out buttons can be found on the Utility category in the Customize dialog box. You can drag these two buttons to any toolbar. The following procedures will help you do this.

1. Select **Toolbar** from the View menu.

2. Click the **Customize** button.

3. Click on **Utility** to bring up the utility buttons.

4. Drag the **Zoom In** and **Zoom Out** buttons to your active toolbar.

A FINAL THOUGHT

In this chapter, you learned to customize Excel in a variety of ways. Of course, there are no limits to the ways you can work with Excel and you should now have a good start on that journey of exploration. In the next chapter we will explore Excel's toolbars and ways to customize them to your liking.

CHAPTER 15

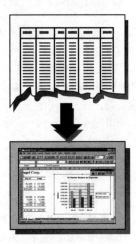

SWITCHING AND CUSTOMIZING TOOLBARS

♦ Displaying and positioning toolbars

♦ Creating custom toolbars

♦ Designing custom toolbar buttons

As you have seen throughout this book, toolbars are often the fastest and easiest way to initiate Excel tasks. With a click of the mouse, you are off and running with an operation that might otherwise take several mouse clicks or keystrokes.

You can make toolbars even more useful by customizing them to include just the buttons you use most often for a particular type of operation, or by creating custom buttons.

DISPLAYING AND POSITIONING TOOLBARS

Excel automatically displays the Standard and Formatting toolbars and positions them at the top of the screen. You have also seen Excel display other toolbars such as the Chart toolbar when editing charts, and you have displayed the Drawing toolbar by clicking on the **Drawing** button on the Standard toolbar.

Let's see how you can choose other toolbars and position them wherever you want them on the screen.

1. Start Excel, if it isn't already running, and make sure there is a worksheet on your screen.

    You don't need to have any particular workbook open since you are displaying and moving toolbars without actually using the buttons.

    The shortcut menu is the fastest way to choose which toolbars are displayed on your screen. There is also a Toolbars dialog box which makes additional toolbars available, as well as a few extra options. Start with the shortcut menu.

2. Right-click on any of the toolbar buttons on either toolbar to display the toolbar shortcut menu, as shown in Figure 15.1.

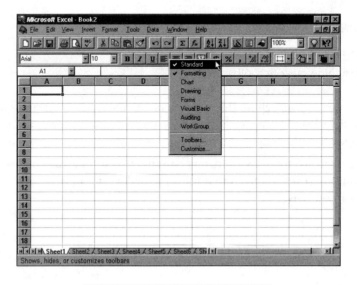

FIGURE 15.1 THE TOOLBAR SHORTCUT MENU.

The toolbars that are currently displayed have a check mark in front of their names on the shortcut menu. You can remove a toolbar from the screen by clicking on its name. Clicking on a toolbar name without a check mark will cause it to be displayed.

If you frequently switch to other Microsoft applications, you find that the Microsoft toolbar is one of the most useful and time saving toolbars included with Excel. With this toolbar you can instantly switch to any of your other Microsoft programs at the click of a button. Most newer Microsoft applications also have Microsoft toolbars available so you can easily switch from them back to Excel or another program.

Let's display the Drawing toolbar now.

3.   Click on **Drawing** to display the Drawing toolbar, shown in Figure 15.2.

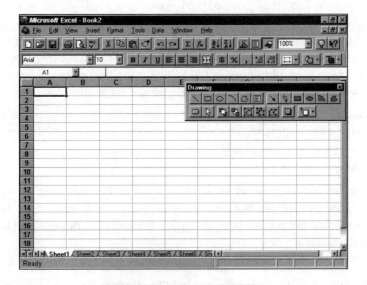

FIGURE 15.2 THE DRAWING TOOLBAR.

All the available toolbars and their respective functions are listed in Appendix C. You can mix and match buttons to create your own custom toolbars using any of the buttons, or create your own custom buttons.

N O T E

As with other toolbars, you can see what the function of each of these buttons is by simply moving the mouse over a button and reading the

ToolTip. The lower-left portion of the status bar displays a longer description of the button.

Toolbars can be moved by moving the mouse pointer to one of the areas between a toolbar border and the buttons and then dragging. However, if the toolbar is floating, it is easier to move it the same way you move other windows—dragging it by the title bar. You can remove a toolbar by clicking on its name in the shortcut menu or by simply clicking on a floating toolbar's close box in its upper-right corner.

Often, having a toolbar floating on the screen obscures important information or is distracting, even if you move it out of the way. One solution to this problem is to dock it in one of the docking positions.

There are four docking locations: the top, bottom, and sides of the screen. In fact, the Standard and Formatting toolbars are docked at the top of the screen now. You can dock a toolbar by moving it to one of the docking areas. The exception is that you cannot dock a toolbar to the left or right side of the screen if it has buttons with drop-down lists (such as the Zoom Control button on the Standard toolbar) or buttons with tear-off palettes (such as the Borders button on the Formatting toolbar).

4. Drag the Drawing toolbar by the title bar to the bottom of the screen until you see the outline of the toolbar. Now release the mouse button.

The Drawing toolbar is now docked on the bottom of the screen, as shown in Figure 15.3.

The horizontal position depends on where the outline was when you released the mouse button. You can move the toolbar right or left by positioning the mouse over any space between the buttons and the edges of the toolbar.

NOTE

For a toolbar with very few buttons, such as this one, it's a good idea to position it at the far left or right of the docking area so there will be room for another toolbar, should you decide to add one.

The Standard and Formatting toolbars, which are docked, can be undocked or docked in another position by dragging them to where you want them. Let's undock the Formatting toolbar and position it as a floating toolbar near the top of the worksheet.

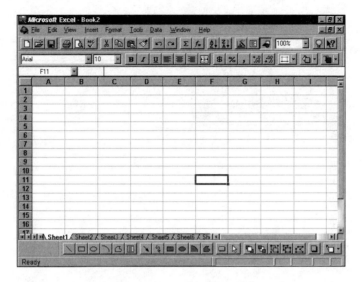

FIGURE 15.3 THE DRAWING TOOLBAR DOCKED ON THE BOTTOM OF THE SCREEN.

5. Move the mouse pointer into the Formatting toolbar (but not on top of a button) and drag it down so the top edge of its outline is just below the column headings. Now release the mouse button.

   The Formatting toolbar should be positioned approximately like the one in Figure 15.4.

   You may want to change the size and shape of the toolbar. There is a solution. Let's change it so there are fewer rows of buttons and the toolbar can fit comfortably in a corner of the worksheet.

6. Position the mouse pointer over the right border of the toolbar so it is a double-headed arrow. Drag it across about an inch and release the mouse button.

   The Formatting toolbar should look approximately like the one in Figure 15.5. If your toolbar is taller or wider, you can grab one of the borders and resize it until it is just the way you want it.

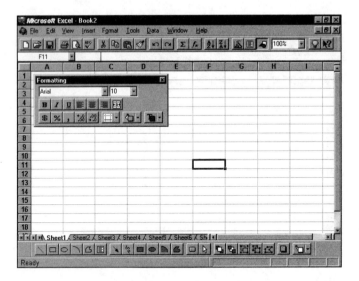

FIGURE 15.4 THE UNDOCKED FORMATTING TOOLBAR POSITIONED NEAR THE TOP OF THE WORKSHEET.

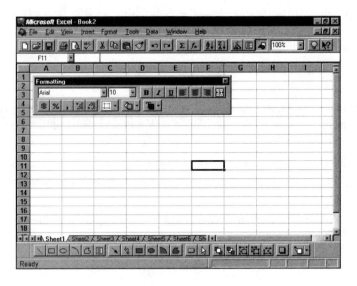

FIGURE 15.5 THE RESIZED FORMATTING TOOLBAR.

Before moving on, let's redock the Formatting toolbar so it will be in its normal position the next time you use Excel.

7. Move the Formatting toolbar up to the top of its outline in the Formula bar, and release the mouse button to redock it below the Standard toolbar.

   Now let's check out the Toolbars dialog box, which is used to choose toolbars and change some of their options.

8. Choose **View**, **Toolbars** to display the Toolbars dialog box, as shown in Figure 15.6.

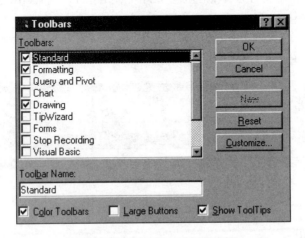

FIGURE 15.6 THE TOOLBARS DIALOG BOX.

You can use the check boxes in the Toolbars dialog box to choose which toolbars to display. Notice that if you use the scroll bar to scroll down the list of toolbars there are more toolbars to choose from in the dialog box than are available from the shortcut menu.

The check boxes across the bottom of the Toolbars dialog box allow you to change several toolbar options.

The Color Toolbars check box lets you choose whether the toolbar button faces are displayed in color or black and white. You might want to use this option if you are using Excel on a laptop or notebook computer with a black-and-white screen.

The **Large Buttons** option lets you display extra-large toolbar buttons. This option can be useful if you use a high-resolution screen driver. Standard Windows resolution is called VGA (Video Graphics Array) and uses a resolution of 640 dots by 480 dots. In standard resolution, the buttons are usually large enough to see the detail without using too much screen real estate.

Many computer/monitor combinations are capable of higher resolutions, such as 800 x 600 or 1024 x 768. If you are using one of these higher resolutions, you already know that the trade-off for the finer detail in the higher resolution is a smaller image, which can cause some difficulty in making out the detail of some screen elements. If you have a very large monitor (17" or more), you may find that the screen image, even at high resolutions, is large enough. If you have difficulty discerning the detail of the buttons, choose **Large Buttons**. Let's try it now to see its effect.

9. Click the **Large Buttons** check box and then click **OK** to enlarge all the toolbar buttons, as shown in Figure 15.7.

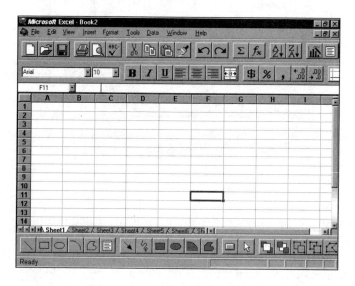

FIGURE 15.7 LARGE TOOLBAR BUTTONS.

N O T E With large buttons in standard resolution, some of the buttons on the docked Standard and Formatting toolbars are not visible. At higher resolutions this is not a problem. If you want to display large buttons in standard resolution, just undock the toolbars. Of course that creates another problem: a great deal of your worksheet is obscured by toolbars.

One way to solve this problem would be to remove a few buttons so that all the remaining buttons are visible in their docked position. You learn how to do this in the next section, "Creating Custom Toolbars."

Before we move on, let's return to normal-sized toolbar buttons.

10. Choose **View**, **Toolbars**, or choose **Toolbars** from the toolbar shortcut menu to display the Toolbars dialog box.

11. Click the **Large Buttons** check box to remove the check mark.

    Before closing the dialog box, let's talk about the last check box in the dialog box. The Show ToolTips check box lets you turn off the ToolTips feature, which shows what a button does when the mouse pointer is positioned over it. My advice is to leave this option checked. I can't think of any reason why you might want to turn this feature off.

12. Click **OK** to remove the dialog box and return the toolbars to their normal size.

CREATING CUSTOM TOOLBARS

Now that you know how to display and position the toolbars supplied by Excel, let's look at how to customize toolbars. There are several ways to modify toolbars to suit the way you work. You can alter existing toolbars by adding, removing or changing the position of buttons. You can also start from scratch with a new toolbar equipped with your choice of buttons.

With the Toolbars or Customize dialog box on the screen, you can remove or reposition any button on a toolbar that is currently displayed by simply dragging it:

♦ Off the toolbar

♦ To a new position on its toolbar

♦ To any other visible toolbar

Let's try removing and repositioning some buttons. We use the Customize dialog box to perform some additional customization. You can open the Customize dialog box by clicking the **Customize** button on the Toolbars dialog box or from the toolbar shortcut button.

1. Right-click on any of the toolbars to display the toolbar shortcut menu and then click **Customize** to display the Customize dialog box, as shown in Figure 15.8.

   The Customize dialog box contains all the existing buttons you can use to add to a toolbar. The buttons are separated into logical categories to make it easy to find the button you want.

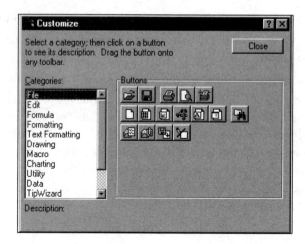

FIGURE 15.8 THE CUSTOMIZE DIALOG BOX.

Before we add any buttons, let's make some room on the Formatting toolbar so we won't obscure any buttons when we add a new one to it.

Let's say you decide that you don't need the Bold, Italic, and Underline buttons because you have already memorized the keyboard shortcuts (**Ctrl-B** for bold, **Ctrl-I** for italic, and **Ctrl-U** for underline). Let's remove these buttons from the Formatting toolbar now.

2. Drag the **Bold** button from the Formatting toolbar onto the worksheet and then release the mouse button. Repeat the process for the **Italic** and the **Underline** buttons so the toolbar looks like the one in Figure 15.9.

Let's add buttons for Double Underline, Strikethrough, and Rotate Text Down. All of these buttons fall within the Text Formatting category but you could, of course, add buttons from different categories.

3. Click **Text Formatting** in the Categories list to display the Text Formatting buttons, as shown in Figure 15.10.

NOTE You cannot see the ToolTips when you move the mouse pointer over a button in the Customize dialog box, but you can see a description of the button's function by clicking on it. The description appears in the Description area at the bottom of the dialog box.

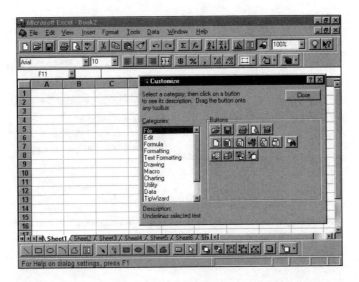

FIGURE 15.9 THE FORMATTING TOOLBAR WITHOUT THE BOLD, ITALIC, AND UNDERLINE BUTTONS.

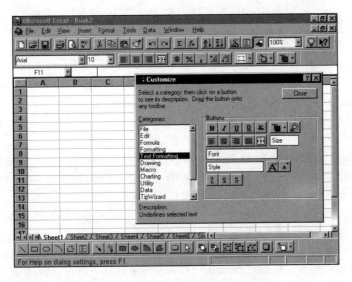

FIGURE 15.10 THE TEXT FORMATTING BUTTONS.

4. Drag the **Double Underline** button (its description is "Double underlines selected text") up to the Formatting toolbar, so its outline is between the Font Size and the Align Left buttons, as shown in Figure 15.11.

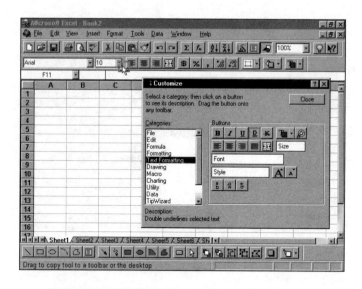

FIGURE 15.11 THE OUTLINE OF THE DOUBLE UNDERLINE BUTTON
READY TO BE PLACED ON THE FORMATTING TOOLBAR.

5. Release the mouse button to accept the placement of the new button.

   If the button ended up to the left or right of its intended position, you can simply drag it left or right to reposition it where you want it.

6. Drag the **Strikethrough** button (its description is "Draws a line through selected text") to the position just to the right of the Double Underline button and release the mouse button.

7. Drag the **Rotate Text Down** button (its description is "Rotates text sideways, reading top to bottom") to the position just to the right of the Strikethrough button and release the mouse button.

   The Formatting toolbar should now look something like the one in Figure 15.12.

   Now let's create a custom toolbar with just the buttons we want. We can simply drag a button from the Customize dialog box onto the worksheet to create a new toolbar named Toolbar 1, Toolbar 2, etc. However, it usually makes more sense to enter a name for the new toolbar before creating it, which is done from the Toolbars dialog box.

8. Click the **Close** button to remove the Customize dialog box from the screen.

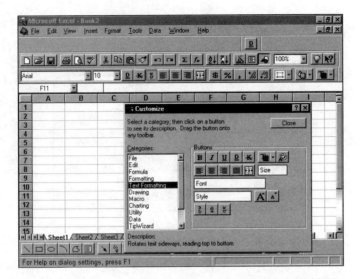

FIGURE 15.12 THE FORMATTING TOOLBAR WITH ITS THREE NEW BUTTONS.

9. Choose **View**, **Toolbars** or click on **Toolbars** from the toolbar shortcut menu to display the Toolbars dialog box.

   When you create a new toolbar, choose a name that denotes the group or category of buttons you plan to add to it. If you are creating a toolbar with a conglomeration of buttons with no particular relation except for the fact that you want them on a toolbar, a name such as "My Toolbar" might be a good way to designate your toolbar. In fact, that's exactly what we'll do right now.

10. Select the text in the Toolbar Name text box by dragging the mouse over it and type **My Toolbar**.

    The Toolbars dialog box should look like the one in Figure 15.13.

    Notice that as soon as you enter a name in the text box, the New button becomes available.

11. Click the **New** button. The blank new toolbar appears and the Toolbars dialog box switches to the Customize dialog box, as shown in Figure 15.14.

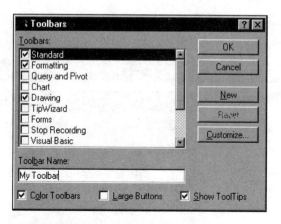

FIGURE 15.13 THE TOOLBARS DIALOG BOX WITH THE NAME OF OUR NEW TOOLBAR ENTERED IN THE TOOLBAR NAME TEXT BOX.

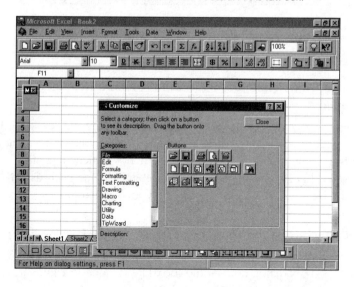

FIGURE 15.14 THE BEGINNING OF THE NEW TOOLBAR NEXT TO THE CUSTOMIZE DIALOG BOX.

The toolbar will widen and lengthen as you add buttons to it. The way you see it now, it isn't wide enough to fit the entire title, "My Toolbar." If you only plan to add one or two buttons to a toolbar, use a very short name.

N O T E

Let's add several buttons from several categories to the new toolbar. As you add them, don't worry too much about getting them positioned just right since you can always reposition them. Also, we are going to position the buttons in a single row. If some of them end up stacked vertically, you can resize the toolbar by dragging a border.

12.   From the File category of buttons, drag the **Open** button onto the new toolbar and release the mouse button.

Just because a button is already in use on one toolbar doesn't mean you wouldn't want it on another. You may want to equip My Toolbar with your most often used buttons so you won't need to display any **N O T E** other toolbars when it is displayed.

13.   Click on **Drawing** in the Categories list and then drag the **Arrow** button (its description is "Adds an arrow") to the right of the Open button on the new toolbar and release the mouse button.

14.   From the Charting category, drag the **ChartWizard** button (its description is "Creates embedded chart or modifies active chart") to the right of the Arrow button and release the mouse button. The new toolbar should now look like the one in Figure 15.15.

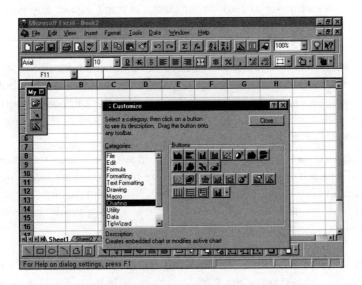

FIGURE 15.15 MY TOOLBAR WITH THE THREE BUTTONS ADDED.

The new toolbar will be listed on the toolbar shortcut menu and in the Toolbars dialog box, so you can display and remove this toolbar from your screen as you would any other toolbar.

Let's leave the Customize dialog box on screen as we will be using it in the next section.

DESIGNING CUSTOM TOOLBAR BUTTONS

If putting together your own collection of buttons does not provide you with enough customization, you can change the image of any of the buttons on any toolbar. The simplest approach, if you can find an existing image you like, is to copy the image to the button you want to change.

If you need an even more custom image than that, you can edit a button's image or design your own using the Button Editor or just about any other paint-type graphics program you like, including the Paintbrush program that comes with Windows.

WARNING

I'm not very creative when it comes to graphic design. On second thought, "not very creative" is an overstatement. Drawing stick figures is about as far as I got in art class. So don't expect any great-looking (or even good-looking) button images from these examples.

The first thing to do is to replace the image of one of the buttons on My Toolbar with one from the Customize dialog box. To do this, click on the button you want to use in the dialog box and copy its image to the Clipboard, then click on the button with the image you want to replace, and then paste the image from the Clipboard. It is easier than it sounds.

Let's replace the image on the Open button with an image from the Custom category. The Custom category buttons are normally used to attach macros, as you learned in Chapter 12, "Automating Your Work with Macros." However, we can copy any image we want. Since these do not already have functions assigned to them, they are a natural choice.

1. Scroll down the Categories list until the Custom category is visible, then click on it to display the Custom category buttons, as shown in Figure 15.16.

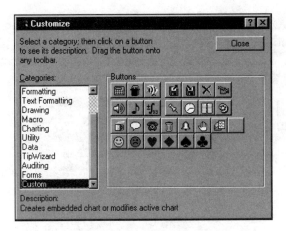

FIGURE 15.16 THE CUSTOMIZE DIALOG BOX WITH THE CUSTOM CATEGORY BUTTONS DISPLAYED.

Let's use the heart image on the bottom row of buttons for our new image.

2. Click on the **heart** button just to the right of the frowning face button on the bottom row.

3. Choose **Edit, Copy Button Image**. The heart image is now stored on the Clipboard and ready to be pasted on top of another button.

4. Click the **Open** button on My Toolbar and then choose **Edit, Paste Button Image**.

   The Open button in My Toolbar should now look like the one in Figure 15.17. With the Customize or Toolbars dialog box open, right-clicking on a button displays a special shortcut menu for customizing the button. Let's edit the heart button to customize it even further.

5. Point to the heart button on My Toolbar and right-click to display its shortcut menu, as shown in Figure 15.18.

6. Click **Edit Button Image** to display the Button Editor dialog box, as shown in Figure 15.19. Each small box in the Picture portion of the dialog box represents one dot or pixel of the image. You can click on a color in the Colors portion of the dialog box and then apply that color to any dot in the picture by simply clicking on it. If you want to apply the color to a series of dots, you can drag the mouse over the dots to paint the color.

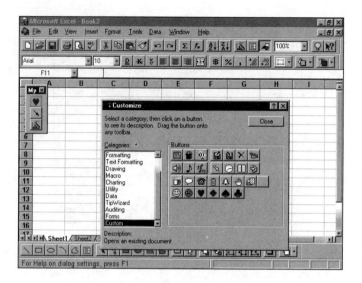

FIGURE 15.17 Now My Toolbar has a heart.

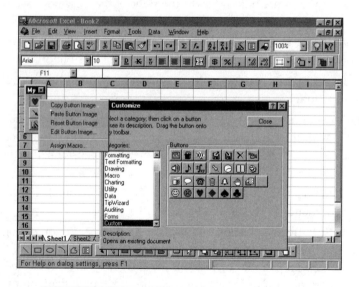

FIGURE 15.18 The shortcut menu for customizing a button.

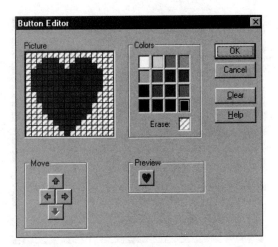

FIGURE 15.19 THE BUTTON EDITOR DIALOG BOX.

Clicking on the **Erase** box allows you to erase any of the dots that are filled with color by dragging or clicking on them.

You can use the arrow buttons in the Move portion of the dialog box to move the entire image up, down, left, or right, if the image doesn't already extend to the edges of the Picture box.

The **Clear** button lets you remove the entire image so you can start fresh and create your own image.

Let's add a black horizontal line on the top and bottom rows and erase a few dots in the middle of the heart to create an open heart.

7. Click on the black box in the Colors portion of the dialog box and drag across the top and bottom rows of the Picture portion of the dialog box. If you make a mistake, you can remove black "dots" by clicking on them again.

The Preview portion of the Image Editor dialog box shows, in actual size, what your button will look like as you edit it.

N O T E

8. Click the **Erase** box and erase a few dots in the middle of the heart so the picture portion looks like Figure 15.20.

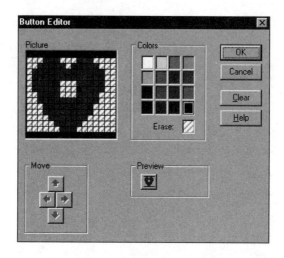

FIGURE 15.20 THE OPEN HEART WITH TOP AND BOTTOM BORDERS.

9. Click **OK** to close the Image Editor dialog box and accept the modifications.

10. Click the **Close** button to remove the Customize dialog box.

The Image Editor doesn't offer a wide variety of graphics tools to create complex images. If you want more design flexibility, consider using a more sophisticated paint-type program, such as Paintbrush, to create an image. You can then copy your design to the clipboard and paste the image onto the button of your choice using the technique just described.

Before we finish this chapter, let's get the screen back to normal. We'll remove the Drawing toolbar, delete the "My Toolbar" toolbar, and reset the Formatting toolbar back to its original configuration.

11. Choose **View**, **Toolbars** to display the Toolbars dialog box.

12. Scroll down the Toolbars list until you can see the Drawing and "My Toolbar" check boxes.

13. Click on **My Toolbar** in the Toolbars list to remove the check mark and, if you want to delete the toolbar, click the **Delete** button to display the message dialog box shown in Figure 15.21.

14. Click **OK** to confirm the deletion of My Toolbar.

15. Click on **Drawing** in the Toolbars list to remove the check mark so the toolbar won't be displayed when the Toolbars dialog box is closed.

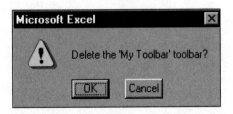

FIGURE 15.21 THE MESSAGE DIALOG BOX CONFIRMS THE TOOLBAR DELETION.

16. Finally, scroll back up the Toolbars list and click on **Formatting** twice so it is still checked and is highlighted. Then click the **Reset** button to return it to its default setup.

17. Click **OK** to remove the Toolbars dialog box. Your screen should be back to the way it looked before you started this chapter.

A FINAL THOUGHT

In this chapter, you learned to display, position, and customize your toolbars to make them work as efficiently as possible for you. Don't forget to refer to Appendix C for a complete listing of Excel's toolbars and their button functions.

The next chapter covers some techniques for customizing your Windows environment.

CHAPTER 16

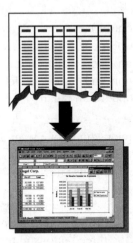

CUSTOMIZING WINDOWS

♦ Taming the mouse

♦ Straightening the desktop

♦ Color your world

You learned in Chapter 2, "Getting Started—Excel and Windows Basics" to use Windows productively. In this chapter, you will explore several ways to make Windows behave just the way you want.

We will use the Control Panel, a program that comes with Windows, to alter mouse operations, the desktop environment, and Windows' colors.

TAMING THE MOUSE

The Control Panel is a Windows program that provides options for customizing such aspects of Windows' environment as fonts, sound, keyboards, and printers. You can find detailed information about these options in the Windows documentation and by using Help. There are also many good books that cover all these options and many more in depth.

We are just going to discuss a few of the more useful Windows customization options. One of the most useful options is customizing the mouse so you can work with it more easily. Let's start the Control Panel application and customize the mouse now.

1. If Excel is running, minimize the program window by clicking on the **Minimize** button in the upper-right corner of the screen (the left-most of the three buttons in the corner of the screen).

    The Control Panel icon is normally found in the My Computer window. Let's open that window now.

2. Double-click on the **My Computer** icon to display the My Computer window, as shown in Figure 16.1.

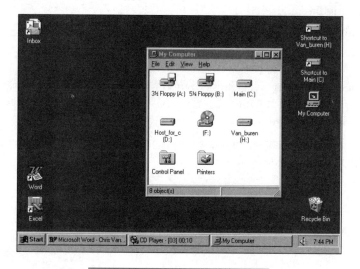

FIGURE 16.1 THE MY COMPUTER WINDOW.

3. Double-click on the **Control Panel** folder to see the Control Panel icons, as shown in Figure 16.2.

FIGURE 16.2 THE CONTROL PANEL WINDOW.

To enter one of the Control Panel's customization areas, double-click on its icon to open a dialog box. Let's go into the mouse dialog box now.

4 Double-click on the **Mouse** icon to display the Mouse dialog box, as shown in Figure 16.3.

The Mouse dialog box provides options for changing the mouse pointer speed (how fast the pointer moves across the screen as you move the mouse), changing the double-click speed (how much time you can pause between two clicks and have Windows interpret it as a double-click instead of two single clicks), and swapping left and right mouse buttons (which may be useful for left-handed computer users). Other options are available in the various tabbed pages of the Mouse dialog box.

In the Motion tab is another feature called *Mouse Trails*, which leaves a temporary trail of mouse pointer images as you move the mouse pointer. This feature is often useful for laptop computers with LCD (Liquid Crystal Display) screens. The mouse pointer on some LCD screens has a submarine effect which can obscure the pointer as you move it from one place on the screen to another. Using the Mouse Trails feature can help you keep track of the mouse pointer in these situations. For standard desktop-type screens, this feature is usually more of an annoyance, though it can be amusing to try it out for a few minutes.

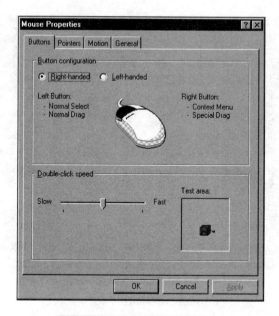

FIGURE 16.3 THE MOUSE DIALOG BOX.

Let's try changing some of these options now to see what effect they have on mouse operations. We'll start with the tracking speed. If the tracking speed is too fast, you may have a difficult time accurately positioning the mouse pointer precisely. If the tracking speed is too slow, it will slow you down, causing you to make unnecessary mouse movements.

6. Move your mouse back and forth several inches on your desktop and notice how rapidly the on-screen pointer moves compared with how rapidly you move the mouse.

7. Click on the **Motion** tab in the Mouse dialog box. Then move the scroll box in the Pointer Speed portion of the dialog box all the way over to the fast (right) side of the scroll bar and repeat step 5 to see the difference.

8. Move the scroll box in the Pointer Speed portion of the dialog box all the way over to the slow (left) side of the scroll bar and, once again, repeat step 5. Notice that the mouse pointer moves much more slowly.

9. Reposition the Pointer Speed scroll box so the tracking speed is comfortable for you.

Next let's take a look at the Double-Click Speed setting. The goal here is to set the double-click speed as fast as possible but not so fast that you cannot double-click. Most people have a tough time double-clicking when it is set at the fastest speed.

etting the double-click speed too slow can be an equally bothersome problem. For example, you might click on one screen element then move to another element and click on it, and have Windows interpret that as double-clicking on the first element. You certainly don't want the double-click speed set so slow that you have to consciously wait before clicking again to avoid having the two clicks be a double-click.

9. Click on the **Buttons** tab in the Mouse dialog box. Then point to the Test Area box and double-click.

If you double-clicked fast enough, the Jack-in-the-box will appear, as shown in Figure 16.4. The next double-click puts the little fellow away.

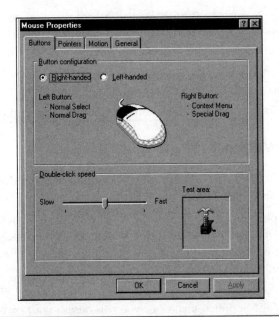

FIGURE 16.4 THE MOUSE DIALOG BOX WITH THE TEST AREA ACTIVATED.

10. If you had to try double-clicking several times before you could get the Jack-in-the-box to appear, move the Double-Click Speed scroll box a little to the slow (left) side. If you had no difficulty double-clicking at the current setting, move the scroll box to the fast (right) side until you do have some trouble and then back it off just enough that you can double-click comfortably.

If you want to use the Swap Left/Right Buttons, click the **Left-Handed** or **Right-Handed** options in the Buttons tab of the dialog box.

WARNING

If you swap the left and right mouse buttons, you won't notice the change until you exit the Mouse dialog box by clicking **OK**.

12. Click **OK** to accept any changes you made and close the dialog box.

STRAIGHTENING THE DESKTOP

The Control Panel's Display Properties dialog box provides several options for enhancing the appearance of your Windows display, such as adding background graphic images, changing screen colors, and more.

You can also choose from several screen savers which will blank your screen and display moving images after a specified time of inactivity.

Let's take a look at these options and discuss their pros and cons.

Patterns and Wallpaper

1. Double-click on the Control Panel's **Display** icon to display the dialog box, shown in Figure 16.5.

   Two Display Property options allow you to add a background to surround your windows: patterns and wallpaper. *Patterns*, as the name suggests, are designs made up of dots. These are generally not very intricate but can add a bit of visual appeal.

   Wallpaper is actually a graphic file used as background. The graphic can be one of the supplied images or you can design your own in a paint program. Like the toolbar buttons we discussed in the previous chapter, wallpaper graphics can be extremely intricate. In fact, because wallpaper is displayed in a much larger size than toolbar buttons, you can use much more elaborate images for your wallpaper and still easily discern the details.

   Let's start our desktop delving by choosing a pattern. To select a pattern, click on the desired pattern name in the Patterns list that appears in the Background tab of the dialog box. You may then edit the pattern if you wish.

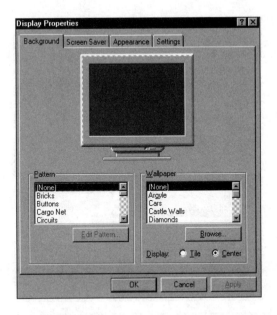

FIGURE 16.5 THE DISPLAY PROPERTIES DIALOG BOX.

2. Click on the **Background** tab (if it's not already active).

   You can use the scroll bar to see additional pattern choices, but for now, choose one of the patterns near the top of the list.

3. Click on the **Cargo Net** pattern.

   You can immediately see what the affect of the patter selection is by looking at the sample screen, as shown in Figure 16.6.

4. With Cargo Net selected, click **OK** to close the Display Properties dialog box and display the pattern, as shown in Figure 16.7.

N O T E   If you can't see the pattern, you may need to reduce the size of some of your open windows. For example, if you have Excel maximized, none of your desktop will be visible, so you won't see the pattern, just as you wouldn't be able to see the top of your desk if you had papers completely covering its surface.

5. Double-click on the **Display** icon in the Control Panel window to display the Display Properties dialog box once again.

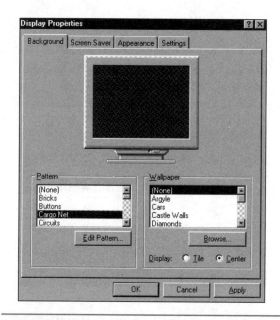

FIGURE 16.6 THE SAMPLE SCREEN SHOWING YOUR SELECTED PATTERN.

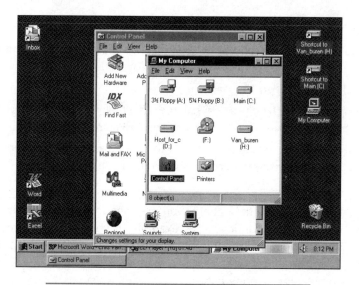

FIGURE 16.7 THE CARGO NET PATTERN COVERING OUR DESKTOP.

6. Click on the **Edit Pattern** button to display the Pattern Editor dialog box, as shown in Figure 16.8.

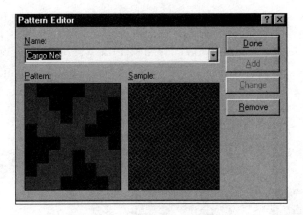

FIGURE 16.8 THE PATTERN EDITOR DIALOG BOX.

From this dialog box you can choose different patterns to edit by using the Name drop-down list. Choosing **None** from the list lets you create your own pattern from scratch.

Each small square in the middle box of the dialog box represents one dot or pixel of the pattern. The Sample section on the left side of the dialog box lets you see what your modified pattern will look like as you make changes. Clicking the mouse in the large box adds a black dot if there isn't already one there, and removes a black dot if there is one there.

The Add button lets you add a new pattern to the list after you enter a new name in the Name box. The Change button saves the changes you make to the pattern. The Remove option lets you delete a pattern from the list.

We won't change the pattern, but let's see what a couple of the other supplied patterns look like in the next two figures.

7. Click **Done** to close the Pattern Editor dialog box.

8. In the list of patterns, choose **None**.

Next, let's take a look at the wallpaper portion of the dialog box. The wallpaper images are color images and can add significantly greater visual appeal than the simple patterns we just looked at. If you want to edit one of the wallpaper images, you need to use another program, such as Paintbrush.

You can use the Center and Tile options to position the image on screen. The Center option centers the image on your screen. If the wallpaper image you use is large enough, this is a good choice. However, if you are using a small wallpaper image, it could be hidden behind some of your open windows. The Tile option places as many copies as required to fill the screen and reduces the chance that the wallpaper will be hidden.

Choosing a wallpaper image is just like choosing a pattern. Click the arrow to display the drop-down list of wallpaper images and choose the one you want. Figures 16.9 and 16.10 show two different wallpapers.

FIGURE 16.9 THE ZIG ZAG WALLPAPER.

9. Be sure that the Tile option is chosen, then click on the desired wallpaper name in the list, as shown in Figure 16.11.

N O T E

All the wallpaper file names have a .bmp extension, which stands for bitmapped. This is a particular type of file format that can be created by most paint-type graphics programs. If you want to create your own wallpaper file, you need to save it as a .bmp file. You also need to save it in your main Windows directory, usually C:\WINDOWS, so that it will appear in the list of wallpaper files.

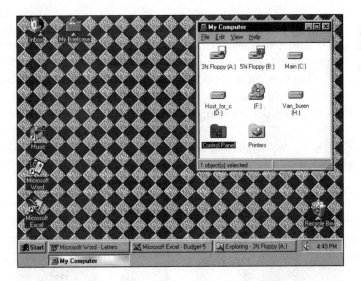

FIGURE 16.10 THE DIAMONDS WALLPAPER.

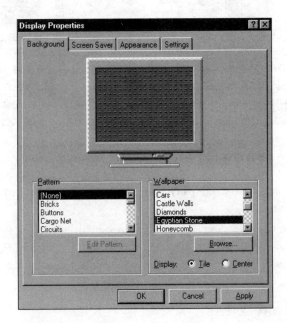

FIGURE 16.11 THE EGYPTIAN STONE WALLPAPER.

WARNING Windows performance can suffer if there isn't enough memory available, and using wallpaper uses memory. The more complex and larger wallpaper images use more memory than the smaller, simpler ones, but they all use memory. If you want to conserve as much memory as possible for your Windows programs and maximize performance, consider avoiding wallpaper.

10. Click **OK** to see what the wallpaper looks like on the display screen. Figure 16.12 shows the Egyptian Stone example.

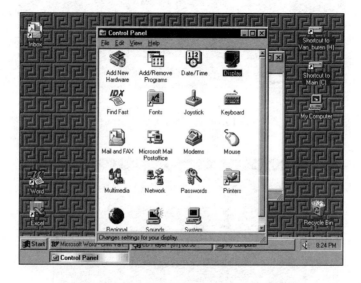

FIGURE 16.12 THE EGYPTIAN STONE WALLPAPER IN ACTION.

11. Double-click on the **Display** icon, then choose **None** from the wallpaper drop-down list.

We'll discuss the next several features in the Display Properties dialog box without performing any actions. Leave the Display Properties dialog box open so you can refer to it as we look at the next few options.

THE SCREEN SAVER TAB

At one time, screen savers were vital for protecting your screen from phosphor burn-in, which could occur if the same image remained on screen for long periods of time. Phosphor burn-in caused the image that was burned into the screen to appear as a ghost image even when another image should have been the only one on the screen.

Newer color monitors are much less susceptible to phosphor burn-in and make screen savers unnecessary. With standard VGA monitors, an image can remain on the screen for days or weeks without causing any problems. Also, like wallpaper, screen savers can decrease performance by using some of your computer's resources to monitor periods of inactivity. For example, if you set the screen saver to activate after ten minutes of inactivity, the computer must constantly time the length of inactivity.

My advice is to forget about screen savers unless you have a fast enough computer that the performance decrease is unnoticeable. To choose a screen saver, select from the list of screen saver names in the drop-down list in the screen saver portion of the Desktop dialog box and then specify the number of delay minutes (the number of minutes of inactivity Windows will wait before starting the screen saver). You can use the Preview button to see what each of the screen savers looks like. The Settings button lets you specify some options for the screen saver that you have chosen.

There is one genuine advantage to using screen savers. They can help you protect confidential information by requiring a password to clear the screen saver. Normally, any keyboard or mouse activity clears the screen saver. However, with password protection enabled, you (or anyone else trying to use your computer) would need to enter the password that you had specified. This can be a nice little security feature.

Figure 16.13 shows the settings dialog box for the Flying Windows screen saver.

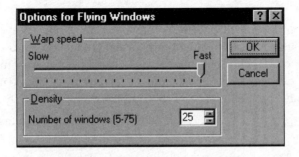

FIGURE 16.13 THE FLYING WINDOWS SETUP DIALOG BOX.

The setup dialog boxes for other screen savers provide different sets of options depending on the characteristics of the particular screen saver.

Figure 16.14 shows the Change Password dialog box.

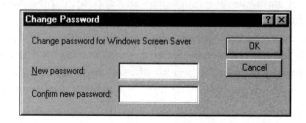

FIGURE 16.14 THE CHANGE PASSWORD DIALOG BOX.

For security purposes, asterisks appear as you type your password. This way, if someone is looking over your shoulder, they won't see your password. Also, you are told to type the same password twice, once in the New Password text box and once in the Repeat New Password text box. This ensures that you actually typed the password you intended to type. Also, if you already had a password set, type the old password in the Old Password text box.

If you decide to set a password, make sure it's one you can remember. Otherwise, you will not be able to get back into Windows once the screen saver is activated.

WARNING

COLOR YOUR WORLD

The Appearance tab in the Display Properties dialog box lets you change the colors of various screen elements. Although the colors you choose are primarily an aesthetic decision, choosing unwise color combinations can make it hard to read portions of the screen. For example, if you choose black menu text and black menu bars, the menu text will be completely invisible.

Windows provides a variety of color combinations that make it easy to spruce up your screen.

Let's take a look at the colorful options the Display Properties dialog box provides.

1. Double-click on the **Display** icon in the Control Panel (if it's not already open) then click on the **Appearance** tab to display the screen shown in Figure 16.15.

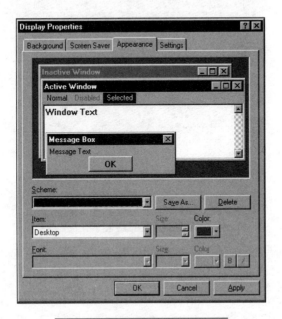

FIGURE 16.15 THE APPEARANCE OPTIONS.

The easiest way to make color changes is to choose one of the available color schemes from the Schemes drop-down list. To choose one of the color schemes, click on the arrow next to the Schemes box. Let's do that now.

2. Click on the arrow next to the Schemes list box to display the list of available color schemes, as shown in Figure 16.16.

I won't show you figures of different color schemes, since the figures in this book are in black and white. Try choosing several of the schemes to see their effect. When you click on a color scheme, you can see its effect by looking at the sample screen section at the top of the dialog box.

3. Click on **Windows Standard** (or whatever scheme was already in effect) to retain that as the color scheme.

You can also create custom color schemes and even custom colors by selecting colors for various screen elements from the Color Palette. Let's take a look at the Color Palette now.

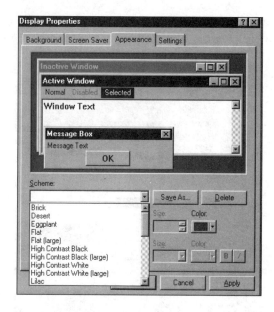

FIGURE 16.16 THE LIST OF COLOR SCHEMES.

4. You can change a screen element's color by choosing the element from the drop-down list of screen elements under Item, as shown in Figure 16.17. Click on that list now.

SHORTCUT Instead of choosing from the drop-down screen element list, you can simply click on the element you want to change in the sample portion of the dialog box. When you do, you'll know if you clicked on the correct element because the element's name will appear in the Screen Element box.

Having chosen the screen element you want to change, just click on the color in the color palette you want to use for that element. As you change colors for various screen elements, you can see the changes in the Sample Windows area at the top of the dialog box.

After you change all the screen elements you want to change, you can close the dialog box and the changes will remain in effect. However, if you later choose a different color scheme, your changes will be lost unless you save them with a color scheme name.

FIGURE 16.17 THE DROP-DOWN LIST OF SCREEN ELEMENTS.

To save a color scheme, click on the **Save As** button to display the Save As dialog box, as shown in Figure 16.18.

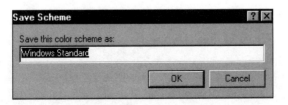

FIGURE 16.18 THE SAVE SCHEME DIALOG BOX.

You can then enter a name for your new color scheme. This name now appears on the color scheme drop-down list, so you can choose it in the future.

5. Click **OK** in the lower-left corner of the Color dialog box to close it and accept any color changes you made.

6. Close the Display Properties dialog box by choosing **OK**. Close the Control Panel window by clicking in the **Close** box in the upper-right corner.

A FINAL THOUGHT

In this chapter, you learned to customize your Windows environment in several ways. The Control Panel offers other customization options that you might want to explore. Windows' Help facility includes information on the other Control Panel features, as does the Windows documentation.

CHAPTER 17

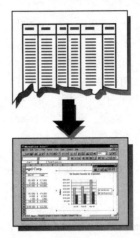

USING EXCEL WITH OTHER PROGRAMS

- ♦ Why use other programs with Excel?
- ♦ An Office overview
- ♦ Choosing which Office program to use
- ♦ What is OLE and why should I care?
- ♦ Linking samples

No program is an island. Gee, that sounds familiar. But seriously, few computer users rely solely on one program. If you are using Excel—and I think it's safe to assume you are since you're reading this book—you have other programs at your disposal.

If you have Microsoft Office, which includes the Word for Windows word processing program and the PowerPoint presentation program, you have the ability to create compound documents using parts of two or more of the programs. Even if all you have is Windows and Excel, you have the miniapplications that come with Windows, such as WordPad and Mailbox.

379

WHY USE OTHER PROGRAMS WITH EXCEL?

For as long as people have been creating paper documents, they've been adding bits and pieces of various types of information together—cutting out a picture from one place and pasting it into another, cutting out a chart here and pasting into a report there. In computer jargon, documents that include pieces from several applications are called *compound documents*.

The technology to create computerized compound documents has been like the Holy Grail—very elusive. Finding such a technology would mean far greater computer productivity. The possibilities seemed endless, but the search for a means to accomplish it seemed never ending.

In several places throughout this book, I have mentioned the value of using other, more specialized, programs for accomplishing certain tasks. For example, you can create and edit toolbar buttons with the Button Editor. However, using a more flexible program, such as Paintbrush, allows you greater freedom of expression and control.

Certainly Excel isn't the best tool for every job. It's an incredible spreadsheet program and excels at creating and formatting number-oriented documents. But when it comes to creating text-oriented documents, you'll want to use a word processing program with all the tools for formatting words such as Word for Windows.

"Use the best tool for the job" may just sound like common sense. And it is. Of course you would use a word processing program if you were writing a report for your company proposing to hire some new employees for your department. You want to format the report so it is as attractive—and persuasive—as possible.

But words alone probably won't make this proposal fly. The words will likely need to be backed up by some numbers demonstrating the various costs and benefits these proposed new employees will bring. I hope you know by now that the best tool for that job is a spreadsheet program such as Excel.

You can create and print the report with your word processing program. Then you can create and print a worksheet (and perhaps a chart for emphasis) from Excel and insert the worksheet and chart pages into the report. But imagine how much more professional-looking and convincing the report is if the worksheet and chart were integrated into the body of the report.

Right there, smack dab in the middle of a beautifully formatted word-processed page, you place your worksheet and your chart, as if you had used scissors and paste, but without the muss and fuss. And the worksheet and chart can be linked to the report document so, when the data is changed in the worksheet, the changes are instantly reflected.

AN OFFICE OVERVIEW

Microsoft Office is a combination or suite of programs including Excel, Word, PowerPoint, and, in the Office Professional version, Access. Other, smaller programs may also be present in your version of Office, such as Binder and Schedule +. Word is a word processing program. Word processing is the single activity performed by more computer users than any other. From simple memos to complex reports or even books, word processing programs provide the tools for entering, formatting, editing text, and printing documents.

PowerPoint is a presentation graphics program that provides all the tools necessary to create dazzling presentations using overhead transparencies, 35mm slides, or your computer screen.

Access is a relational database program used for creating, editing, viewing, querying, and reporting all sorts of information.

There are some tremendous advantages to using Office instead of a mish-mosh of programs from other companies. First, all the Office programs are arguably the best programs available in their respective categories.

As you work with the Office programs, you find that several major consistencies jump out at you. The menus for the programs are almost identical. Of course the options within the menus are appropriate for the particular program you're working with. Microsoft also ensures that dialog boxes, toolbars, shortcut menus, and program help all operate consistently. There's even a consistent shortcut for switching among the Office programs. There are also hundreds of minor consistencies that give the group of programs a unified feel.

This consistency makes learning the second and third programs much easier than the first. After you've learned any one of the programs, you find yourself guessing, often correctly, about how to perform a task in one of the other programs. After a short while it all starts to feel natural and automatic.

Notice the similarity among the screen elements in the screens from Word and PowerPoint as shown in Figures 17.1 and 17.2.

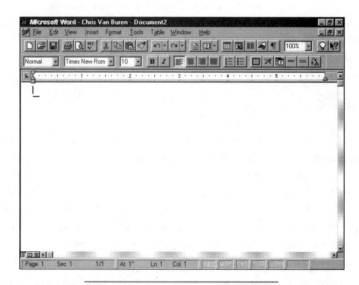

FIGURE 17.1 A WORD FOR WINDOWS SCREEN.

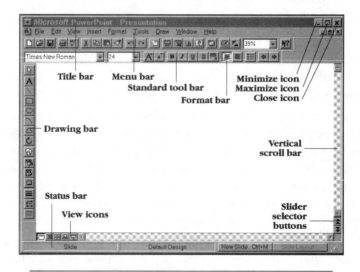

FIGURE 17.2 THE MAIN POWERPOINT SCREEN WITH COMPONENTS LABELED.

The Microsoft Office Manager (MOM)

When Microsoft Office is installed in the normal manner, the Microsoft Office program starts automatically when you start Windows. The Microsoft Office toolbar appears in the upper-right corner of the screen.

Figure 17.3 shows the Microsoft Office Manager Shortcut bar.

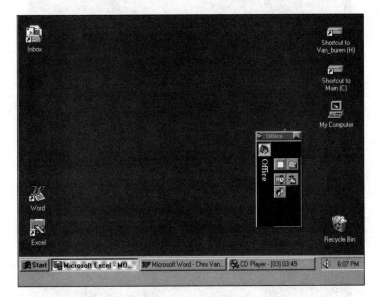

FIGURE 17.3 THE MICROSOFT OFFICE MANAGER SHORTCUT BAR.

To add program icons to your Shortcut bar, click on the control menu and access the Customize option.

1. Click on the Shortcut bar's control menu in the upper-left corner. The screen should look like Figure 17.4.

2. Choose **Customize**.

3. Click the **Buttons** tab. See Figure 17.5.

4. Click to place a check mark beside any application you want to add to the Shortcut bar. Click next to **Excel** and **Word** to add these icons.

5. Click **OK**.

To start or switch to any of your Office programs using the Microsoft Office Manager Shortcut bar, just click the button for that program. If the program isn't already running, it may take a while to start. If the program is already running, clicking on its Microsoft Office Manager Shortcut bar button switches you to that program almost instantly.

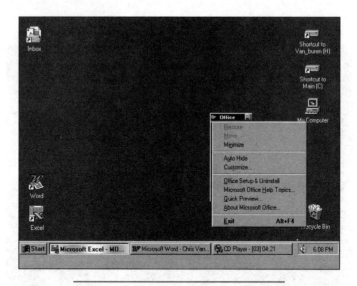

FIGURE 17.4 THE SHORTCUT BAR'S CONTROL MENU.

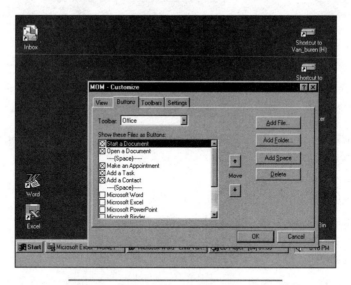

FIGURE 17.5 ADDING ICONS TO THE SHORTCUT BAR.

Remember, if you don't know which Microsoft Office Manager tool-bar button belongs to which program, position the mouse pointer over the button to see a ToolTip for the button that tells you the name of the program.

N O T E

The Microsoft Office Manager is so convenient, I recommend that you always keep it running, except, perhaps when you are giving on-screen PowerPoint slide show presentations where the toolbar could be distracting.

The Right Tool for the Job

Deciding which of the Office programs to use for a particular task or project is the first—and often the most difficult—challenge. There is some overlap in capabilities, so many projects could be completed using any of the programs. Choosing the best one for the job, however, makes the job go more smoothly and gives you greater flexibility to do it the way you want to.

Picking the correct program might seem to be a matter of common sense—working with words, use Word; manipulating numbers, use Excel; creating a presentation or a chart, use PowerPoint; manipulating data, use Access. Well, it's not quite that easy because there's a shared set of capabilities among the members of the Office ensemble.

Word, for example, has a table feature for manipulating rows and columns, and can even perform calculations like Excel. Word also has the ability to create charts. Excel, in addition to its extensive number handling capability, can also create dazzling charts. Access might appear to be the best choice for data management, but Word and Excel also have the ability to create databases and to sort and select portions of the database that meet certain criteria. PowerPoint also lets you work with text and create charts.

The path to the best choice becomes even murkier when you take into account the ability to link portions of any of these programs to any other. So how do you decide?

As a general rule, Word is the best choice for primarily text-oriented documents. When you need to work extensively with numbers and calculations, Excel is usually the preferred tool. Excel also makes the most sense for charts, especially those that reflect data in an Excel spreadsheet. PowerPoint is normally the tool to turn to for presentations that pull together elements from the other two programs. Access is the best choice for complex data management.

Ultimately, the best advice I can give is to learn the capabilities, strengths, and weaknesses of all the Office programs. It also helps if you know what elements you want to include in your document. If you know what the programs can do, and what you want to accomplish, choosing the right one can be as easy as picking the correct socks to go with your shoes. Actually, I sometimes have trouble with that myself.

The following are some more concrete examples of tasks and which program is best suited to each job.

Word makes putting together almost any written document a breeze. From business and personal letters to book-length manuscripts, simple memos to annual reports to almost any legal document, Word has the tools to make them appear just the way you want.

For number-oriented documents, from simple household budget worksheets, to forecasts for multinational corporations, from a cash flow analysis for a sandwich shop, to a portfolio analysis for a multimillion dollar pension fund, Excel provides tools for deftly manipulating the numbers to answer the questions you are posing and finds the best solutions when you are wondering *what if....*

Excel is also the first place to turn when you want to transform the numbers from your Excel worksheets into charts. A column chart showing the relationship between income and expenses is a sure way to clarify the numbers. A pie chart to compare the contribution each division is making to the company makes a stronger statement than numbers alone. A line chart showing the ups and downs of the various investments in the pension fund can help make better choices than staring at a bunch of numbers.

The complex database management tasks Access excels at include accounting systems where the various pieces of the system are tied together. For example, you could have accounts receivable or accounts payable entries automatically posted to the general ledger.

The word-oriented documents created in Word, the number-oriented worksheet documents created in Excel, forms or other portions of data created in Access, as well as the related charts, can all be used as parts of a presentation. The point of most documents created in Word, Excel, and Access is to persuade and enlighten, so it makes sense that by simply putting them together you can create a persuasive presentation. True enough. But if we want to use the right tool for the job (that is the heading after all), PowerPoint is the likely choice.

Let's say you are making a presentation to the board of directors to convince them to recommend the acquisition of another company. You might use Word to create an analysis of the proposed acquisition, but you could also use salient portions of the analysis, as well as Excel charts, to create slides for the presentation. Within PowerPoint itself, you might add slides with bulleted lists of important points, as well as speaker's notes for you to use during the presentation.

PowerPoint lets you add music, digitized speech, and even video clips to create a multimedia presentation with the kind of production values you would expect to find in a Pepsi commercial. If you can't convince the board with all those tools at your disposal, maybe it's time to move on to the next project.

The next two sections describe some of the nifty new features in the latest versions of Word and PowerPoint. I won't give Access any further discussion here since it isn't used nearly as often as the other two programs.

A Quick Look at Word for Windows

When it comes to word processing programs, there are none with more capabilities—combined with incredible ease of use—than Word for Windows 95. Of course this new version includes all the features you expect in a world class word processing program. However, some of its new features truly set this program apart from the competition. Figure 17.6 shows a text document in Word for Windows.

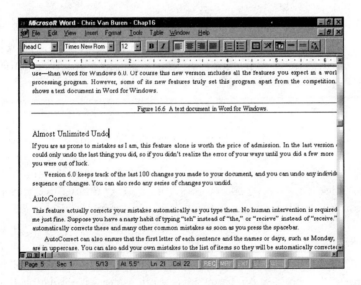

FIGURE 17.6 A TEXT DOCUMENT IN WORD FOR WINDOWS.

Almost Unlimited Undo

If you are as prone to mistakes as I am, this feature alone is worth the price of admission. In the last version of Word, you could only undo the last thing you did, so if you didn't realize the error of your ways until you did a few more editing steps, you were out of luck.

Word 95 keeps track of the last 100 changes you made to your document, and you can undo any individual change or sequence of changes. You can also redo any series of changes you undid.

AutoCorrect

This feature actually corrects your mistakes automatically as you type them. No human intervention is required, which suits me just fine. Suppose you have a nasty habit of typing "teh" instead of "the," or "recieve" instead of "receive." AutoCorrect automatically corrects these and many other common mistakes as soon as you press the **Spacebar**.

AutoCorrect can also ensure that the first letter of each sentence and the names or days, such as Monday, Tuesday, etc., are in uppercase. You can also add your own mistakes to the list of items so they will be automatically corrected.

AutoText

This feature is similar to the Glossary feature in earlier versions of Word. You can use AutoText to store passages of text or graphics and then retrieve them with a mouse click or keystroke.

AutoFormat

Wouldn't it be great if you had your own personal design expert to format your documents professionally? Word does! AutoFormat can analyze your document and apply the formatting it thinks is best suited to the content. Of course, AutoFormat doesn't always make a good guess, so you have the opportunity to choose from several format templates, or reject the changes altogether.

Shortcut Menus

Just as in Excel, clicking the right mouse button on almost any object on the Word screen displays a shortcut menu of options for manipulating that object. This can be a tremendous time saver. Rather than a variety of menus to find the appropriate options, they are right there in one place. The other Office applications also make use of shortcut menus.

Wizards

Word's Wizards present you with a series of dialog boxes to aid you in creating a variety of types of documents. You can create the structure for several types of letters, memos, newsletters, fax covers, and tables by simply answering questions in the Wizards dialog boxes. With Wizards, you can create sophisticated documents, even if you don't know how to use most of the features involved in their creation.

A Quick Look at PowerPoint

If you make presentations, whether to small or large groups, you may wonder how you ever got along without PowerPoint. This program provides all the tools necessary to create dazzling presentations using overhead transparencies, 35mm slides, or your computer screen.

Your presentations can incorporate text, charts, graphics, and even sound and video, if your computer has the equipment to add these niceties. You can even print your presentation to hand out to your audience. You can also create speaker's notes to help the presenter remember what to say as the presentation progresses.

Of course, you can also easily incorporate documents and pieces of documents created in your other Office programs into your presentations. Figure 17.7 shows a PowerPoint screen with several slides from a presentation.

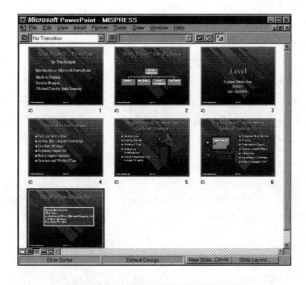

FIGURE 17.7 A POWERPOINT PRESENTATION.

One of PowerPoint's best features is the way it can lead you by the hand through the entire process of creating a presentation. All you need to worry about is what exactly you want to present, and PowerPoint does the rest.

Even if you've never used the previous version of PowerPoint and have no idea where to begin creating presentations, there's no need to panic. PowerPoint makes creating presentations easy, even for novice users. And, as Microsoft points out, if you know how to use Excel 95 or Word 95, you already know how to perform more than 100 tasks in PowerPoint.

In addition to the new features that have been added to Word and Excel—such as shortcut menus for any object on the screen, ToolTips, and Wizards—PowerPoint adds a number of unique features.

The AutoContent Wizard

Word and Excel have Wizards, but PowerPoint's AutoContent Wizard is special. This Wizard provides a brief interview and then creates your entire presentation for you—almost. Just add your own specific text, add any graphic objects, change the "look" with the Pick a Look Wizard, and your presentation is complete.

The Pick a Look Wizard

The Pick a Look Wizard guides you through the formatting of your presentation so you'll end up with a presentation that looks professionally designed.

The ClipArt Gallery

The ClipArt Gallery provides a new, easier way to add the expanded collection (more than 1000 pieces) of included graphics to your presentations. Just pick from the groups of thumbnail sketches.

Free Rotate

You can now freely rotate text or other objects 360 degrees. You can also edit rotated text and objects.

Freehand Drawing

As you give electronic presentations on your computer screen, you can now use the freehand drawing tool to add temporary annotations to your slides.

Some PowerPoint Terminology

♦ **Slides** are the heart of every presentation you create in PowerPoint and can be presented as overheads, 35mm slides, or electronically on screen. Slides can contain text, graphics, charts, and even sound and video.

♦ **Outlines** contain the text of your slide presentation. You can enter text for your slides directly on the slides or in the outline.

♦ **Speaker's notes** provide the presenter with a page that corresponds to each slide and contains a small image of the slide along with any additional notes.

♦ **Audience handouts** are printed copies of your presentation. You can have two, three, or six slides per handout page and you can add additional elements, such as other text or graphics. For example, you might want each page of the handout to include your company logo.

♦ **Placeholders** let you quickly add the type of element you're likely to want in a particular portion of the slide. When you pick a layout for your presentation, placeholders for such elements as text, graphics, and charts are included. Just click or double-click in the placeholder (depending on the type of placeholder) to add or edit the element.

♦ **Objects** are the individual elements that make up presentations. Text elements—such as titles or bulleted lists, graphics, and charts—are each individual objects and can be moved, sized, rotated, and even overlap other objects in a presentation.

WHAT IS OLE AND WHY SHOULD I CARE?

There are three ways to insert information from another Windows programs into a document:

♦ Paste from the Clipboard

♦ Embed an object

♦ Link an object

When you select information in a document and then choose **Edit**, **Cut**, or **Copy** (or use a keyboard shortcut or toolbar button to cut or copy), the information is stored on the Clipboard. The Clipboard is a temporary holding area that stores information until you cut or copy something else. The Clipboard only holds the last thing you cut or copied and replaces it with the next thing you cut or copy.

You can retrieve the Clipboard's contents by positioning your insertion point where you want the information to go—whether in a different location in the same document, a different document in the same program, or even a document in a different program—and then choosing **Edit**, **Paste**.

Cutting or copying and then pasting information is simple and straightforward, but has some limitations. Typically, the information you paste is treated as ordinary text or graphics that either can't be edited at all, or must be edited using the available tools of the program in which you pasted it.

In Chapter 13, "Linking Worksheets," you learned how to use a simple form of linking to tie several source worksheets to a dependent worksheet. This is a valuable form of linking, but is only the beginning.

Dynamic Data Exchange—Baby Steps

With the advent of Windows version 3.0, a technology called DDE (Dynamic Data Exchange) was introduced, enabling users to create truly compound documents. Not only could these compound documents include information from multiple applications, but the data could be updated as the source data changed. DDE was a step in the right direction, but hardly a panacea.

Creating compound documents with DDE could be intimidating, often requiring writing a bit of programming code, and could be dangerous. It was common for DDE documents to cause applications, and Windows itself, to crash. With DDE, you learned to save your work often or suffer the consequences.

OLE 1.0—The Holy Grail? Not Quite

The first implementation of OLE 1.0 after the release of Windows version 3.1 removed many of the obstacles to creating compound documents. Using OLE, embedded data was more easily edited and linked data was less likely to cause system crashes. Also, for the first time, you could create useful compound documents without a degree in Rocket Science.

OLE isn't really a separate technology from DDE, just an evolutionary progression. In fact, OLE is based on the underlying DDE technology. It just added a friendlier interface and additional features.

As wonderful as OLE 1.0 was, it still suffered from some of the same instability problems as DDE. It was more stable, but not stable enough. Links to source data were still easily broken. While it made embedding data easy, editing embedded data still had to be done in the source application, away from the document where the object was embedded.

OLE 2.0—The Genuine Article

OLE 2.0, the latest version of OLE, which is supported by all the main Office applications and many other Windows applications, has everything computer users have been searching for—almost. Links created using OLE 2.0 are much more stable. You do not have nearly as many lost links or system crashes as you once had to put up with.

Perhaps best of all is the way you can edit embedded objects. Embedded objects can now be edited in place, sometimes called *visual editing*. With in-place editing, you edit the object right in the document where it's embedded, surrounded by the other parts of the document. This way, you can see your edits in context, which greatly enhances efficiency.

When you edit an embedded object, the menus and toolbars of the application the object was created in usually replaces the menus and toolbars of the application the object is embedded in. You're able to edit the embedded object without ever leaving the document.

You'll see how in-place editing works with WordArt later in this chapter.

In Windows 95 there are quite a few programs that support OLE 2.0, and more are appearing all the time. The really good news is that Microsoft Office is the first suite of programs that supports OLE 2.0. If you have Office, lucky you! It makes sense that Office is the first OLE 2.0–compatible suite. After all, it was Microsoft that developed OLE 2.0.

WARNING

Documents using OLE require more of your computer's resources than simple documents created in one application. If you have a slower computer with relatively little memory, you may be better off avoiding OLE. Trying to create compound documents with your weakling computer may take more time and patience than it's worth.

On second thought, the benefits of OLE are so compelling you would be wise to upgrade or replace your computer so you have enough muscle to make working with OLE bearable.

Linking or Embedding? That's the Question

When creating a compound document, the first decision you have to make is whether to link the data to or embed the data in the document. Let's take a look at the differences.

Linking places a representation of the data from one document in another. The primary advantage is the data in the representation is updated when the data in the source document is updated.

Linking would be the right choice if you were putting a portion of an Excel worksheet, such as a budget, into a Word document where you wanted to be certain the Word document always reflected the latest budget numbers.

One disadvantage to linking is that the data isn't quite as easy to edit. You don't have the advantage of in-place editing. When you double-click on the linked data, the source document appears in its original application. It is not a big problem, just a bit less convenient.

Another disadvantage to consider is that the document containing the source data must be available in order to edit the linked data. If you delete the source document, you are not able to edit the linked data.

Choose embedding if you don't need the data updated from a source document. A graphic image, such as clip art or some WordArt, does not usually have to be updated and is a perfect candidate for embedding.

Embedding makes editing easier by allowing in-place editing. The menus and toolbars are replaced with the menus and toolbars of the application the embedded document was created in. In the example of an Excel worksheet in a Word document, the Word menus and toolbars would be replaced with the Excel menus and toolbars. This allows you to edit the worksheet data in the context of the Word document, but using Excel's tools.

The primary disadvantage of embedding is that it makes the document larger by roughly the size of the source document. For example, if you embed a 15,000 byte Excel worksheet into a 15,000 byte Word document, the result is a Word document of about 30,000 bytes. Linking, on the other hand, adds very little to the size of the document.

OLE Samples

Describing how OLE works isn't nearly as effective as actually seeing a couple examples of OLE in action. First, we'll show you an example of an Excel worksheet in a Word for Windows document. Then you'll see some WordArt text linked to an Excel worksheet.

N O T E

The WordArt program lets you create fancy text with a virtually unlimited variety of effects. You can use WordArt to add dazzling titles or to draw the reader's attention to a particular portion of a document.

Technically, WordArt is included with Word. In fact, if you purchase Word separately from the Office package, you get WordArt as part of the deal. But WordArt, like all the supplemental Office programs, can be used with any of the Office programs.

A sample Word for Windows document with a portion of our Spokane Locks and Bagel budget worksheet is displayed in Figure 17.8.

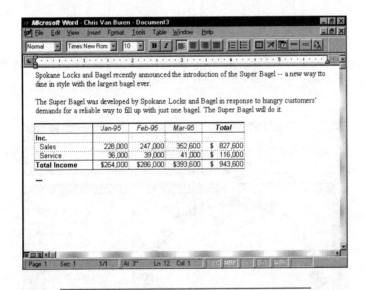

FIGURE 17.8 WORD DOCUMENT WITH AN EXCEL WORKSHEET.

The worksheet looks like it's just part of the Word document. But double-click anywhere on it and—zap! As you can see in Figure 17.9, the Excel menus, toolbars and formula bar are available and you can edit the worksheet as though you were in Excel.

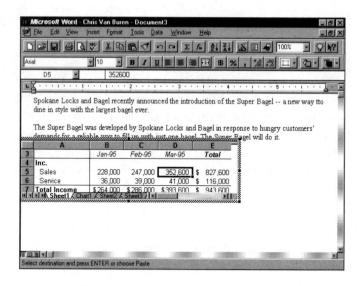

FIGURE 17.9 THE EMBEDDED WORKSHEET READY TO BE EDITED.

The Excel program with our budget worksheet on screen but with the title replaced with some fancy WordArt text is displayed in Figure 17.10.

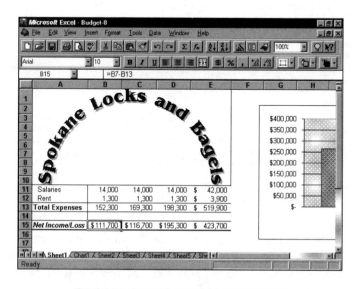

FIGURE 17.10 EXCEL WITH LINKED WORDART TEXT.

The same worksheet after double-clicking on the WordArt text is displayed in Figure 17.11. The WordArt program menus and dialog box replace the Excel menus and toolbars.

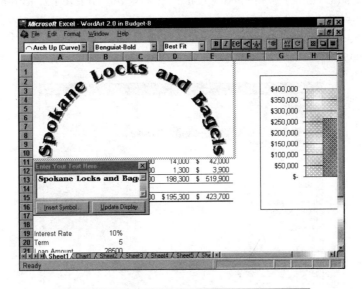

FIGURE 17.11 WORDART TEXT IN EXCEL, READY TO BE EDITED.

Using OLE

Here are the steps for creating OLE objects on your own. We'll embed a WordArt object into an Excel worksheet.

N O T E

If you don't have WordArt, you may be able to follow along using another program. Although embedding objects from the supplemental programs included in Office works exactly the same way in all the Office programs, this isn't necessarily the case when using other Windows programs.

Some other programs may not support the latest version of OLE (2.0 as of this writing). Others may not support OLE at all. If the program in which you want to embed an object doesn't operate in exactly the same way as described in this chapter, don't panic. Refer to that program's documentation to see how, and if, it handles OLE objects.

1. Start Excel, if it is not already running.

2. Open the Budget workbook if it is not already on your screen.

3. Be sure cell A1 is the active cell and press the **Delete** key to remove our sheet's title.

4. Choose **Insert**, **Object** and the Object dialog box appears, as shown in Figure 17.12.

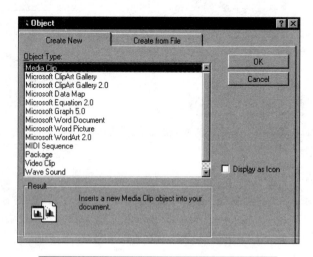

FIGURE 17.12 THE OBJECT DIALOG BOX CREATE NEW TAB.

5. If the Create New tab of the Object dialog box isn't displayed, click on the **Create New** tab.

   The names in your Object Type list may differ from the figure, depending on how your programs are installed on your computer.

   You'll also notice a check box in the lower-right portion of the dialog box to **Display as Icon**. This option lets you display a small icon (picture) representing the type of embedded object.

6. Scroll down the list to **Microsoft WordArt 2.0** and click on it.

   The Result portion of the dialog box shows you what happens with this object type.

7. Click the **OK** button.

   The title bar still says Microsoft Excel, but Excel's menus and toolbars have been replaced by the WordArt menus and toolbar. Also, the WordArt text entry box appears on the screen, as shown in Figure 17.13.

NOTE If Microsoft WordArt 2.0 doesn't appear in your list, you may need to run the Word setup program to install the application. Start Word Setup by double-clicking the **Word Setup** icon in the Program Manager group that contains your Office icons. The screen prompts tell you what to do to add to your installation. If you want further instructions, the documentation that came with the Word program has complete setup instructions.

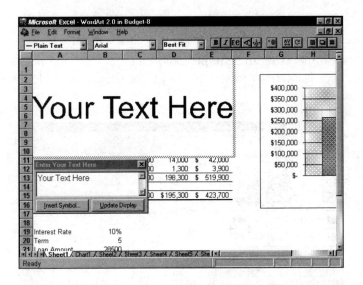

FIGURE 17.13 THE WORDART MENUS, TOOLBAR, AND DIALOG BOX IN EXCEL.

The first step in creating a WordArt object is to type your own text. All you have to do is start typing, replacing the text in the text entry box that says "Your Text Here" (unless of course you want your text to say "Your Text Here").

8. Type **Spokane Locks and Bagel Corp. First Quarter Budget**.

The text you type in the text entry box doesn't replace the WordArt text above the dialog box until you apply an effect or attribute, or click the **Update Display** button in the WordArt text entry box.

After typing your text, you can use the menus and toolbar buttons to specify how your text should look, by selecting fonts and font attributes, curves and shapes, alignment, and shadows. Unlike Excel and the other main Office programs, not all the toolbar functions are accessible from the menus or vice versa, so you may have to use both menus and toolbar buttons.

You'll notice that the WordArt toolbar doesn't provide ToolTips like the toolbars in Excel and the other main Office programs do. Refer to your Word documentation for what each of the buttons does.

N O T E

One of the first things you may want to alter is the shape of the text.

9. Click on the **Line and Shape** toolbar button (the one next to the box that says Plain Text) to see the variety of shapes available, as shown in Figure 17.14.

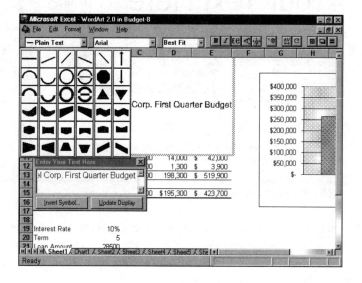

FIGURE 17.14 THE PALETTE OF SHAPES.

10. Click on the half circle just below the straight line that is highlighted on the shapes palette.

The text appears curved and "Plain Text" has been replaced with "Arch Up (Curve)" on the toolbar, as shown in Figure 17.15.

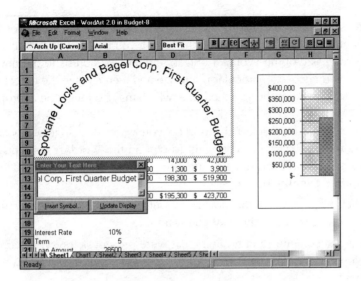

FIGURE 17.15 THE WORDART TEXT WITH ITS NEW SHAPE.

N O T E

You can have any amount of text you want in a WordArt object, but some of the shapes require two or three lines of text to be displayed properly. For example, the Button shape requires three lines—one for the top curve, one for the middle line, and one for the bottom curve. You could use just one line for this shape, but you'd only have the top curve, which would defeat the purpose of choosing this shape.

You can click on the **Font** button to choose another font for your WordArt text. Be aware that all the text in a WordArt object must use the same font and size, as well as any other attributes. You can't have a single word bold, for example. If you use the bold attribute, all the text is bold.

11. Click on the font down arrow on the toolbar. It's next to the box with Arial in it.

12. Click on **Times New Roman**. You may need to scroll down the font list to find Times New Roman.

Use the **Shading**, **Shadow**, and **Border** buttons to add shading, shadows and borders to your text. These options just affect the text, not the box that surrounds the text.

NOTE Although you can choose a specific point size for your WordArt text, the Best Fit option is often the best. If you use Best Fit, you can change the size of the WordArt object, and the text adjusts to the new size. If you choose a particular point size and then change the object size, the text remains the specified size, which may no longer be appropriate.

To edit the text, select the portion you want to change, or position the insertion point where you want to type in the WordArt text entry box. If you've already added the attributes you want to the text, click the **Update Display** button.

13. Click anywhere on the document outside the text entry box after your WordArt text looks the way you want it to.

The Excel menus and toolbars that were present before you started using WordArt reappear, and your WordArt object is a part of your Word document.

You can resize the object by using the handles surrounding it. You can move it to another part of the document by positioning the mouse pointer inside the object and dragging.

The embedded WordArt object with font, shading, and size changes is shown in Figure 17.16.

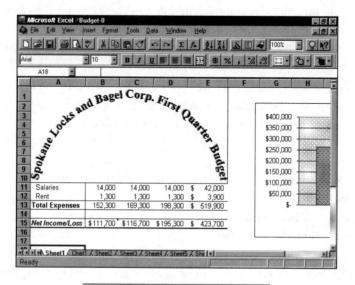

FIGURE 17.16 THE EDITED WORDART OBJECT.

If you want to edit the WordArt text after you've left WordArt, double-click in the WordArt object, or choose **Edit WordArt 2.0** from its shortcut menu. The text entry box and WordArt's menus and toolbars will reappear.

Linking an Excel Worksheet into a Word Document

You can link or embed an entire document into another, or just a portion. There are fewer steps to linking or embedding the entire document, so that's what I'll cover. For this example, I'll provide general, rather than specific, instructions.

To link an Excel worksheet to a Word document:

1. Start Word and open the document you want the Excel worksheet linked to.

2. Position your insertion point where you want the worksheet data to appear.

3. Then choose **Insert**, **Object** and click the **Create from File** tab.

   Figure 17.17 shows the Create from File tab of the Object dialog box.

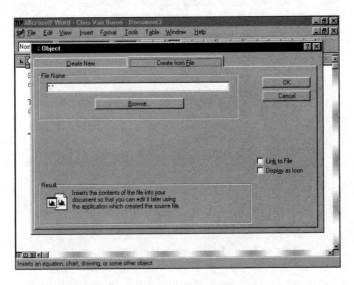

FIGURE 17.17 THE CREATE FROM FILE TAB OF THE OBJECT DIALOG BOX.

4. Click the **Link to File** check box in the lower-right portion of the dialog box.

This check box tells Word to create a link to the file rather than embed it. The Result portion of the dialog box tells you what happens when you click in the Link to File dialog box.

5. Click **Browse** to locate your file using the browser. Change to the drive and directory where the Excel worksheet is stored, click on the worksheet's name in the File Name list, and then click **OK**.

Excel doesn't have to be running to link or embed a worksheet. It does, of course, have to be available to run.

N O T E

After a while (it could be several minutes if you have a slow computer), the worksheet appears in the Word document, as shown in Figure 17.18.

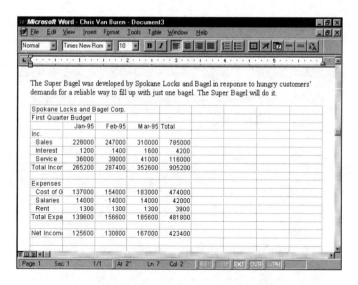

FIGURE 17.18 AN EXCEL WORKSHEET IN A WORD DOCUMENT.

The worksheet is now an object in the Word document that can be moved and sized. You can move the worksheet by clicking on it so handles appear surrounding the object, then positioning the mouse pointer anywhere in the object and dragging. Resize it by positioning the mouse pointer over one of the handles so it becomes a double-headed arrow and then drag.

To edit the worksheet data, double-click on the object. The worksheet appears in a separate Excel window. You don't have to exit Excel to see the results of any changes you make. Just switch back to Word to see that the data is updated. Don't forget to save any changes you make to your worksheet data in Excel.

You can see the problem of inserting an entire worksheet. It can take over the whole document, leaving little room for the surrounding text. For this reason, you may choose to insert just selected cells rather than the entire worksheet. There is a way to insert an entire worksheet, or a large portion of a worksheet, without having it overwhelm the document. You can insert the worksheet as an icon.

To insert a worksheet as an icon, follow the above steps, but click on **Display as Icon**. After the file is linked, it appears as an icon, as shown in Figure 17.19.

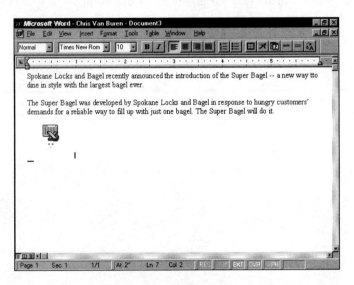

FIGURE 17.19 A LINKED WORKSHEET DISPLAYED AS AN ICON.

The icon lets the reader know that there is additional information available. To see the worksheet, simply double-click on the icon. The worksheet appears in Excel just as if it were a normal nonicon link.

WARNING

The Display as Icon option is only a good idea if the intended reader of the document will be reading it on a computer that has Excel (and the document) available. If you print a document with a linked file that is displayed as an icon, the icon prints just as it appears on the screen. If the reader views the document on a computer that doesn't have Excel, of course, the data won't be visible.

A FINAL THOUGHT

In this chapter, you learned some of the basic concepts of using Excel with other programs and using OLE to share data between applications. This just scratches the surface of Excel's ability to work with other Windows programs. Combining Excel with other programs adds up to more than the sum of the programs and greatly enhances your ability to create complex documents. I hope this book has helped you to gain the skill and confidence to produce usable worksheets that make your life easier and more enjoyable.

APPENDIX A

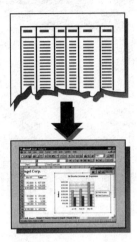

FOR LOTUS 1-2-3 USERS

There are many Lotus 1-2-3 users switching over to Excel, so Microsoft has included some tools to help former 1-2-3 users over the hump. If you are one of these, you'll be delighted at how easy it is to learn Excel. In fact, you won't even have to learn too much of Excel. You can just let Excel's help for 1-2-3 users guide you through your Excel tasks.

The first place to go to see what sort of help is available to you is the Excel Help system. Choosing **Lotus 1-2-3** from the Help menu displays the Help for Lotus 1-2-3 Users dialog box, as shown in Figure A.1.

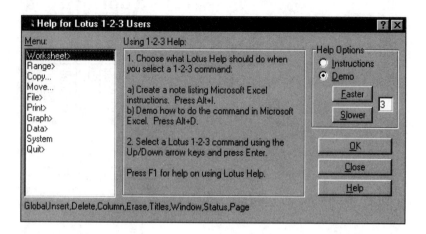

FIGURE A.1 THE HELP FOR LOTUS 1-2-3 USERS DIALOG BOX.

In the Help Option area of the dialog box in the upper right, you can specify whether Excel gives you instructions or demonstrates how to perform a 1-2-3 task in Excel, leading you by the hand as the task is carried out. You can also enter a number in the box just below the two option buttons to specify how quickly or slowly Excel carries out the demonstration.

If you choose **Instructions**, the steps for carrying out the task appears in the middle portion of the dialog box.

In either case, you choose the command you want to learn about from the Menu list. For example, if you want to learn how to perform the /Worksheet, Insert, Column command in Excel, you would click on **Worksheet** and then **OK** (or double-click on **Worksheet**) to display the list of Worksheet commands. Next, double-click on **Insert**, and then on **Column**.

If you have chosen the **Demo** option, you are be asked to confirm or change where the columns are to be inserted, as shown in Figure A.2.

After entering the required information, clicking on the **OK** button causes Excel to carry out the task, using the Excel procedures.

If you have chosen the Instructions option, a note appears on your screen telling you how to perform the task, but letting you do it on your own.

Figure A.3 displays an example of an instruction note.

You can drag the note to any portion of the screen you want so it is not in the way. When you are finished with the note, you can clear it from the screen by pressing **Esc**.

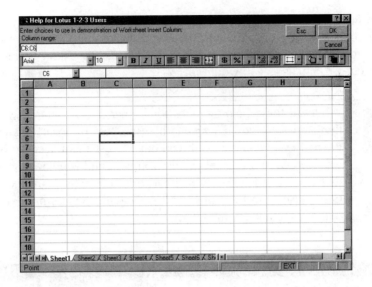

FIGURE A.2 A LOTUS 1-2-3 DEMO HELP DIALOG BOX.

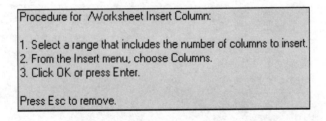

FIGURE A.3 AN INSTRUCTION NOTE FOR INSERTING COLUMNS.

If even this much help is not enough, you can have Excel use your actual 1-2-3 commands to carry out tasks in Excel. You can even set up Excel to allow you to enter formulas in the 1-2-3 format and have Excel translate them for you. All these options are specified in the Transition portion of the Options dialog box, as shown in Figure A.4.

In the Settings area of the dialog box, you can choose the **Lotus 1-2-3 Help** option to have Excel display the 1-2-3 help dialog box when you press the **Slash** (/) key. The Transition Navigation Keys check box lets you use 1-2-3 keyboard navigation keys in Excel.

The Sheet Options area of the dialog box lets you specify how you want formulas handled. Choosing **Transition Formula Evaluation** causes Excel to evaluate formulas entered in Excel using 1-2-3's rules. Transition Formula Entry lets you enter formulas as you would in 1-2-3.

WARNING

While all these help facilities for former 1-2-3 users are very nice, they can slow down your learning process by insulating you from the real Excel commands. If you need to use them because you have been forced to use Excel against your will and you have to get a project completed before you have time to really learn Excel, fine. Otherwise, bite the bullet and stick with the normal Excel commands. You'll thank me later.

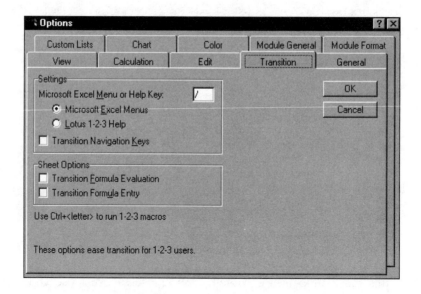

FIGURE A.4 THE TRANSITION PORTION OF THE OPTIONS DIALOG BOX.

In addition to all the help facilities, you'll be pleased to know that all the 1-2-3 files you have created can be opened directly into Excel. You are prompted with a dialog box asking if you want to open the 1-2-3 version *xx* file. That's all there is to it. All the formatting and formulas you used in 1-2-3 are retained. You can even use most of the macros you created in 1-2-3 version 2.01 and some from 2.2.

APPENDIX B

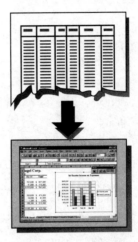

KEYBOARD SHORTCUTS

Excel provides keyboard shortcuts for almost everything you can do with the mouse. I concentrated on the mouse actions to accomplish most tasks in the book. However, you save time if you use some of the keyboard shortcuts, particularly if you are a touch typist. Good typists find that removing their hands from the keyboard to use the mouse slows them down. Using keyboard shortcuts allows you to keep your hands on the keyboard.

This list of keyboard commands is not comprehensive. These are just some of my favorites. You'll find a complete guide to the keyboard commands in Excel's help facility. To view the keyboard commands in help, choose **Help**, **Contents**, click on **Reference Information**, and then on **Keyboard Guide**. You are then able to choose among a variety of keyboard guides in different categories.

Function Keys

To	Press
Get help	**F1**
Get context sensitive help	**Shift+F1**
Edit cell	**F2**
Display Info Window	**Ctrl+F2**
Display the Function Wizard	**Shift+F3**
Switch between relative and absolute reference while editing	**F4**
Repeat last action when not editing	**F4**
Close active windows	**Ctrl+F4**
Close application	**Alt+F4**
Display Go To dialog box	**F5**
Check Spelling	**F7**
Calculate all sheets in open workbooks (when manual calc is turned on)	**F9**
Calculate active sheet	**Shift+F9**
Save As	**F12**
Save	**Shift+F12**
Open	**Ctrl+F12**

Inserting, Deleting, Copying and Moving

To	Press
Cut selection	**Ctrl+X**
Copy selection	**Ctrl+C**
Paste selection	**Ctrl+V**
Clear selection contents	**Del**
Undo last action	**Ctrl+Z**

MOVING AND SELECTING

To	Press
Extend selection one cell	Shift+Arrow
Move up or down to edge of current data region	Ctrl+Up Arrow key or Ctrl + Down Arrow
Move left or right to edge of current data region	Ctrl+Left Arrow key or Ctrl +Right Arrow
Move to beginning of row	Home
Select to beginning of row	Shift+Home
Move to last cell in worksheet	Ctrl+End
Select entire column	Ctrl+Spacebar
Select entire row	Shift+Spacebar
Select entire worksheet	Ctrl+A
Move down one screen	Page Down
Move up one screen	Page Up
Move right one screen	Alt+Page Down
Move left one screen	Alt+Page Up
Move to cell A1	Ctrl+Home

MOVING WITHIN A SELECTION

To	Press
Move down	Enter
Move up	Shift+Enter
Move left to right	Tab
Move right to left	Shift+Tab

FORMATTING DATA

To	Press
Apply Currency format	**Ctrl+Shift+$**
Apply Percent format	**Ctrl+Shift+%**
Apply Date format (Day+Month+Year)	**Ctrl+Shift+#**
Apply two decimal place format with commas	**Ctrl+Shift+!**
Apply or remove bold	**Ctrl+B**
Apply or remove italic	**Ctrl+I**
Apply or remove underline	**Ctrl+U**

APPENDIX C

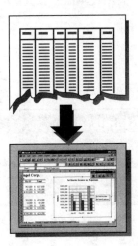

TOOLBAR REFERENCE

Here are all the toolbars included with Excel. Each button is labeled with its tooltip. Don't forget that you can create your own custom toolbars using these and many other buttons available in the Customize dialog box.

THE STANDARD TOOLBAR

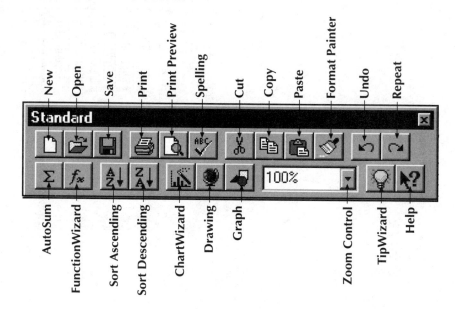

THE FORMATTING TOOLBAR

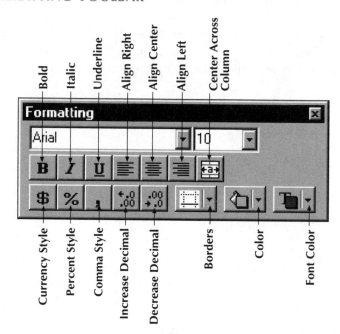

THE CHART TOOLBAR

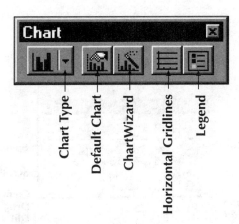

Chart Type
Default Chart
ChartWizard
Horizontal Gridlines
Legend

THE DRAWING TOOLBAR

Line
Rectangle
Ellipse
Arc
Freeform
Text Box
Arrow
Freehand
Filled Rectangle
Filled Ellipse
Filled Arc
Filled Freeform

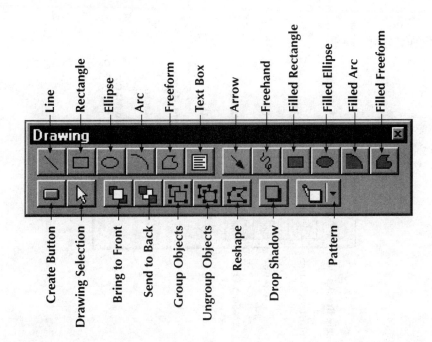

Create Button
Drawing Selection
Bring to Front
Send to Back
Group Objects
Ungroup Objects
Reshape
Drop Shadow
Pattern

THE FORMS TOOLBAR

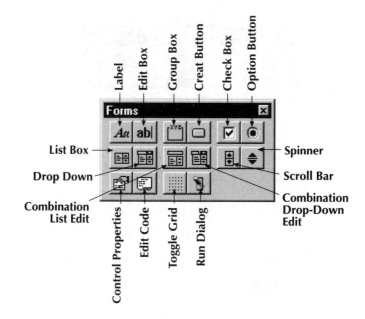

THE VISUAL BASIC TOOLBAR

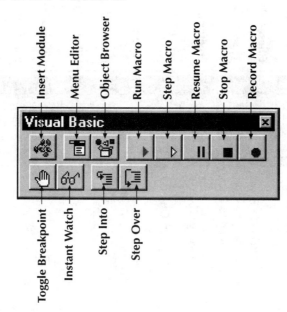

THE AUDITING TOOLBAR

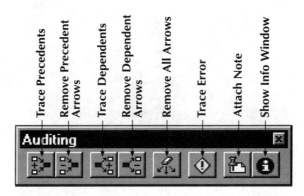

THE WORKGROUP TOOLBAR

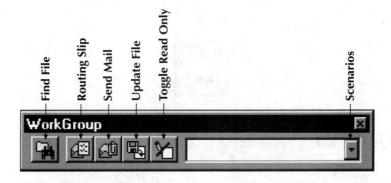

THE MICROSOFT TOOLBAR

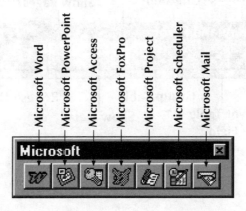

THE FULL SCREEN TOOLBAR

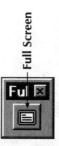

THE STOP RECORDING TOOLBAR

THE QUERY AND PIVOT TOOLBAR

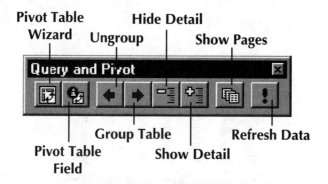

GLOSSARY

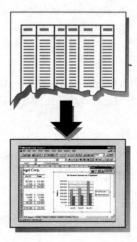

active window

The window that is currently in use or selected.

active cell

The worksheet cell that is currently selected.

application window

The window containing the menu bar for an application.

cell formatting

Appearance changes applied to cells, such as alignment, fonts and borders.

cell

The rectangular area on a worksheet that is the intersection of a column and a row.

comparison operators

Symbols used to compare values, such as > (greater than), = (equal to) etc.

comparison criteria

A set of search conditions used to find the data you're looking for in a list or database.

Control menu

The menu that contains commands for manipulating the active window. The Control menu is opened by using the Control-menu box.

Control-menu box

The icon in the upper-left corner of a window used for opening the Control menu. Double clicking on the Control-menu box closes the window.

data series

A group of related data points that are plotted in a chart.

data point

A piece of data that is represented in a chart.

default

Settings that are preset. Excel comes with default settings for many options, such as column width. Most defaults can be changed.

dependent worksheet

A worksheet that uses linked data from one or more source worksheets.

document window

A window within an application window. An Excel workbook is a document window. There can be multiple document windows within an application window.

drop-down menus

A list of commands that is opened by choosing its name from the menu bar.

field names

> The label in the first row of an Excel database list used to name the fields.

field

> A category of information in a database list. A column in an Excel database is a field.

fill handle

> The handle in the lower-right corner of the active cell or selection used for moving, copying, and filling data from the cell or selection into other cells.

group icons

> Icons containing program icons, usually in Windows' Program Manager.

header row

> The first row in an Excel database containing labels for the field names.

hotkey

> The keys used to initiate a command. The sequence of underlined menu letters are hotkeys.

icon

> A pictorial representation of an object or element. Excel is started from an icon. The toolbar buttons are icons.

insertion point

> The flashing vertical line indicating where text is inserted. The insertion point is sometimes called a cursor.

link

> A reference between two worksheets. Useful for summarizing or consolidating data from multiple worksheets or workbooks.

macro

> A series of actions that has been recorded, or programmed, and named, which can be executed by running (playing) the macro. An Excel macro is really a small program within Excel.

mouse

> A hand-held pointing device that you move across your desktop to control the on-screen pointer. A mouse usually has two or three control buttons.

name list

> The list of names assigned to cells or ranges of cells on the worksheet. The name list is opened from the name box on the left side of the formula bar.

Personal Macro Workbook

> A workbook for storing macros that you want to be available all the time. The Personal Macro Workbook is usually hidden, but is always opened when you start Excel.

point

> A size measurement, usually referring to font size. One point is approximately .72 inches.

program

> A sequence of instructions that can be run by a computer. Excel is a program.

proportional fonts

> Fonts with variable-width characters. Proportional fonts usually look more professional than monospaced fonts, in which each character occupies the same width.

record

> A collection of fields pertaining to one database entry.

relative reference

>A cell reference that determines its position relative to the original location. Relative referencing allows formulas to work properly, even when they are copied to other areas of the worksheet.

restore button

>A double-headed arrow button in the upper-right corner of a window, used to restore the window to its previous size.

scroll bars

>Devices used for navigating vertically and horizontally in a window. Vertical scroll bars are usually on the right side of the window. Horizontal scroll bars are usually on the bottom.

shortcut menu

>A list of commands that is relevant to a particular area of the screen. Shortcut menus are opened by right-clicking on that area.

sort key

>The field used as the basis for a database sort. Up to three sort keys can be used at one time in an Excel sort.

source worksheet

>A worksheet with linked cells or ranges that provide variable information to the dependent worksheet.

tool tip

>A short description of a toolbar button that appears just below the mouse pointer when it is on a toolbar button.

TrueType fonts

>A particular type of font that is scalable to practically any size on the page and the screen.

user interface

The kind of menus, dialog boxes, and other elements used to interact with the program. Windows is a graphical user interface because it incorporates many graphical elements for your interaction.

VBA

Visual Basic for Applications. This is the primary programming language used for Excel macros.

workbook

A collection of sheets (worksheets, chart sheets) that is saved with one file name. A workbook can contain up to 255 sheets.

x-axis

The horizontal plane of a chart. Sometimes called the category axis.

y-axis

The vertical plane of a chart. Sometimes called the value axis.

INDEX

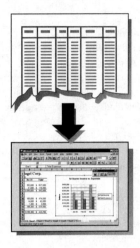

427

C

calculations
    Manual option, 319
    on active worksheet only, 319
    on all open workbooks, 319
    Options, 318-320
    Precision as Displayed option, 319
    Recalculate Before Save option, 319
cells
    active, 421
    Alert Before Overwriting Cells option, 317
    aligning (*See* alignment)
    blank, testing for, 84
    borders, 141-142
    defined, 21, 421
    entering formula into, 52
    finding, using Go To, 26
    Format Cells dialog box
        Alignment, 129-132 (*See also* alignment, main entry)
        creating styles in, 151
        Font, 141
        Number, 135-136
        Protection, 147
    hiding to protect data, 147-149
    Info Window option, 321
    locking to protect data, 147-149
    multiple lines of text in, 132
    names, 113-116
        Define Name dialog box, 115
        Insert Names dialog box, 114
        name list, 115, 424
        used in formulas and functions, 115-116
        using adjacent text, 114-115
    ranges, 105-107
        non-contiguous, selecting, 106
        rectangular, selecting, 107
        select by dragging, 105-106
        selecting to print, 159
        selecting using Go To, 107
    reference notes, 49-51
    unlocking, 149
center (*See* alignment)

charts, 169-199
    3-D, 173, 174, 177-178
    activating, 187, 197
    adding new data series 193-194
    area charts, 177-178
    bar charts, 173-174
    changing chart type, 191-192
    changing data, 189-191
    Chart toolbar, 186, 417
    column charts, 172-173
    combination charts, 179-180
    copying, 188-189
    creating in chart sheets, 196-197
    creating with Chart Wizard, 180-186
        adding a legend and title (Step 5), 185-186
        Back button, 183
        choosing category of chart (Step 2), 183
        choosing subcategory of chart (Step 3), 184
        Finish button, 183
        preview (Step 4), 185
        Range text box (Step 1), 182
        selecting elements from worksheet, 180-181
        sizing chart, 181
    data point, 170, 422
    data series, 170, 422
    data series orientation, 195-196
    deleting, 188
    doughnut charts, 175-176
    drag and plot, 193-194
    editing, 192-196
    elements described, 170-172
    embedded, 171, 198
    empty cells in, 330-331
    enhancing, 201-224
        axes, 204-208
        customizing the plot area, 211-212
        Format Chart Title dialog box, 209-210
        labels within, 214-215
        text, 208-209
        tick marks, 207
        with color, 206-207, 213, 324
        with fonts, 206, 209-211

DISK TO ACCOMPANY

TEACH YOURSELF... EXCEL FOR WINDOWS 95

Following are directions for installing and enjoying the disk that accompanies this book:

1. From Windows 95, start Excel.
2. In Excel, use the **File-Open** command to view the files on this disk. You may need to select **Drive A:** or **Drive B:** in the Open dialog box.
3. Choose the desired file from the disk and click **Open** to bring it into Excel.
4. Use the file as desired.

These files are excellent examples of Excel in action—and can give you a better understanding of Excel's features. You may even want to use and/or customize some of the files for your own personal data. Following is a brief description of the contents of this disk:

BUDGET files

These files contain different version of the BUDGET worksheet that is used as an example throughout this book. You can see the various stages of this worksheet and compare it to your own sample as you work through the lessons in the book.

SHAREWARE directory

This directory contains various shareware files for Excel. Some of these are self-running programs that are ready to hold your personal data. Others are simple tools to help you get more out of Excel. Instructions are available within the files. Shareware is available as public domain software and is subject to the licensing agreements specified within each file.

CALENDAR

This file provides a perpetual calendar created in Excel. You can examine the formulas to see how they were created. Choose months and years to view—and print the calendar for any month of any year. Add your own ideas to improve this worksheet or customize it for your own needs.

INCOME/EXPENSE

The Income/Expense worksheet is a simple log of your income and expense transactions. It uses Excel's database features to track these transactions and present data that you want. You can view all your expenses for a particular category for tax purposes. Or, use the other worksheets in the workbook file to get reports from the data. You can get a quick summary of all your income and expense totals for each account, plus, balance your checkbook. Instructions for each worksheet page are available through the Instructions buttons.

NOTE: THIS DISK CONTAINS EXCEL DATA FILES THAT CAN BE USED ONLY FROM WITHIN EXCEL. IT DOES NOT CONTAIN ANY PROGRAMS OR STARTUP FILES.